NORTH OF FAMILIAR

Caitlin Press Inc.
8100 Alderwood Road
Halfmoon Bay, BC V0N 1Y1
www.caitlin-press.com

Images courtesy of the author unless otherwise noted
Design by Vici Johnstone
Typeset by Demian Pettman
Printed in Canada

Caitlin Press Inc. acknowledges the Government of Canada, the Canada Council
for the Arts, and the British Columbia Arts Council for their financial support for
our publishing program.

Canada Council   Conseil des Arts   BRITISH COLUMBIA   Funded by the   Canadä
for the Arts   du Canada   ARTS COUNCIL   Government
                                                              of Canada

Library and Archives Canada Cataloguing in Publication

Milos, Terry, 1951-, author
North of familiar : a woman's story of homesteading
and adventure in the Canadian wilderness / Terry Milos.

ISBN 978-1-987915-45-7 (softcover)

1. Milos, Terry, 1951-. 2. Women—British Columbia—Atlin—
Biography. 3. Frontier and pioneer life—Atlin—British Columbia.
4. Atlin (B.C.)—Biography. 5. Autobiographies. I. Title.

FC3849.A86Z49 2017   971.1'8503092   C2017-902294-6

A WOMAN'S STORY
OF HOMESTEADING AND ADVENTURE
IN THE CANADIAN WILDERNESS

NORTH OF FAMILIAR

TERRY MILOS

CAITLIN PRESS

This book is dedicated to my son Travis,
who brings such joy to my life through his love,
and in memory of my dear son Brett Matthew Milos,
who remains in my heart forever.

CONTENTS

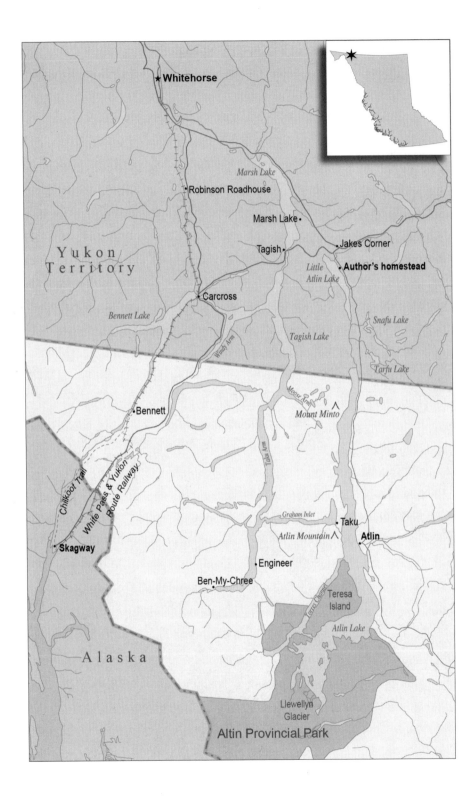

INTRODUCTION

I was born in Coral Gables, a southern suburb of Miami, Florida. The city was a 1920s planned community designed almost entirely in the Mediterranean Revival Style. Many of its middle-class homes were built on the edge of man-made canals dug through coral rock to the Atlantic Ocean. My father played football for the University of Miami and worked in administration there until his retirement. My entire childhood was spent basking in warm weather, dancing under swaying palm trees, playing on beautiful white sandy beaches, waterskiing, boating, picnicking and taking trips to the Caribbean.

Every summer my dad was given a month off and my mom, dad, older sister Cheryl, younger brother Matt and I would travel north to see my grandparents in West Virginia and Wisconsin. The morning our family's journey began, we were always packed and ready early to avoid heavy traffic. In the early days we would have a bed made up in the back of our station wagon so we could nap. When my dad bought our first VW Beetle we wrapped up my newly born brother Matt and put him into the compartment behind the back seat. These were the days before seat belts—safety-preparation involved my mother yelling "duck!" All of us kids loved the long drive, but we were easily bored.

As soon as we reached the mountains of the Carolinas I really came alive. They just seemed to grab my soul and call to me. I would search out old cabins as we drove, and instead of seeing a dilapidated old shack with a caved-in roof, I would see it as I imagined it to be years ago when there were no roads, only a trail. I could see the homestead alive; I could almost hear the voices of the people that once lived there, see the children playing, see myself playing with them.

Although I longed to experience a pioneer lifestyle from an early age, I never imagined in my wildest dreams that I would eventually live in a small, cozy cabin in the bush in the southern Yukon and have the opportunity for so many wonderful northern adventures. Alaska was always touted as being the last great wilderness in the United States, but I was drawn to the vast land to the east of Alaska, the land that had not been tarnished by American politics and settled by wealthy southerners with their "lower forty-eight" ideologies.

I wanted the true bush experience I felt only Canada could offer. This is the story of how my wildest dreams came true.

Down by the Creek

In the spring of 1973, my boyfriend Stan and I were sitting next to a stream in Marin County, California, when he asked me to immigrate to Canada with him. We were in a quiet redwood glade catching the warm rays of the morning sun filtering through the trees. "I've been thinking," he said. "I've been wondering what you'd say if… I've been thinking we should move up to Canada."

From a very early age, I had watched movies of wagon trains and the migration of the pioneers to the West and learned how the early settlers lived, built their cabins and survived their many hardships. The old homesteads I saw from the back seat of the car, face pressed to the window, on those family vacations to West Virginia had reinforced my yearning for a pioneer lifestyle.

After high school, I had left Florida and moved to San Francisco to continue my schooling. I was now, at twenty-one, living in rural California, caught up in the sixties "back to the land" hippie movement, planting gardens and learning how to preserve food. And I was in love with a man who was asking me to start a new life with him in the far northernmost reaches of Canada.

I was definitely caught off guard, but not completely surprised. Stan was twelve years older than me, and I knew that for years he had wanted to move north again. Instead of returning to Alaska, where he was born and raised, he wanted to live in the wilderness of Canada to experience real bush living. I also knew that he had never found the right woman to live out his dream with until now. Although it was my dream too, we had known each other for only a short time; maybe a month. We had never even discussed our future together. I was still in college and would graduate with a BA the following June, and I wasn't sure what career I wanted to pursue. I was leaning towards being a teacher, as working with and caring for young people appealed to me. Stan was a carver, but he made a living as a carpenter and could likely get a job anywhere.

The author, aged eighteen.

So when the question of immigrating to Canada popped up, breaking the silence of that peaceful and fateful morning, I said, "Wow, I'd love to." Why not go to a new country and start a life there? It sounded incredibly exciting, especially because I was so madly in love with Stan. He seemed to be the man of my dreams—not only handsome, strong and well built, but someone who loved nature and being in the outdoors as much as I did, someone who shared my beliefs and was willing to give up his very independent life and move away from his friends and all that was familiar to him to start a new life with me.

Also, I was against the Vietnam War so I was excited about the prospect of living in Canada. I was not thrilled with the Nixon administration and the fact that so many of my friends had been sent to Vietnam, some of whom never returned.

Stan seemed stunned that I said yes. He just looked at me, a sheepish smile inching across his face. "Really?" he said.

My head quickly started nodding up and down as a smile widened across my face. "Yes, yes, I really want to… I'd love to!" I was so excited I jumped up and held my arms out to him. Stan, joining in my enthusiasm, jumped up too and we hugged and hugged each other, laughing and looking into each other's eyes. We walked hand in hand back up the trail feeling jubilant and ready to face the unknown together.

Little did I know then that this was to be an adventure that would stay embedded in me for the rest of my life; one that would help to shape the person I've become.

I called my mom and dad with the wonderful news of our plans, but the conversation didn't go anything like I'd imagined it would. My parents were not the least bit excited. They didn't know this man threatening to carry their daughter off to God knows where. Canada was far away, and I wasn't even married yet. "How could you even consider this?" they asked me. "What are you thinking? What about continuing your education, your career?" I was trying to explain myself, hoping to convince them that I wasn't completely crazy, when Stan started waving his arms to get my attention, which I totally ignored since I was so engrossed in my conversation with them.

I hung up, depressed but determined. Stan asked, "Why didn't you tell me you were calling your parents and telling them about our plans?" Then, hesitantly, he added, "I've been meaning to talk to you. I… I was going to… I think we should get married."

We were married on May 1, 1974, a month before my twenty-second birthday. Our ceremony took place in a field of wildflowers on the hill behind our pan abode log cabin, not far from the sleepy little village of Nicasio, California, where we had been living while I was finishing college. The cabin was in a valley that had forested hillsides of oak, bay and fir trees above it, and a babbling creek with stands of magnificent redwoods below it.

I carried a bouquet of wildflowers and wore a wreath of them on my head made by a friend who had lovingly picked them that morning. Stan had his newest blue jeans on and a denim shirt hand-embroidered with flowers and designs. After the short ceremony, in which we exchanged non-traditional vows, we went back to the house, changed our clothes and went on what we enjoyed most: a long hike in the nearby hills.

Within weeks of our marriage we received a letter stating that our immigration status had been approved. I was still in school, with only a month to finish my BA, and I could hardly concentrate I was so excited. In the days that followed, we spent all our spare time getting ready for our move north, which was to take place immediately following my graduation.

Canadian customs required a list of all the items we intended to bring into Canada with us. The things we couldn't squeeze into our brown 1954 Ford pickup and carry with us into our new lives were either given away to friends and neighbours or donated to local charities. Stan hesitated to suggest that we might not be able to fit my loom in—he knew how much it meant to me, as I was a textile artist. But I was adamant: leave anything but my loom and spinning wheel! Bags and boxes were jigsawed in and taken out in what seemed like a hundred attempts to get it right. In the end, we managed somehow to shoehorn everything in, including my two most precious items. Every nook and cranny of the truck bed had been filled, stacked so high you could not even see out of the back window. When we noticed it was sitting a lot lower on its springs, we exchanged glances and our eyebrows rose, but we said nothing, knowing better than to tempt fate. After it was all tarped and tied down, we collapsed, exhausted, but with huge smiles on our faces. We were ready to go.

Upon our arrival at the Canadian border in the summer of 1974, a very serious customs officer requested all our paperwork and the list of items we were bringing into the country with us. My heart kept beating faster and faster. We were so nervous and excited, praying everything was in order, desperate for things to go smoothly. As the border guards searched our truck, they kept looking at our list, never saying a word or giving us any indication of what they were thinking. Finally, with a nod, the officer handed back our list and indicated we were through; we could now enter Canada as official Canadian immigrants. I wanted to jump up and down and yell with joy, but instead I got into the truck and waited until we had driven down the road before letting out yelps of delight.

We headed first for Peace River, a town in northwestern Alberta, to see the parents of a friend. They'd written our letter of sponsorship, which was required for immigration, and had offered us a place to stay until we decided where we wanted to settle. We had never met them, but we wanted to go and see them and thank them personally. And besides, maybe the Peace River region would be the place. I hoped I could get a teaching job in one of the small rural schools somewhere, even though I didn't have an education degree or teacher's certification, which would have taken one more year of university. I had been so anxious to move to Canada that I decided to skip my fifth year of education, despite the fact that I had a scholarship.

Our friend's parents greeted us warmly and showed us our accommodations. They were a kind, hard-working couple that cared for mentally handicapped children in town. We set to work helping them around the place and, over the next week or so, tried to find ourselves other work to hold us over until we figured out just where we were going to settle ourselves.

The Peace River area was beautiful in its own way, but not like I had envisioned the northern wilderness. Instead, this part of Canada was relatively flat land and had an abundance of bog land, or muskeg, as it is called in western Canada. Walking in the wet muskeg was like walking on a big sponge with little trees growing out of it. With each step I took, my foot would sink deeply into the moss-covered earth, filling my boots with brackish water and causing nearby trees to tip and come precariously close to knocking me in the head. Anything that wasn't bog was either ranch or

Stan and Terry on their wedding day near their cabin in Nicasio, California.

farmland. I wanted wilderness with forests to wander through and cascading creeks to splash in.

We only had a small amount of cash, a little less than a thousand dollars when we entered Canada. Luckily, Stan found a job right away working in the hay fields at a nearby ranch owned by Dutch immigrants. I was invited to help out in the kitchen. Every day, I soon learned, from the minute the men went to work in the fields, the women started preparing food for the midday meal, which, in that part of the world, was the main meal of the day. Bread was set out to rise, desserts baked, veggies gathered from the garden and meat prepared. I enjoyed this time and appreciated everything the women taught me. They were friendly, down to earth and easy to talk to. They told stories of happenings on the ranch and laughed easily amongst themselves.

But working on a ranch and preparing food in the kitchen, day in and day out, was not getting us any closer to our goal of finding our own place and settling down. And to make matters worse, I found out that without a degree and a teaching certificate, it was impossible to get any kind of teaching job in Alberta, or Canada, for that matter.

To entertain ourselves on Stan's days off, we would drive around the backcountry roads looking for deserted cabins and old homesteads to explore. But this only made us want our own place even more.

So we were ecstatic when we stumbled upon a TV program publicizing the new Atlin Provincial Park in British Columbia. The film of the park showed the most stunningly beautiful area we had ever seen in our lives. It was like a fairy-tale northern setting with a pristine lake, mountains and glaciers. We were so impressed that we immediately quit our jobs, packed up and headed northwest to see Atlin, BC, for ourselves, already knowing in our hearts that this might just be where we wanted to settle.

NEW TERRITORY

During the journey we were either choking from the dust or nearly sinking in the huge mud holes peppering the Alaska Highway. The Alcan, as Americans call it, was a long and arduous drive in the never-ending days of early summer on the winding mountainous roads of northern BC. There were so many mosquitoes that we had to keep our windows rolled up, even though it was boiling hot, to avoid either breathing them in or being bitten to death—or both. In 1974, the Alaska Highway was only partially paved and was endlessly riddled with sinkholes, frost heaves, washboards and cracks. But it was spellbinding to me: an exciting adventure with spectacular scenery, fascinating folks and wildlife in abundance.

We drove for endless hours through the expansive wilderness dotted only here and there with small communities, often little more than a handful of cabins, a gas pump, lunch counter and garage. If you were lucky, you could get a tire repaired or find a replacement at one of the abandoned vehicles lined up behind a garage; if not, you might be stuck for days. Beyond Fireside, the Alaska Highway then wove in and out of BC and the Yukon seven times, twisting and winding through a diverse mix of forest, meadows, wetland and more mountain ranges. We often drove for hours without seeing another vehicle. All the while we were mesmerized with the incredible views, each turn in the road creating a different scene to absorb, yet there was not enough time to do so as the next bend moved our view and senses in a different direction. We stopped often to take in the beauty, the scents, and to feel the wind on our faces.

The road to Atlin begins approximately a hundred kilometres east of Whitehorse, just after turning south from Jake's Corner off the Alaska Highway. It is the only road connecting the community of Atlin, BC, with the Alaska Highway, Whitehorse and the outside beyond. The Canadian Army built it in 1950–51, part of what was then called the Northwest Highway System.

After stopping in the town of Watson Lake for gas, we drove past the communities of Rancheria, Swift River and Morley River, which all

Original sign at Jake's Corner, the turnoff for the Tagish and Atlin Roads, with the Land of the Midnight Sun motto on it.

consisted of collections of buildings clustered around a lodge. As we neared Jake's Corner, where we would turn off for the Atlin Road, our hearts began racing a bit faster. Aside from what we'd seen about Atlin Provincial Park on TV, we didn't know anything about the town; to us it was a tiny dot on the map. Was it really going to be as beautiful as it had looked onscreen? How big was it? Were there facilities? What would we do when we got there? We knew for sure we did not want to live in Peace River, Alberta, so we hoped and prayed that this was what we were looking for—our dream place.

Almost immediately after turning at Jake's Corner our wide-eyed gazes settled on a beautiful lake nestled in the bottom of a vast valley rimmed with snowcapped mountains to the southwest. As our truck laboured up a hill above the boat launch and picnic area on the eastern shore of Little Atlin Lake, we found ourselves looking at a large swampy area, teeming with little pools and wet areas filled with beaver dams and waterfowl. We crested the hill and drove by the "KM 6" sign that would soon figure so importantly in our lives. Little did we know this sign marked the entrance to our future home.

Continuing down the narrow gravel road twisting its way along Little Atlin's eastern shore, we eventually ascended a long hill that took us up to a broad plateau. Then, moments after crossing the swath bisecting the forest that marked our entry into BC, our entire picture changed. We came over a rise and to our wonderment, had our first look at breathtakingly beautiful Atlin Lake, which was seemingly a lake with no end. To the west, beyond its northern edge, an almost symmetrical mountain towered boldly. Now known as Mount Minto, we later learned it was an old volcano sacred to the local Taku River Tlingit First Nation because it was where their forefathers moored their boat after the Flood, according to legend. We passed several lovely lakes, but nothing prepared us for the first view from the town of

Atlin sitting on the edge of Atlin Lake. We saw the regal Coast Range with its snowcapped mountains and glaciers stretched to the north and south as far as you could see. The quaint little colourful town sat on the lake's edge in the midst of this splendour, a jewel in a crown. The lake sparkled a rich aquamarine colour in the sunlight and the grandeur was spectacular. It's no wonder Atlin is called "the little Switzerland of the North!" The Tlingit named it *Ah-tlen*, meaning "Big Water"—which is very appropriate for the largest natural lake in BC.

Exploring the town was like taking a step back in history. This was a gold-rush town that had refused to die—an almost-but-not-quite ghost town. We walked down Atlin's historic Pearl Avenue and other side streets that were rebuilt in 1917 after a fire destroyed the downtown core. There were many old abandoned buildings as well as restored ones, including Taylor's Photo Shop, a mortuary, the Globe Theatre, Garrett Store, Moose Hall, Kershaw's Hardware, Atlin's first fire hall, general store, and numerous cabins, homes and small barns. Several of these homes, the Aurora House, for example, were reputed to have been brothels.

Some of the buildings were tilted and slanting and looked as if you could push them over; others still stood sturdily and were decorated with gingerbread or had bay windows, porches and balconies. All were wooden, mostly log or board construction. The Eggert Jewelry Store, with a barn-style roof, had the town clock, its hands frozen in time, proudly standing in front. Some of the gold-rush days' stores and buildings had been conserved by the historical society, as evidenced by signs and plaques. Many were renovated, too, all in keeping with the flavour of the early days. Next to the courthouse, which was built in 1900, was a cute little cabin with a widow walk and long dormer in the front. The main street had several buildings with false fronts. Flowers sprang out from window boxes and overgrown gardens. The former schoolhouse, built in 1902, was now a museum, the yard filled with remnants of the gold rush, including an old steam shovel used at one of the creeks. Fireweed was growing everywhere, tangled with wild roses. Rhubarb was abundant, having gone wild from the many gardens it once belonged in.

My excitement mounted as we walked towards the lake. Almost immediately we could feel a cool breeze and hear waves gently lapping the pebble-strewn beach. The foreshore was speckled with old boats. On the opposite shore stood Atlin Mountain, and we would soon learn that its three prominent peaks could be recognized from anywhere in the area.

Town of Atlin lit up by the afternoon sun with Monarch Mountain behind.

South of Atlin Mountain, on the other side of Torres Channel, stood another mountain with a pointy peak resembling a swirl on an ice cream cone (Years later, after admiring this mountain and its swirl for so long, I landed on it by helicopter and got to take a short walk around). The white of snow and glaciers peered from behind and to the south of this mountain. There was water everywhere here. I was drawn to the water, having always lived by it, and wanted nothing more than to jump on a boat and explore this vast lake.

During our walking exploration of the town we also met many "locals." Everyone was very friendly and willing to chat and answer questions. We stopped and talked to one old-timer called "Whispering Bill" near the lakeshore who sat hunched over on a bench in his bib overalls chewing on a piece of grass. He delighted in telling us some stories and giving us a bit of the town's history. As he spoke he looked off in the distance as if he was seeing the scene he was describing. We leaned near him to listen carefully to each word. Using his hands as he described the old days when boardwalks lined the streets, he told how on Sundays the ladies would dress in their finest and promenade around town. There were stories of gold too, and we were fascinated.

Our conversations got us excited about trying our hand at making and selling our art here in this friendly little community set beside this magnificent lake. We wanted to call this place home. After a bite to eat at the Atlin Inn, we drove past a craft store where we witnessed Diane, the owner, who we had just met when we stopped in, jumping in her car and driving away with a dog in the front seat and one in back. Others followed her down the street all the way around a corner and into town. It was hilarious!

We turned onto the Warm Bay Road, which ran down the east side of Atlin Lake, and stopped at a lookout for the Llewellyn Glacier. The glacier flows into the southwestern tip of Atlin Lake from the Juneau Icefield. It is one of the largest icefields on the continent, spreading from the Atlin region almost to the salt water at Juneau. Its tongues of ice melt into Atlin Lake, the sediments giving the lake its incredible aquamarine hue. The scene in front of us was undoubtedly the most beautiful we had seen yet. I felt transported to some magic place, as though I was in a fairy-tale land.

Our next stop was the warm springs where there was a pool about four-and-a-half metres across and about one metre deep, with very warm water bubbling from its gravel bottom. Just up the road was "The Grotto," a cave-like hole with surprisingly warm water flowing out of it at a fairly high rate. The flora and fauna intrigued me. There seemed to be so many extraordinary plants flourishing around the springs that I hadn't seen growing anywhere else.

Diane told us we could stay in an old granary that had been skidded into town and put on her property. It was a very small wooden building that really only had room for a bed. But we were ecstatic to have a place to stay in town for a couple of days so we could continue exploring.

All of our experiences in this new land solidified our desire to move to this area, but some tough decisions had to be made. After finding out I could not teach without proper certification, I now saw the value in continuing my education so I could both teach and create my artwork in this small community. It was a difficult decision, but in order to realize our dream, we had to make some plans to ensure our future. We had only our 1954 Ford pickup, our clothes, art supplies and a few dollars in our pocket. So in the end, we decided it would be best for my husband to go back to work on the ranch at Peace River and for me to continue my education.

View of Llewellyn Glacier from a float plane, one of many glaciers in the Juneau Icefield, showing chunks of ice breaking off from the edge of the glacier, the melt water eventually finding its way into Atlin Lake.

Our New Home

We were ready to head back to Canada: me with two credentials in my hand and Stan, who had flown down from Peace River earlier in the year, packed up and anxious to go. But we didn't have as much money as we had hoped to start our new life in Atlin. In fact, we had only a few hundred dollars—enough for gas and food for the trip if we were lucky. Apprehensively, we headed north anyway.

I put in a call to Diane at the craft store in Atlin and spoke with her about our predicament. She graciously offered us a little cabin on Grayling Lake, which was twenty-seven kilometres from Atlin. It was ours until we could get settled. She also offered to sell some of my woven wall hangings, which would help generate more income for us. Our first home in the North was waiting for us!

We soon discovered the cabin was more like a shack. It was small—maybe three-and-a-half metres by four-and-a-half metres—and had two windows, a makeshift counter, a bed and two chairs. But it was home. The lake was small and had grayling in it, but not too much else besides leeches and bugs. We couldn't even drink the water, but no matter, it was a place to live. And not only did we have a home, we were lucky enough to get jobs immediately as well. Stan applied and was hired for a job from a Local Initiatives Program (LIP) grant with some other locals to build playground equipment at the park. He was paid $2.85 an hour and had to provide his own tools. I procured a job for $2.50 an hour (below the then-minimum wage) to work in the other craft store in town. My responsibilities included waiting on customers, gluing small gold nuggets onto charms and making parkas.

I had been sewing since my early teens, but I had never made anything like a parka, which had a liner made of duffle and a shell with pockets, a hood and decorations sewn onto it. However, a job is a job and I was pleased to have one. There was one small inconvenience; it all had to be done on a treadle sewing machine. So there I sat, day in and day out, pumping the treadle on the machine, sewing parkas that sold for a minimum of $300.00

while I was getting only $2.50 an hour. I also had to wait on customers in between and make sure the cases were filled with souvenirs and gold jewelry. It could have been worse—we were finally in Atlin and I was employed. Besides, the owner was very kind and the job gave me an opportunity to meet a variety of townsfolk and tourists.

Meanwhile, back at the cabin, we ate oatmeal for breakfast, peanut butter sandwiches for lunch and beans and rice for dinner almost every day. We went to the warm springs and collected watercress, picked wild rhubarb, strawberry blithe (greens) and managed to get some moose meat every once in a while from our new friends.

Saturdays were washdays and I would spend the entire day at the cabin doing our laundry. I sorted all the clothes, dragged out the big round washtub and hauled water from the lake, heating some of it on our little stove. I used a toilet bowl plunger to agitate the water and then put the clothes through a hand wringer washer I had picked up at a secondhand store and into another tub. The washtub was too big to pick up or dump so I had to bail out some of the water in order to tip it over. Down to the lake I would go to haul more water and fill the tub to rinse everything, not once but twice. I had to repeat the whole process before I was able to hang them on the clothesline. A few Saturdays of doing this and I was starting to wish there was a laundromat in town.

Our time in the cabin was a bit of a novelty, but it definitely had its drawbacks. There was the constant problem with water disposal; everything from the washbasin and more went into a slop bucket. It would begin to smell in the heat of the summer and had to be cleaned regularly, which meant hauling and heating yet more water. The slop bucket also served as the pee bucket if you couldn't manage to run outside in the middle of the night. That meant it had to be cleaned even more often. After a while I would just start throwing water directly from the washbasin out the door to avoid the slop bucket completely. When it was nice out and bugs weren't trying to eat me alive I would even do dishes outside. I never thought I would miss a sink with a drainpipe so much!

As fall began to close in, I continued to explore the possibility of teaching. I applied for a BC teaching credential and met with the principal of the small school in Atlin, offering to help out where I could. I hoped it would help lead to a job. My seasonal employment ended at the craft store and Stan, along with a friend, Alex, whom he met on the park job, got work clearing trees on Yukon's Dempster Highway. Alex's wife, Sylvia, and I became very close and set ourselves to the task of preparing for the winter in the men's absence.

Firewood was first on the list. There was a sawmill outside of town that gave away their discarded slabs and waste from logs just for hauling away. Every day Sylvia and I would load her two very young kids in their Divco (an old bread truck of sorts) and head out to the mill where we would stuff it full of slabs, some of them even sticking out the windows, while taking care of the kids. The men at the mill just looked at us and shook their heads. They couldn't believe what we were doing, but we didn't care.

The second thing on our list was gathering food for the winter. We picked strawberry blithe for greens and buckets of berries while we had the kids continually honk the horn to scare away the bears. When our guys returned they laughed at our pile of slabs and how we acquired them, but were appreciative. Nevertheless, they still had to go out and cut "real wood." Many years later, Sylvia and I still laugh about this episode.

One day Stan and I had just finished stacking wood at our little cabin at Grayling Lake and were inside taking a break when we heard a noise outside. We looked out the window and there were two riders on horseback, a man and a woman. The man had on a fringe coat with a rifle across his saddle and the woman wore leathers and had a jug slung over her shoulder. They looked like something out of a movie set. We soon learned that they lived in a teepee nearby. They were concerned about us mistaking their dogs for wolves and wanted to make sure we wouldn't shoot them. Bonnie, who had a front tooth missing, carried a jug of "hooch" and every once in awhile Dixon would ask for a slug. They were quite the characters. We found out that Dixon was an ex-biker from the Los Angeles area, and Bonnie was quite a city gal at one time. Now they lived in the bush, almost exclusively off of the land, with Dixon earning extra money from the sales of his artwork. We learned later that he was a very talented artist. He painted, sketched and produced very detailed pen and ink drawings. He sold some of his work through the local stores and gallery and some independently.

We ended up becoming friends and visited frequently during our first fall. At dinner in the teepee one night we chuckled, wondering what people in other parts of the world were eating as we sat and feasted on our meal of fresh fish and moose smothered in freshly picked mushrooms with sautéed greens, and blueberry pie with homemade ice cream made from local cow milk for dessert.

Dixon Pagnella with his horse at the tepee. Photo courtesy of Bonnie Pagnella.

As the leaves changed to brilliant hues of amber, copper, rose and gold, then floated off the trees, Stan and I began to get even more excited about our first winter in the North.

But we were just settling in when things took a dramatic turn for us. I was offered a teaching job at the Atlin Elementary Junior Secondary School a few weeks after school had begun. A new half-time position entitled "learning assistance" had been developed, intended for experienced teachers who would provide support for students with learning difficulties. Since I was the only one to apply for the job, it was reluctantly offered to me, a first-year teacher. And of course I accepted—at twenty-three, this would be my first employment as a professional teacher. I was ecstatic and ready to go.

Two months after I was hired, the grade three/four teacher applied for maternity leave. Her job was posted, I applied and was hired as a full-time teacher. As my new position entitled us to housing, we packed up our few possessions, said our goodbyes to the Grayling Lake cabin and moved into town. I was thrilled. Our new home was the little house next to the government building with the widow walk that I had noticed when we first visited Atlin. It had a living area, a separate kitchen with a wood cookstove, two bedrooms and a small, empty bathroom-size room. It had electricity and was close to the school and all the stores in Atlin, but there was no running water. And, like many of the houses in town, it had an outhouse. There wasn't much privacy with everyone's outhouses in the backyards, and I often found myself waving to my neighbour as I traipsed in my housecoat in the early morning to use it.

After a couple of months, we were offered a small modular home, or teacherage, next to the school. Even though we were advised by some of our friends that we might not want to live right by the school, we took it. After all, it had all the conveniences, including running water and five appliances. The new job and home definitely changed our lives.

It was amazing how many friends we suddenly had. People would stop by under the pretense of wanting to say hello or have a beer, when what they really wanted was to use a real bathroom or maybe even do a load of laundry. At that time, Atlin still didn't even have that laundromat I'd dreamed about at Grayling Lake. So we accommodated as many as we could.

I soon found out why this was the most undesirable teacherage. The kids were always there, and everybody in town knew what you were doing. When we had a party, the parents stopped by unannounced. The first parent to ever come by and knock breezed by me when I opened the door, turned and asked, "What qualifies you to teach my son?" The good news is that eventually Stan and I became friends with him and his wife. I guess I'd passed the test. The bad news is we had other people we hardly knew stopping by at all hours of the night looking for a party.

The kids were always playing in the streets until late, still used to their summer schedules. Parents had difficulty getting them to bed at a reasonable time, which impacted waking up in the mornings. I could hear kids whining and begging with their mom or dad to be able to play longer. Black plastic bags covered many of the children's bedroom windows to create darkness and coerce sleep as the still-long days of fall continued.

When the first snows arrived, covering the hill behind our teacherage, the kids delighted in sliding down on anything they could come up with. I would awaken to happy kid noises and look at my clock and see that it was only 6:00 in the morning. I would put my robe on, walk outside and yell nicely at the kids to go back to the village and back to bed—or at least go eat breakfast and let their parents know they were up. It didn't always go over well. I felt grumpy and tired and was greeted by smiling, happy kids who just didn't understand why they had to go home. It often took a lot of persuasion, resulting in my day beginning earlier than desired.

As the days got shorter and shorter and the temperatures dropped, the lake began to freeze. The fog and clouds enveloped the islands in front of town, creating a mystical effect. The mountains sometimes poked through high above the fog and clouds, framed by blue sky, while rays of light searched for openings, shooting light onto the lake. Every day the scene changed, and as the water near the shore and shallow parts of the lake began to freeze, you could see pockets of open water. Some days the fog was so thick it covered the entire town, creating a dark and dismal feeling. At times it was depressing to wake up to no sunshine for days on end knowing the sun was shining brightly just out of town away from the lake. The smaller lakes froze early and became playgrounds for skaters, cross-country skiers and snowmobilers. People swarmed out of town to enjoy the first of the winter sports on the weekends. Meanwhile, I woke up day after day in the dark, taught school with grey overcast skies and returned home in the dark.

But then it happened. I woke up one day to sunshine and not a cloud in the sky. The lake had finally completed its freezing. It was magic—an instant winter wonderland. As I gazed out towards the mountains and the beauty of the frozen wilderness I quickly forgot I was ever depressed.

CHRISTMAS EXCHANGE

The Christmas holiday was just around the corner, and I was very excited that our friends Jon and Susan, who lived in the bush at the north end of Atlin Lake, had invited us to visit them.

Stan and I had never been to the cabin before, but we had a map they had drawn with directions. Our fresh food gifts were carefully wrapped in our down bags and items were arranged in our packs so as not to expose or crush any of them. I made their son a gift and packed that, as well as some emergency gear. Not wanting to leave our car on the road during the Christmas break, we arranged for another friend of ours to drop us off at the north end of Atlin Lake. However, by the time we arrived there, it was much later than we had anticipated. Darkness was setting in fast, especially since it was only a week after the winter solstice—the shortest and darkest day of year! We were on cross-country skis and as we set out anxiety was creeping in with the cold. We dreaded the thought of spending a night outside, as we had no tent and had hoped to arrive before dark

We quickly realized that making it to Jon and Susan's that day would be impossible. With the loss of the sun and the darkness came the biting cold. Each breath we took formed a cloud in front of our faces that quickly turned to frost. Icicles were forming on Stan's moustache, white covering his brows and eyelashes. It spread over us like a blanket. As we trudged along the lakeside trail through the snow, each step we took made squeaking sounds, which we had learned snow makes only in very cold temperatures. Looking for a suitable spot to set up camp, we suddenly came across two cabins practically camouflaged by the thick bush. In no time we were peeking into the windows and checking the doors—they were abandoned. One appeared to be a sleeping cabin, and the other could have been an old trapline or squatters cabin. Much to our delight, it contained a small, rusty wood-burning stove, two single bed frames with old worn-thin mattresses and a table. Critter droppings and squirrel stashes suggested no one had been there for a while, but the stove worked and that was all we cared about. Kindling was neatly stacked near the stove waiting for the next occupant to use. Very quickly the sound of crackling wood filled the cabin and we laid our insulated pads and sleeping bags out on the bed frames by flashlight. We fell asleep chatting about how lucky we were to find this place and what an adventure we had ahead of us!

We awoke early but stayed in our bags until a vague light of dawn began to illuminate the frosted windowpanes. The cabin was still relatively warm from the fire the night before, so we got up, repacked and checked our map. Before leaving we replaced the kindling for the next person who needed the warmth of a cabin and headed out, turning to smile at the little home that had made all the difference to us.

But we soon realized something wasn't right. At a point where the map told us to turn off to the right, the trail looked as if it hadn't been used in quite a while. We backtracked, had no luck and again returned to the same turnoff in the trail. We knew that Jon would have recently taken in supplies for Christmas; if this were the right trail, we'd see fresh tracks. It was very cold, but it hadn't snowed in a while and there were none. We were hesitant to head up this trail, so we continued on the main trail until we came to a second turnoff, slightly less used than the first. It was already midday and we knew we had better get moving if we wanted to find the right trail and get to the cabin before another nightfall crept up on us. Stan decided the only logical thing to do was to follow the obviously used main trail to see where it led—hopefully to Jon and Susan's.

Tracks were everywhere, telling one story after another. Tiny mouse paths running sporadically from one hole in the snow to the next, rabbit prints crossing over the mouse and vole tracks to a nearby bush where bark had been stripped from the branches. Wing-feather marks in the snow, specks of blood and the obvious halt of scurrying tracks told of an owl swooping down for a meal. Chickadees seemed to dance in the trees, moving from one snow-laden bough to another making cheery sounds. I was amazed at how these cute, little tiny birds with their toothpick legs could remain warm in such bitter temperatures. In contrast, the ravens made loud cawing sounds as they flew overhead, seeming to follow along with us down the trail.

After continuing on for what seemed like only a couple of hours, once again darkness was beginning to descend upon us. We picked up our pace and all of sudden things brightened as we came from our forested trail into a beautiful meadow with the most picturesque sight I have ever seen. A log cabin sat in a clearing with light spilling out of the windows and smoke trailing from the chimney. There was a small barn and a shed for hay. Horses were grazing against a backdrop of magnificent snowcapped mountains. The scene reminded me of a "Leanin' Tree" country Christmas card.

We were making our way towards the cabin when a stern-faced man appeared from inside. "Hi," we said. "We're looking for Jon and Susan's cabin and we seem to have missed the trail. Do you know where it is?"

"Oh no," he said, an almost painful expression passing over his now-friendly face. "You're not their friends from Atlin, are you? Susan's mother sent them airline tickets to visit them for Christmas. They left here about a week ago."

We couldn't believe it! I think we both stood there for a minute with our mouths open wide. We just didn't know what to say, let alone what to do. Why hadn't they called us?

Tim, as we later learned was his name, said, "Well, come on in." That was the beginning of our friendship with Tim and Eve. We unpacked our treasures and showered them with fresh veggies and baked goods. We took out the wine and the rum and stayed two days and two nights. We all shared a small, one-room log cabin and got to know each other almost intimately in a very short time. Eve was eight months pregnant and was happy for the diversion. She listened to alcohol-induced stories and we learned all about what brought them to the bush and their dreams and plans for the future.

Tim had a horse-drawn buggy that he used to take Eve over the lake to get to their truck so they could to go into town for her doctor's appointments. She was due soon and when the contractions started, they would make their way to the Atlin Road and on to Whitehorse.

We thoroughly enjoyed our stay and meeting these wonderfully warm, independent folks, but it was time to move on and head back to Atlin. The third morning we said our goodbyes to Eve, went on a tour of the surrounding area and then Tim took us through a trail to the north shore of the lake. We put on our skis and headed out onto the lake for our journey south back to Atlin.

Shortly after leaving Tim and Eve's, skiing on the lake ice became very difficult. There was a lot of overflow—water that flows from cracks and pressure points out over the ice. The water was quickly freezing on the bottom of our skis, hindering our progress. We had to stop frequently to scrape the ice off and start out again.

As we trekked down the middle of the lake, the shortest distance to the next point, we kept hearing loud booming sounds like a cannon going off under the lake, and the ice would shake. We had heard of this phenomenon and had been told that the freezing and contracting of the ice caused the loud noise, but even knowing what it was and that we were safe, we were still unnerved. The sounds were eerie and stopped us in our tracks each time. Even though we knew the lake was frozen solid, we stopped periodically to chop into it to check the thickness of the ice.

Eventually we headed for the western shore, where we took off our skis and fashioned a toboggan of sorts by cutting willow branches growing nearby and clipping them onto our ski bindings to keep all four skis together. This allowed us to put our backpacks on our little sled and begin walking. We traded our ski boots in for the much-warmer snow packs (insulated winter boots) we carried with us. This was how we trudged through the snow on the lake to the first tendril of land beneath towering Mount Minto, which Stan and I had seen when we first saw Atlin Lake .

Once again, the light began to fade and dusk crept over us, bringing a freezing chill to the sky. We found a little clearing on the shore of the lake to set up camp under the magnificent mountain. We knew we had just passed the Yukon-BC border, so we figured we had travelled about fifteen kilometres. Gathering wood was the first and most important task before dark. There was an abundance of driftwood and dead wood that was ready to collect, thank goodness! We soon had a pile higher than we were tall. Feeling satisfied, we broke off branches from the nearby fir trees to make our beds. We had read that a bough bed was a marvelous source of insulation when sleeping out in the cold. We laid the boughs out a bit longer and wider than our sleeping bags and close to a metre high. We put our drop cloths down and laid our sleeping bags on the beds; we hadn't yet figured out that a two-person sleeping bag was the best for keeping warm in conditions like these. The fire was blazing and we were able to cook a meagre dinner and drink some hot chocolate. It is an amazing and frustrating thing that happens when you are sitting in front of a fire (in somewhere around thirty below zero, or colder). You absolutely burn in the front and freeze in back. As soon as you move a little bit away from the fire so your eyebrows are not being singed, your behind is so cold that even with extra clothing on, you can't stand the discomfort. When we couldn't stand it anymore, we decided to climb into our sleeping bags. Every so often Stan would sneak out of his bag and throw another piece of wood on the fire, then we would doze a while, put more wood on and sleep some more, until finally all of the wood was gone. I knew then that it must be almost morning. I asked Stan what time it was. He looked at his watch, looked again and said, "You're not

Susan Jennings with the author and her dog Kodi in front of the Jennings cabin at the north end of Atlin Lake.

going to believe it, but it's only 8:00 pm." Our early stop at dusk (about 3:30 pm) and the fact that wood burns much faster at colder temperatures would make this an exceptionally long night.

That's when it hit me. What are we doing? Are we insane to be out in the middle of the bush in the cold with no means of communication, no way to get to the road, no tent or anything else? The answer was simple: Yes, we were pretty foolish but here we are. I knew it was going to be a hell of a long night as we were too cold to think about getting up and gathering more wood. Tucking my head in the bag and zipping up as tightly as I could, I shivered all through the night until daybreak.

Wolves howled in the distance as it was beginning to get light. I was never so excited to see morning; the sunlight meant warmer temperatures. Gathering more wood and lighting a fire, we had a quick breakfast of camp coffee and granola bars. Camp coffee is very simple to make and tastes as good as any coffee dripped or perked. You simply fill up your pot with cold water, throw a handful of grinds in, let it come to a boil, take the pot off the heat, add a bit of cold water to settle the grinds, pour and drink. Some camp-coffee specialists add a bit of salt to the pot too. Picking up our weary, cold bones, we packed up and headed out, staying close to shore. Since we were travelling down the west side of Atlin Lake, we decided to continue on and drop in on some other friends living in a trapline cabin at Logger Bay.

Pink clouds embellished the sky as we came upon Nan and Jack's cabin. Light pouring from its windows assured us that they were home. As we ambled up the trail, we heard a loud, "Happy New Year!" Until that moment, we hadn't even realized it was New Year's Eve. What a night to celebrate the new year coming in! Even more surprising was that the loud greeting came from Peggy, Nan's mother, an artist we had met in Atlin. Jack and Nan weren't even there. We walked into the warm and cozy cabin filled with wonderful smells from something cooking on the stove. "You're just in time for dinner," Peggy said. "I'm cooking up some lynx stew!"

I had heard that trappers occasionally ate the lynx they caught in their lines. I'd never eaten it, but what the heck, I was cold and hungry. In addition to the meat, the stew was graced with dried wild mushrooms. It was delicious! The lynx tasted like rabbit. To be in a warm cabin with a full belly and good company was more than anyone could ask for. We had a delightful evening and toasted the new year, falling asleep in a warm, comfortable bed.

The next morning, after a fabulous breakfast, we put on our skis and headed out again. We planned to cross the lake and continue up the shoreline all the way to Atlin. The crossing was good in some places and bad in others, with overflow, jagged ice and changing snow conditions, but we made it to an area with access to the Atlin Road. At this point, we took off our skis and crossed a patch of bush to the road to catch a ride. We figured getting a ride wasn't really cheating too much. We had hoped to complete the return trip entirely on foot or skis but we were tired, cold and not too far from town.

The first vehicle to drive by was the snowplow. The driver stopped to talk to us (everybody knows everybody in the area) and said he wasn't allowed to give us a ride, but if we hopped in the back where nobody would see us, he would let us out just outside of town. It was a catch-22; a ride to town, but in the back of a dump truck bed with sand flying around, not to mention the wind and cold. It was not what I envisioned when we talked about catching a ride to town! But I endured it and we made it home.

Another adventure now behind us, we were none the worse for wear, with plenty to tell our friends—especially Jon and Susan, who had neglected to tell us they wouldn't be home!

OLD-TIMERS AND TRAIN TRACKS

Atlin had so much to see and do. We explored endlessly around the area, following mining roads into the backcountry to the old mines where we'd wander aimlessly, taking pictures and finding discarded remnants of times long ago and wondering what life was like back then.

We had learned that Atlin was born in the last great gold rush of 1898, and when gold was discovered there, it was one of the richest offshoots of the Klondike gold rush. Some locals believe that a man named George Miller and his partner Lauchlin "Lockie" MacKinnon first discovered gold on Pine Creek in Atlin in the summer of 1897 while driving cattle into Dawson City. Evidently Miller passed on the information with a rough map to his brother, Fritz, in Juneau, who decided to investigate the area on the map with his business partner Kenneth McLaren. They entered the area by way of Taku Inlet and the Atlintoo River, crossing the still-frozen Atlin Lake in early spring. They were able to locate the creek and staked claims around July 1898.

Information concerning the new strike reached Alaskan ports and Victoria, BC, in early August and resulted in a rush to the area. At its height, there were as many as ten thousand people living in the area from Pine Creek and the shores of Atlin Lake to the nearby boomtown, Discovery, where mostly placer gold was mined. Total placer gold production exceeded $23,000,000. Placer gold is gold that has weathered from the host rock where it was formed and been "placed" either on a hillside or streamed by the action of water, glaciers or other geological forces. Past the town of Discovery to Surprise Lake, mines popped up everywhere on all of the creeks, where they are still active today.

There were a number of placer gold operations on the creeks in the Atlin area, with larger placer deposits including Otter, Wright, Boulder, Birch, Ruby, Spruce and Pine. The mining operations on these creeks continued to produce significant quantities of gold into the late 1980s. Spruce Creek, the richest stream, produced more than 40 per cent of the gold. Twenty-one other creeks in the area also continued producing gold as well.

Our neighbour in town, John Harvey, owned one of the largest operations in the Atlin area, on McKee Creek. Most of his claim had been hydraulically mined previously. His operation utilized a D8 cat for stripping and moving channel gravels into a pit for washing. Then a monitor, an incredibly powerful water cannon, was used to break up the clays and free the gold from the gravels that get washed into a sluice. The tailings were piled and two settling ponds caught the suspended sediments. Rewarded with an impressive 36.88 troy ounce nugget from his operation one summer day, he showed it off in town, loving the attention. As impressive as it seemed, John's paled in comparison to the huge 84-ounce "West" nugget discovered on Spruce Creek in 1899; apparently it contained over 50 ounces of pure gold.

When my mom and dad came to visit, we were invited to see a small gold mining operation that used a loader and sluice and belonged to my friend's husband on Pine Creek. Scooping loads of gravel from the surrounding area, he would place it on a large screen that allowed the smaller gravel to emerge from the other side. This went into a sluice box with water being pumped through to separate the lighter gravel (tailings) from the heavier materials (gold and black sand). This works because gold is nineteen times denser than water and much heavier than the other materials.

John Harvey (right) and his partner Harvey Evenden with the 36.88 troy ounce nugget found on their claim on McKee Creek. Photo courtesy of the Brad Smith collection.

When you run the water through the sluice, the gold will "fall out" as the other materials continue through. After running a load of gravel through, Jim stopped the water flow and checked the sluice for the gold. We were astounded to see several small wet nuggets glistening in the sun.

There were many operations like this one that started out as "mom and pop" operations as opposed to those with big equipment, lots of employees and twenty-four-hour shifts. Another man we knew who worked a claim in Boulder Creek, off Surprise Lake, had only four or five employees at the peak of his operations.

We met and spoke with many old-timers. One such fellow was Bob Fraser, who intrigued us with stories and spun yarns of times past. Bob was a real character in his holey jeans with his long johns poking through and wisps of hair sticking out beneath his old felt hat. His beard, moustache and eyebrows were stark white with tinges of yellow from a lifetime of smoking. He usually had a hand-rolled cigarette between his fingers or was chewing tobacco. When someone bought him a beer, it would be in his other hand.

Over time, we developed a relationship with Bob. One day he invited us out to the Noland mine where he was working to teach us how to pan for gold. It was an underground operation located on the richest bedrock gravel field in the Atlin area, and it was where the bulk of the gold along Spruce Creek was recovered. Here, gold grades averaged 0.54 ounces per cubic yard. In more recent years, the shallowest portions of the so-called "yellow gravel" were using mechanical open pit operations. Mechanical extraction is a dry method to extract minerals involving drilling and blasting to break rock and then direct removal by excavators. Some underground methods were still used too.

We sat for hours with our feet in rubber boots and our hands in the cold water of a stream panning at this historic mine. Our gold pans were well-used metal ones like those used in the gold rush days. First Bob had us fill the pan about three-quarters full of gravel. Next we removed any of the bigger rocks that were mixed into the gravel. He then had us submerge the pan just under the surface of the water and shake it vigorously back and forth and side-to-side. He directed us to begin moving the pan in a circular motion, which makes most of the dirt and clay wash out of the pan. Again we removed rocks or large pieces of gravel. Next we put the pan back under the water, making sure it was fully submerged, tilted it away from us and began swirling the pan side to side again using a slight tossing motion so the lighter, smaller gravel slipped out of the pan. This was the hard part; if you flipped it forward too hard, you not only removed the lighter gravel but some of the heavier material at the bottom of the pan, which, if you were lucky, contained the gold. We continued this process until only the heavy materials or black sand remained at the bottom. My feet and hands were freezing, but I was so thrilled that we were finally getting down to where we might see gold that I persevered. Lifting the pan from the stream with a few centimetres of water left in it, I continued to swirl the water slowly in a circle like Bob had showed us. Sure enough, we saw some colour, and the black sand sparkled with flecks of gold. You would have thought we had found nuggets the way I jumped up and down. We were rewarded with mostly flakes, but to me, flakes were better than nothing! My fingers were so numb I could hardly remove the flakes from the pan and put them into a little magnifying container we had brought with us. It was a great experience. I thought about the many hours of panning it must have taken in the gold rush days to recover enough gold to make it all worthwhile.

After warming ourselves up in the truck, we continued exploring the mine site. There was an old abandoned steam shovel, along with a drill, water wheel and numerous cabins. I loved going into the cabins to see how they were set up and to imagine being there, looking out the windows, feeling what it would have been like to have lived there, struggling and enduring the harsh winters.

I always knew when a woman had lived in one of the cabins. Everywhere we travelled, whether it was mining camps, on the shores of Atlin Lake or on traplines, one could easily see the female influence. Evidence of hand-painted wallpaper was a dead giveaway, as was shelf paper or part of an old iron bed instead of a few boards on some stumps, or an overgrown garden. The newspaper that insulated the walls was a gift to us explorers too, as it had dates on it and gave us insight as to the time periods. The articles told of discoveries and the frenzy of excitement surrounding them, and the ads proved to be a good source of humour—we were amazed at the prices.

Bob would become a constant in our lives for many years. He would stop by or we would have a drink at the pub with him. The older he got, the more precious he was, always laughing, forever telling stories.

One night, he and his friend Joe came by. They were in town and on a roll, drinking endlessly, after Bob had sold a few gold nuggets. Sometimes when they were winding down, they would drop in, knowing they could get a good meal and a place to crash before heading back out again. This particular night, Bob and Joe needed a couple of days' rest and some good

Bob Fraser, gold miner and one of Atlin's "old-timers," with the author's boys, Travis and Brett.

food so they could regroup, pick up supplies and go back to Bob's cabin on Joe's property near Surprise Lake. You could smell Bob the minute he came in the door—I'm not sure how long it had been since he had bathed.

Well, I made a deal with Bob. I would feed him, let him have a few more beers and stay the night or as long as he wanted, but only if he took a bath. You would have thought I was asking for the world—he was like a little kid, hemming and hawing and making up excuses and carrying on. I shoved him towards the bathroom and shut the door. A few minutes later, I could hear him calling me quietly. The door was open a crack, and he was standing in his long underwear. Now this was not the middle of winter, but in those days a lot of the old-timers wore their long johns year round, since you were always warm and didn't have to burn as much wood. Well, he couldn't undo the long line of buttons down the front of his long johns (they had the famous flap in the back for allowing one to go to the bathroom). His arthritis had gotten so bad it was nearly impossible for him to undo the buttons. I did it for him and then stood there with my hand through the door waiting for him to give me all of his clothes so I could wash them. He moaned about not being able to put his clothes on when he got out of the bath. I pointed to a robe he could use and he just looked at me and stated, "I don't wear those things."

I said, "Well, today you do, so hurry and get undressed and give me your clothes." So he did, and I got him cleaned up, fed, provisioned with home-canned and baked goodies and sent him and Joe on their way.

In April of my first year of teaching, I wanted to take the twenty kids in my grade four-five class to the historic town of Skagway. Located on the Alaska Panhandle at the northernmost point of the Inside Passage to the southeast, Skagway is about 160 kilometres north of Juneau, the state's capital. We'd been fundraising all year for the trip and I thought it would be fun to take them on the train.

We could board in Carcross, originally Caribou Crossing, a quaint little town just over the Yukon border only 144 kilometres from Atlin. It was once a bustling community and major transportation centre during the Klondike gold rush. The White Pass & Yukon Route Railroad, built in 1898 at the height of the gold rush and completed in 1900, was literally blasted through the coastal mountains in only twenty-six months.

The big day arrived. The class and I drove to Carcross and boarded the train with my husband, who was an additional supervisor. The kids were so excited they couldn't contain themselves. They were jumping around from seat to seat and sharing the candy and little toys they bought at the train station.

The first student to use the toilet facilities created such a distraction that all interest in the scenery instantly evaporated. Loudly proclaiming that you could see the train tracks through the hole in the toilet, he had everyone bolting for the restroom at once. Compelled to step in and establish some semblance of order, I asked for those who really had to use the facilities to raise their hand, which of course almost every student did. Then I allowed them to go one at a time. I also took my turn and was as amazed as they were—not only could you see the railway ties flashing by through the toilet hole, you could feel the air rush up between your legs. Disturbed by the fact that the used paper being dropped in the toilet was quickly blown away, I asked the students to please deposit their paper in the can nearby and not down the toilet. Eventually the novelty wore off, and we all returned to admiring the magnificent scenery.

As the train chugged out of Carcross and climbed up into the mountains, we were transported from spring-like conditions to a totally white landscape. Looking ahead at the tracks from our car, we were able to see the train snaking around huge sweeping bends. It clanked and jerked and swayed back and forth as it crossed the massive bridges spanning the gorges connecting one mountain to the next, and some of the kids grew uneasy as they looked down from their windows. Eventually we reached the summit and then began our descent, the white transforming slowly back into green as the town appeared before us. The kids became excited and chattered eagerly amongst themselves.

The main street of Skagway features historic false-front buildings, wooden sidewalks and a multitude of shops that attest to its colourful history as the gateway to the Klondike gold rush. Tourism was the main industry, but many of the shops and restaurants were closed as no cruise ships were due to arrive and the road from Carcross was closed for the winter. After our walk, the kids wanted to stop at the very first restaurant we passed. Luckily it was open, and the kids flooded through the doors and had a choice of seats. There was a jukebox, and once the students found out what it was and how to use it, they couldn't stop moving with the music, even while eating their dinners.

After our early dinner, all the kids wanted to do was go back to the gigantic gym I had arranged to stay in and play with the equipment. The Atlin School did not have a gym, often using the community hall for team sports, but mostly utilizing the outdoors for all activities. It was almost dark, so I figured it would be good to let them play and hopefully exhaust themselves so they would sleep well and until late in the morning. I called it supervised chaos, but Stan didn't see it that way so he excused himself and didn't come back until they were all asleep. Tired and with little energy, we made the trip home uneventfully.

When we returned to the classroom in Atlin, we studied more about the gold rush and how Skagway, in the winter of 1897, had been the miners' entry point to the White Pass, which led to the Yukon River and eventually the Klondike goldfields. The stampede to the far north, we learned, brought more than 30,000 people. Leaving Skagway, most chose the fifty-three-kilometre Chilkoot Trail that ran along the Dyea River. Struggling towards the summit a mere eleven kilometres away, they climbed over a thousand metres above the Dyea townsite. They then went on to First Sheep Camp, where outfits were weighed by those who could afford packers, and next to the scales, where before the last ascent, Canadian Mounties weighed everyone's loads, duties were paid and men without adequate supplies were turned back. Finally, they proceeded to the brutal thirty-degree incline known as the "Golden Stairs"—fifteen-hundred steps cut into the ice and snow.

Required by law to carry a year's supplies (a tonne or more, including 180 kilograms of flour, 45 kilograms of beans, 45 kilograms of sugar as well as all their mining equipment), the stampeders struggled under the harshest conditions—extreme cold, blizzards, deep snow, avalanches, and sun that was sometimes so bright that snow blindness was a very real possibility. The trail was either so rough or so steep that packhorses could not be used, and those who could afford to hired the local Tlingit people to help them. Those unable to hire packers had to make up to forty trips, travelling up to 250 kilometres to deliver their supplies to the top of the pass. The trip was hazardous and many people lost their lives or gave up, in some cases heading for Atlin, which was closer. Those who accomplished the feat wintered at Bennett Lake, which drained into the Yukon River, the "highway" that would carry them to Dawson City. There they built boats of all kinds and set out on the perilous journey when the river thawed in the spring and the ice went out on the lake.

The students and I went to the government building in town and counted the stairs as we walked up them. We then tried to see how close we could make it to 1,500 steps, going up and down repeatedly. Next, we measured a half-kilometre on the road in front of the school. We walked it twice, then re-walked the distance as many times as possible in an hour to get an idea of the distance the many men and women had to travel.

For years after our trip, my students talked about their train ride to Skagway. In 1982, the train stopped running, but in 1988 it was partially revived as a tourist attraction, running from Skagway to Bennett Lake, about halfway from Carcross. Then, in 2007, the White Pass & Yukon Route once again began providing scheduled passenger service between Carcross and Skagway.

FORTY-BELOW

Not wanting to live full-time in downtown Atlin next to the school anymore, Stan and I rented a wonderful one-room log cabin up on a hill, nestled in the forest outside of town near Pine Creek. But we kept the teacherage too, as the cabin had no facilities. This gave us the best of both worlds; a beautiful little cabin in the bush and a place in town where we could shower and do laundry. We were back to cooking on a Coleman stove, hauling water and using an outhouse, and we loved our return to simplicity. Radio and books were our only source of entertainment. The CBC Radio Mystery Theater was a favourite we looked forward to every weekend. It was a radio drama series full of suspense that ran from 1974 to 1982. It opened and closed with the sound of a creaking crypt door with E. G. Marshall saying, "Come in… welcome," and it plunged us into the world of the macabre.

Stan spent his days walking in the woods and hunting grouse for me to prepare for dinner and working on the rough cuts for his carvings. After grading papers or prepping for the next day at school, I spent endless hours knitting and crocheting items for us to wear and to sell. All of my mitts, toques and socks were created with my handspun, natural-dyed wools and dog hair. They were both colourful and practical. After dinner I would climb up onto our bed with my projects and snuggle in with the kerosene lamp burning brightly to take up where I had left off the night before.

Hearing wolves howling in the night was a treat. We would lie in bed listening to the chorus of their wails fading in and out, mixed with yips and barks. At times they sounded like they were mere metres away, and we felt like we were truly in the wilderness. One winter night I slipped on my shoes and began to trudge to the outhouse before going to bed. Light from the cabin shone on the trail so I never needed a flashlight. I was only a short distance from the porch when I heard a noise and saw movement in the bushes. I knew it wasn't a bear, as they were hibernating. I looked again and saw a dark shape. Quickly I turned and leaped up the steps to the cabin, leaving the door slightly ajar. Grabbing a flashlight, I slowly peered through the partially opened the door and directed the beam towards the bushes near the outhouse. All I could see were two bright green globes glowing in the light. As my eyes adjusted, I made out the form of a large wolf staring intently at me, not moving a muscle. We fixed our gazes on each other silently. And then in a flash he was gone, disappearing into the night. I stood motionless, reflecting on this experience. I felt no immediate fear—only a thrill at having looked so closely into the eyes of this fascinatingly elusive creature!

Our next Christmas in Atlin, Stan and I went to visit our friends Jon and Susan, who were now living in Fort St. John. We had forgiven them for not telling us they were spending the holidays with their family the Christmas before, as we had such an enjoyable experience with their neighbours Tim and Eve. Bonnie and Dixon from the teepee near Grayling Lake had also moved to the Fort St. John area. We hoped to surprise them and spend a fun week with both couples.

The cabin Jon and Susan lived in was extremely small and filled to the brim with their belongings. Bonnie and Dixon came to visit and had planned to spend the night, not knowing we were there. Our presence made sleeping conditions in the house almost impossible, so Stan volunteered us to sleep outside. After our adventure of travelling down Atlin Lake the winter before and sleeping in single sleeping bags, we had had a custom double sleeping bag made. Armed with caribou hides to lie on the snow beneath us and an extra quilt to put over us, we made our way outside. It felt astonishingly cold—each breath of air seemed to burn my lungs and the exposed areas of skin yelled out in protest—but I didn't realize the temperature was hovering at forty-below F (at which Celsius and Fahrenheit thermometer readings converge). How was I ever going to be warm enough? What if I had to get up in the middle of the night to pee? Somehow Stan convinced me it would be an experience to see if we could really manage sleeping outside at forty below; we had managed at thirteen below last winter on our bough beds, so this should be doable. Reluctantly, I climbed in the bag with all my clothes on, including my down jacket. Stan removed most of his outer clothing. Before tucking my head in like a turtle retreating to her shell, I took a moment to gaze at the sky. It was a wonderfully clear night with the Milky Way in full splendour. I caught a shooting star in my peripheral vision and if I hadn't begun to shiver, I would have spent time watching for another and observing the multitude of stars and constellations.

It was a long night. No matter how much we tried to avoid any of the cold air penetrating the sleeping bag, each time one of us turned, a sharp flash of cold air cut its way in. I had a fitful night and I woke up early, needing to relieve myself. I remained motionless, squeezing my legs together, waiting. When finally I heard noises from inside, I made a mad dash to the cabin to warm myself up, then made another one to the outhouse. I didn't want to repeat the experience, so luckily there was room for us to sleep inside the next night.

After a short but satisfying visit with our friends, we flew back to Whitehorse. We did not have a prearranged ride to Atlin, there was no bus service since it was New Year's Eve day and we didn't see anyone we knew at the airport to catch a ride with. As we were bound and determined to make it back to Atlin to party with our friends, hitchhiking was the only alternative. In the winter in the north, nobody gets left on the road. In a very short time, we were picked up by a group of people in a rusty old van that leaked cold air, who were luckily heading to Atlin. We were hoping they would drop us off at the teacherage so we could fire up our vehicle to go to our friend Dick's for the party. He lived in a cabin near Surprise Lake about twenty-four kilometres from Atlin. Well, the folks that picked us up had no place in particular to go, so we invited them to Dick's party and we all drove straight there.

The bridge that went over the creek on the driveway down to the cabin looked like a jumble of boards and logs, and was too unsafe to walk on, let alone drive over. Rumour had it that Joe, the owner, got mad at a guy who was renting the cabin, and one of them—we were not sure if it was the owner or the tenant—hacked at the bridge with a chainsaw to keep the other away from the place. When Joe lived there he just never fixed the bridge, choosing instead to take the fairly long walk up the driveway. When our friend Dick moved in, the bridge was still in a state of disrepair and was getting worse all the time. We had to walk very cautiously across with no flashlights.

I will never forget that night. Loud music penetrated the surroundings from the party, guiding us along until we could see the lights from the cabin. When we stepped inside, everybody was drinking, laughing and dancing wildly. We were immediately dragged into circle formation, arms linked, people swaying to the music as one flowing body moving across the floor. The cabin groaned and shook with each beat of the music. Worry lines crossed Stan's face; he was concerned about the cabin's ability to withstand all the movement. But the cabin stood strong as we greeted the new year and the festivities carried on.

We all made it back across the bridge in the early hours of the morning, exhausted and happy to be going home, the moon shining down on us, helping us to find out way. Driving home on this star-filled night, I was feeling optimistic about the new year.

This was one of the many parties we went to during our first two years in Atlin. Parties at cabins in the bush were a part of the northern life for young people. There was always a sense of adventure involved when you were heading out far from town, especially in the cold, dark winter months.

My optimism was short-lived, though, as a few days later our vehicle broke down. For a long time it had not liked starting in the cold, but now there were other issues, and it was going to cost more to repair than the thing was worth. A friend of ours loaned us his truck, but it had no heater and it was almost as cold inside the truck as it was outside when we drove anywhere. I would bundle up and wrap blankets around myself to stay warm. It was not a pleasant experience. Finally, I gave up on the borrowed truck, deciding instead to get some exercise and mush our dog to school each day.

We'd bought our precious pup Kodiak at six weeks old and trained him to a freight harness early on, as we wanted him to be able to pull a sled as well as be our pet and companion. A long-haired malamute, he was a big dog like his father Lobo, who had weighed a whopping sixty-three kilograms. Kodi was lighter, about fifty-four kilograms, but could pull a surprisingly heavy load—if he absolutely had to.

Each morning after I got dressed and ready for school, I would grab the harness, which was his sign that it was time to run and hide under the bed, where he'd stay until I literally dragged him out. We worked long and hard on this, as he never liked his harness, but we would go every day to school by sled eight kilometres each way. Most sled dogs are chained outside day and night, causing them to be exuberant about getting into their harnesses, hitting the trail and getting some exercise. Not the case with Kodiak, but after we made it down the steep driveway and were on our way he just kept going. We rode through a wonderful old homestead on the trail, Graham's farm, past the old Indigenous graveyard and into town using the back way through the village. Because Kodi was a pet, I simply let him go when I got to the teacherage and he played with the school kids until I was ready to head home.

The ride home was harder for Kodi, as I usually had five gallons of water and groceries. It was a battle of wills, but I won and I loved this time on the sled even though it was often dark. The air was crisp and cold, the evening light lit the snow up with amazing colour and everything sparkled. There was a peace and joy in those late-afternoon kilometres that I truly loved. It was my time to unwind from the demands of teaching two grades in the morning and three in the afternoon.

Terry mushing her dog Kodiak down the Warm Bay Road near her cabin south of Atlin.

Later that winter Stan surprised me with a puppy—a purebred malamute we named Jubilee, after the mountains across from Little Atlin Lake. She was the offspring of one of the lead dogs belonging to Bill Thompson, who bred and ran sled dogs, and who also headed the Commemorative Mail Run from Carcross to Atlin. This was a re-enactment of the sled-dog mail runs that took place during the years of the gold rush.

Jubilee may have been a prized offspring, but she was very difficult to manage. Some say it was due to instinct and some to over-breeding, but whatever the cause, she was very tough to train. She did her business inside the cabin way after normal training time and continued to for years later whenever she felt the need. But she could catch a porcupine by grabbing it on the snout and flipping it over and ripping its insides out without getting a single quill, unlike Kodi who came home repeatedly with his entire snout covered in quills and usually numerous quills in his mouth and on his tongue. Many a day we had to sit on Kodiak to pull quills from his face as Jubilee smirked nearby.

When she was a puppy, I harnessed Jubilee and had her pull around twigs at first and then small logs before graduating her to bigger logs in preparation for pulling a sled and eventually me. Years later, she would be perfectly capable of pulling a sled but remained stubborn and often didn't listen to commands. When let loose, she would run away for days, and if chained, she howled incessantly. Prized or not, she was a pain!

Eventually I gave up on Jubilee as a sled dog. Harnessing both dogs together did not work well either, as Jubilee had a mind of her own, and Kodi did not like another dog next to him. They both reverted to being just pets, with Kodi still pulling a sled occasionally, as he was more dependable and listened better to my commands. I learned you need a lot of patience to train sled dogs properly and that it is best not to make a pet out of a dog you want to be a working dog.

THE THAW

We were heading to a party at Palmer Lake one day when I turned to Stan and asked, "Are you sure we can cross?" I looked at the lake as we parked on the side of the road and hopped out of our rig with armloads of food and drink. It was spring and the days had lengthened significantly, the sun beating down on the frozen landscape. As a result, the lake was slushy on top and everywhere Dick's sled dogs had made a deposit the ice was melted even more, creating a circle several centimetres deep. As we headed towards the trail, there was a sign that said, "Cross at your own risk."

There was another car parked where we had stopped the truck, and no one was in sight so obviously they'd made it. We began to cross, gingerly sidestepping the dog poop holes and walking apart from each other to distribute our weight.

Later, as we sat on the deck listening to music, we heard yelling from the road: "Hey, is it really okay to cross?"

We would respond, "How do you think we got here?" or "No, didn't make it, ha ha." As the evening progressed, more and more people crossed successfully and we all partied late into the night, drinking and dancing inside and out and telling stories and jokes. Joints were being passed around for anyone who wanted a toke, but mostly people consumed huge quantities of beer. As the energy level waned and few remnants of food remained, exhaustion was taking over. When we started thinking about going home, we all suddenly began to consider the state of the ice again.

One of our friends, Bob, had already left without saying a word to anyone. Not good bush etiquette, but that was his way. Every party we ever went to he would leave, just fading away without telling anyone. No one ever knew if he was out freeing himself up for more beer or if he'd gone home. It used to worry us at times, but we got over it. Another friend, Len, used to leave from parties in town the same way, except he never even bothered to put on his shoes.

Tonight, as people were winding down there were jokes about Bob having left in his usual fashion. We wondered how far down the road he'd get before we caught up to him. It was mostly dark, with a scant few rays of moonlight shining through the clouds as we hit the trail to the lake. We worried that, if ice conditions had worsened, we wouldn't even be able to see trouble coming until we were in it.

Most of us headed out at the same time, but paused en masse at the lakeshore. We were indecisive. Do we go before our friend Len or after? (He was a very big man). One of the theories was to let Len go first. If anyone was going to go through the ice, it was him. The other theory was to go first and get the heck out of there. While others were debating, I took advantage of a break in the clouds and practically ran across the lake before the group started out. As I was making my way to the car, I could hear profanities when someone stepped in a slushy hole with dog poop, laughing, yelling and even howling at the moon when it appeared. Everyone made it, including Len, and we didn't find Bob on the road though we heard he got home safely.

Later that spring, one beautiful June afternoon while I was still at school, my husband was betting with some of the locals that he could hike over Atlin Mountain from Torres Channel on its south side to the Atlin River on its north side in one day. I was informed, after the fact, that he had bet that not only could he complete the task, but that his wife could too. He arranged for a boat to take us across the lake when I got out of school the next day, a Friday, to drop us at the base of Atlin Mountain. We would find a camping spot for the night, he'd told his buddies, and then hike over the mountain to the Atlin River where our friend Bruce and his wife lived and a group of people would be waiting for us.

The Atlin River connects Atlin Lake with Graham Inlet on Tagish Lake, another huge lake nearby. Atlin Mountain is a majestic 2,046-metre mountain with three distinct peaks, considered to be in the northern end of the Coast Mountain Range. Its most distinguishing feature is a rock glacier, a tongue of glacial ice overlaid with a body of coarse rock fragments and shattered rock debris that creeps down the mountain's face looking like a slow-motion rock slide. This was the mountain I was supposed to hike over.

All day Friday I kept looking out my classroom window towards the lake and the mountain beyond thinking, "Am I crazy? No, HE's crazy! How could he possibly think we are going to hike over that mountain in one day?" My stomach had butterflies in it, but I also felt a sense of excitement. I had not been preparing for a trip like this or any other hike, for that matter, in a long time. Teaching full-time and doing all of the domestic chores hadn't left time for much else. But there was no going back. I had virtually no time to plan, and that worried me, but I love adventures and exploring new places so I focused on the adventure ahead and told myself I could do it no matter what.

After school I raced home to change clothes. We grabbed our gear, had something to eat and met Joe down at the dock for the ride across the lake. Fortunately, it was a beautiful evening—the air was warm and the lake was calm.

We began our ascent a short way down the channel up the backside of the first small southernmost peak that, together with the three main peaks, gives Atlin Mountain its distinct profile. We had our backpacks and Kodi had his food and a bit of gear in his pack (we left Jubilee at home). Following natural rock slides and drainage areas, we were able to make it quite a ways up until it got too steep and I started to feel really uncomfortable. I mean, hiking is one thing, and rock climbing is quite another—it was something I knew nothing about and was not prepared for. We got ourselves in a bit of a precarious situation and went back down to find a better path up. By this time, 10:00 pm, it was getting to be dusk. The sky would only darken for a few hours in June, but never turn pitch black. We'd made it halfway up the smallest peak on the south side of the mountain and we decided to settle in for the night on a bed of gravel. The ground was steep, so we had to carve out a bit of a niche into the slope, using the gravel to mould a bed around us.

I had hardly noticed the moon, but as I snuggled into my sleeping bag, it shone brightly, illuminating the water below. Our site was high above the trees and we had a perfect view of Torres Channel with the Cathedral Mountains standing tall in their beauty and the top of Teresa Island glowing with moonlight with each ripple of water casting light off of it. It was breathtakingly beautiful; almost incomprehensible. Where we were was pristine wilderness; we had a view very few people will ever have the privilege of seeing. As spectacular as it was from where we lay, we didn't dwell on it for too long, as we needed to get some sleep.

After a bit of a fitful night, we were up at first light, which was 4:00 am. We ate a cold breakfast, packed up and headed off, maintaining our northwesterly course. The walking was easier the higher we went, as the brush thinned out and there were more wide-open areas to traverse. We crested the top of the small peak and headed up the first of the three main peaks. It was a gorgeous day and we were in good spirits.

After rounding the second peak, we began heading up the main peak, the highest point of the mountain. We stopped frequently and snacked, but

Stan was always walking far ahead and, by now tired and out of breath, I had to hurry to keep up. We had planned to skirt the peak and slowly begin our descent, keeping as high as we could, since the walking was easier. As steep as the mountain looks from the shores of Atlin, there were a surprising number of large, open, gradually sloping areas. Snow hugged the ravines and shadowed areas. We rounded a rocky rise and could not believe what we saw: a herd of dozens of caribou at the top of the mountain. Their bodies were silhouetted against the snow, antlers catching the light as they moved their heads up and down, eating something exposed through the snow. We kept Kodiak near us so he wouldn't disturb these amazing animals.

I think Kodi and I must have been watching them for a long time, lost in the moment, because all of a sudden I realized Stan was well ahead of us, and that Kodi and I had better get going. I hurried to catch up, but it was difficult as the descent was fairly steep. About halfway to Stan, I noticed that Kodiak was not following in my footsteps. He remained higher up, seeming hesitant to continue down. I called, then Stan called, but the dog just stood there making shrugging motions until we realized what was happening. I called him frantically to ensure he got to me before his little pack came off but, in no time, it fell to the ground.

Very pleased with himself, Kodi raced down, leaving the pack behind, quite a ways above where I was standing. So of course I had to go back up and get it.

As we climbed down behind the third peak, I was struck by the variety of vegetation. There were plants growing in this surprisingly lush environment that I had never seen in Atlin or the surrounding area, and I made a mental note to check the names when I got back. Along the way we'd started seeing unmistakable signs that there were bears in the area. Droppings, or bear scat, began to appear everywhere but, we were relieved to see, they weren't fresh. All of a sudden, though, I came across still-steaming bear droppings that I imagined came from the biggest grizzly I had ever seen. Boy, did that put a lift in my step!

Unfortunately, trails were virtually non-existent. We would find something that looked like a narrow path through the bush and it would quickly fade, so we started wandering through endless shrubs with no real path. There were many creeks and a main runoff area that was easier to follow than continuing to forge through the thick brush, so we started down this. At one point we stopped, took our boots off and tried walking in the creek, but in the end we just walked through with them on. We weren't too worried

Atlin Mountain, traversed by the author and her husband starting on the left, hiking across the three main peaks and down to Tagish Lake.

about getting our boots wet; it was summer and if we just kept on, we'd make Johnson's that night.

By mid-afternoon, we were on the flats behind the mountain. I was so tired. My mind was working, but my body wasn't behaving properly; it wasn't doing what it was told. When there was a log I had to go over, my leg would not lift that high no matter what I told it to do. I had to physically lift it and place it over the obstacle. I looked at the mountains to the northwest, in the direction of the Chilkoot Pass, thinking of the stampeders and how they struggled on their climb to the summit, wondering how they were able to persevere.

The flats seemed to go on forever. We continued to angle to the northwest so we would come out near the river as close to its mouth as possible across from Taku Landing, or Taku, as the locals called it. Here, decades ago, passengers and freight from Carcross bound for Atlin were transferred to the world's shortest narrow-gauge railway, which ran the three-and-a-half kilometres between Taku Arm and the shore of Atlin Lake, where they were loaded onto another lake boat, the MV *Tarahne*. Our friends lived on a piece of property bought by the railway company.

Our drinking water ran out, as we didn't think we would be hiking for so long. Stan drank from a questionable water source, but I declined. We had to be near the river or the banks of Tagish Lake, and that water was drinkable. It seemed we had been walking forever—it was getting late and we were exhausted!

Finally, we could see light through the trees and then water. Ah, Tagish Lake—the sight gave us extra motivation to continue on more quickly. When at last we broke through the bush and stumbled onto a trail that ran along the shoreline, we couldn't believe our eyes. We were at the sawmill—eight kilometres from where we were supposed to end up. I could have cried.

We had arranged with our friends that when we got to the north end of the Atlin River across from Taku Landing, we would fire three shots from our rifle to alert someone to come and pick us up by boat and take us back to the other side where the Johnsons lived and everyone would be waiting. So even though we were discouraged, we figured if we fired the shots, someone would hear and come and find us. Stan un-shouldered his gun, aimed at the sky and pulled the trigger. I didn't even hear the click because I'd plugged my ears—the gun had misfired. I immediately envisioned grizzly bears attacking, Stan firing that cartridge and *oops*, a misfire. I couldn't believe it. Saying nothing, Stan carefully removed the faulty cartridge and tossed it, to be absolutely sure it wouldn't get mixed in with the others, reloaded and fired off the three shots. We weren't sure if the shots would be heard, so we started to walk the trail along the shore.

Walking the trail was a hundred times easier than being in the bush, but I was so tired I was getting giddy and stumbling around, thinking that any minute I would collapse. We rounded a curve a few kilometres down the trail and came across a trapline cabin. We thought we would take a quick peek at it and have a short stop. The door wasn't locked, as most trapline cabins weren't, so we pushed it open and began to walk in when out of nowhere an arm appeared, scaring the living daylights out of us. In the hand belonging to this arm was a cold beer. Were we imagining it? No, it was one of our friends who had heard the shots and headed this way. He saw us coming and hid in the cabin, assuming we would check it out. It was by far the best beer I had ever drank in my life and I don't even like beer!

Somehow we made it to the boat, across the river and back to our friends where a party was happening. We were the heroes—we had made it, and there was tons of food and drink to celebrate. It was all very wonderful, but I was too tired to eat, drink or really talk to anyone. All I remember is climbing into a tent, taking off my clothes and curling up in my sleeping bag. I don't even know how I got my sleeping bag out or whose tent I was in, but I was done! I woke up off and on hearing laughter and music, but only for fleeting moments. I was out for the night.

MV Tarahne, a propeller luxury liner built in 1917 to transport people and supplies between Atlin and Scotia Bay, now resting on the shore of Atlin Lake.

We later learned that we had hiked over forty-eight kilometres that day. Don't ask me how: youth, ignorance, a sense of adventure, a little of all of it. It certainly gave the town something to talk about for quite a while. There were a lot of people trying to make bets with my husband about future challenges, but I think he had learned that there were to be no bets without my consent from now on. I never wanted to get myself "caught" in another situation quite like that again, but I did manage to get myself trapped into many more adventures.

As much fun as we were having living in the North, by spring of our second year in Atlin we were not as optimistic or content as we had thought we would be. We found many of our friends and so-called acquaintances to be extremely prejudiced towards Americans, and I didn't understand this. After the gold rush in the twenties and thirties, the town survived thanks to tourists, many of them American. Wealthy socialites from Juneau had summer homes in Atlin. Draft dodgers had found their way to Atlin and settled permanently. Like us, other young Americans, most of them very well educated, had chosen to live an alternative lifestyle, becoming an integral part of the community. There was a lawyer living in a tepee, a counsellor on a trapline, doctors who had made their second homes in town—many skilled and accomplished individuals. We were astounded when after a few beers in the local pub these people we knew and whose kids I taught began to rant and rave about Americans. It was discouraging. We just never knew when someone was going to start going on about those "in your face" Americans, and it was definitely beginning to take a bit of a toll on us. One of the worst offenders was my principal, who did not hesitate to express his distaste for Americans, often referring to me and another teacher as "the Americans." He was not blatantly rude, but I couldn't help but feel like he resented having Americans instead of Canadians on staff.

Moving On

As the sun shone later into the evenings, we started thinking more about possibly relocating. We considered Alaska, where Stan's roots were, but another place that had always intrigued us was around Marble Mountain Wilderness in northern California. We researched the area, checked out the real estate listings and found an unbelievable deal on a forty-acre piece of land in the mountains near a little town called Sawyers Bar. Stan was working at Atlin Silver Mine and couldn't get away, so I flew down and checked out the property. The acreage bordered a national forest and had two creeks flowing through it, several springs, meadows of ferns and flowers and some huge old-growth cedar trees. It seemed perfect for us. We bought it and planned to move south after I finished my school year in Atlin.

The end of June came quickly and I was both excited and apprehensive about the move. I had grown very attached to my students as well as many people in town and was going to miss them all. I already felt a void in my heart, a pit in my stomach, each time my attention wavered from my present task of planning a year-end field trip for my students to leaving Atlin. Weather permitting, we were going to hike Monarch Mountain, the mountain that stood behind the town of Atlin to the east.

You couldn't have ordered a better last day of school for a field trip; it was warm and sunny, the scent of wildflowers penetrated the air as we all set out to climb the mountain. The trail heads through sub-alpine to a fabulous viewpoint overlooking Atlin Lake. Out in the middle, Birch Mountain rises out of Teresa Island, which boasts the highest elevation of any fresh-water island in the world. The viewpoint from the approximately 6.5-kilometre trail takes about an hour and a half to reach, with an elevation gain of about 700 metres. The hike is steep, and while some of the students ran up and down like mountain goats, others lumbered up slowly. We identified flowers and wild edible plants and took silly photos. As luck would have it, a leftover patch of snow appeared around the next bend and the snowballs began flying, keeping the students entertained for quite a while. After lunch, Stephan, my volunteer supervisor, suggested we go down to the beach on the lake at Pine Creek. It is a fabulous beach, sandy with the creek running into Atlin Lake. The hot day made it even more enticing, so we headed down.

Officially I was not allowed to let the kids go swimming without a lifeguard, so wading it would have to be. They ran and splashed in the water and played tag and got wetter by the second. What does my supervisor suggest? He proposed they take off all their outer clothing.

I yelled at the kids to keep their clothes on, as ardently as Stephan was telling them it was not a big deal, there was nothing to be ashamed about, that it was natural, and so on. "Mellow out," he told me calmly as he took off his own clothes down to his underwear (of course, they'd have to be the tight Speedo type).

"NO," I shrieked emphatically. "That is not an option here!" Ignoring me, the majority of the kids did in fact take off their clothes down to their underwear and continued to play, racing, rolling and splashing in the shallow waters. I was mortified and feeling helpless. My face was blue from yelling and my voice was hoarse. I was so worried about the parents finding out and the repercussions that I didn't know what I was going to do. Thank goodness time was on my side and the kids had to be home. I was finally able to convince them that we had to go. Reluctantly, they got dressed and we made our way back to school.

Fortunately, I didn't have to face the kids or their parents, as it was the very last day of school, and I can't imagine what I'd have done or said if I had. I drew comfort from the fact that I wouldn't see them the next day or maybe ever again. I was still worried, though, and wanted to leave right away. Stan sympathized with my dilemma so we finished packing up our new three-ton truck and early the next morning we threw the dogs in and headed south as the sun was beginning to appear in the eastern sky. I figured it was best to get out of "Dodge"!

Our California dream did not turn out as we had hoped. Shortly after we moved, even though we were living amidst the beauty of mountains, our longing for the North overtook us. California's wilderness felt far too tame. We missed the vastness of the land, the wild remoteness, the abundance of wildlife, the sound of wolves howling, the warm chinook winds following a bitter cold spell, the northern lifestyle different in so many ways from what we'd experienced in the lower forty-eight.

But we were there now, and while I worked for two months as a teacher in a temporary position in the nearby town of Etna, California, Stan began building a six-by-seven-metre cabin. Constructed out of rough-milled lumber near a stand of old-growth cedar trees and a spring, it was designed with an open plan downstairs and a loft for sleeping.

We easily survived the winter in our partly finished cabin but at 1,524 metres elevation, we were snowed in most of the time. The high mounds of snow were not like the light fluffy snow of the dry north—they were very heavy, making it difficult to do much of anything. We had to snowshoe almost 1.6 kilometres to the main road where we left our truck, or drive to the small town of Sawyers Bar to get supplies or socialize. It became my job after each snowfall to break trail to the road as I was lighter and stayed more afloat on the snow; Stan sank several feet with each step. Our escapades at the local pub in Sawyers Bar formed friendships and memorable times, but our yearning for the northern wilderness remained. We ended up selling our property and cabin "as is" after living there for only ten months and began making plans to head back to the North.

The May weekend before we were scheduled to leave, cars started arriving at our property filled with the people we had met, along with their kids and dogs. There was a huge amount of food and beer, a horseshoe pit was set up and games began with music blaring. Late that night, children, exhausted from playing, didn't bother to argue with their parents about finding a place to sleep. People began dropping onto the floor wherever they could or outside on the ground if they had a sleeping bag. It was a great party that carried on to the next day, and then one by one, people packed up and the cars drove away. Stan and I were overwhelmed with our going-away party and very touched by how much we had come to mean to our new friends in so short a time.

This time it was Alaska or bust, with a stop in northern BC to see our friends. My husband just had to know what it would be like living in "the last frontier"—his roots. As we travelled the Alaska Highway once again, we felt renewed excitement with each turn in the road. The northern wilderness had to be the answer to our dreams. Determination set in and our goal felt within reach.

Well, we almost made it to Alaska, but not quite.

During our stop to visit friends, Stan was offered a job helping to build a house at Marsh Lake, Yukon. Marsh Lake is about fifty-three kilometres southeast of Whitehorse. It is one of five large glacial lakes that flow into the Yukon River along with Bennett Lake, Atlin Lake, Tagish Lake and Lake Labarge. There was a community on its shores and this is where our friend

Theron was building a cabin. It was spring, and we had time to get to Alaska, so Stan took the job to make some extra money.

Setting up a tent right at the lakeshore, we spent our still-lengthening days exploring and visiting when Stan wasn't building. I loved camping next to the lake, listening to the waves lapping on the shore, hearing the birds each morning and seeing the sights at the swamp nearby. Each day I would find a new place to trek, climbing up the hills or skirting the lake. Occasionally bears could be seen strolling lazily along the shoreline, which was thrilling but became disturbing at night when noises nearby would wake me with a start and keep me up.

One morning I stepped out of our tent and almost into the path of my worst nightmare, a black bear lumbering towards me mere metres away. I was so terrified I could do nothing but remain still and silent. The "keep your distance, stand up tall, slowly back away, climb a tree if it is a grizzly or play dead if necessary for a black bear" procedure eluded me completely. I was too scared. Standing motionless as a statue, I watched through squinted eyes as it ambled towards me, sniffing the air with its snout. Passing mere feet in front of me, it continued moseying on down the beach, apparently not interested in me at all. The thought that I might actually get attacked was so real; one chomp with those strong jaws and I could have been a tasty treat. It was that close. Heart racing and nearly hysterical, tears running down my face, I ran to the work site. Stan and Theron dropped everything to see what had happened, as I was in such a state. After trying to alleviate my fears, they went back to work. Hanging around the work site for as long as I could, I cautiously returned to the tent, scanning the entire area to see if the bear was still nearby. I immediately moved the cooking area and all food even farther away from the campsite. I went through everything inside the tent, making sure there was absolutely nothing that might attract a bear, including things like Chap Stick, deodorant, make-up and sunscreen. I had heard recently about a bear that got into a tent and bit into an aerosol can of underarm deodorant and had gone berserk, destroying everything in sight, forcing a couple away from their site for a full day and leaving them in the remote bush with no food or supplies, only a shredded mess. This close encounter left me on edge, and from that day on my fear of bears has run deep. I did not sleep well that night, nor on many nights spent in bear country since then.

Theron had recently decided to sell his log home and wondered if we were interested in buying it. We checked it out reluctantly, but were not interested as we had our hearts set on Alaska. Later that day, Theron's wife took us aside and said to us, "You have to go to Harvey's. He has a place on the shore of Little Atlin Lake below his sawmill site; we go there to swim sometimes. It is absolutely awesome—you have to go and see it. It's not for sale, but we know he wants to sell it. It is a slice of paradise."

So after work one day we headed over to see the place, strictly out of curiosity. A winding driveway took us through the forest past the cabin and sawmill site to an opening with an inviting meadow bordered by a sparkling lake beyond. A quaint log cabin sat amidst the trees, beckoning to us. Wildflowers and berries covered the trail to the lake. The waves were gently lapping on the shore, motioning us to step onto its fine gravel beach. Across the lake were the Jubilee Mountains, and gazing south past the end of the lake you could actually see Mount Minto, the signpost of our winter cross-country skiing adventure down the lake. Looking back towards the cabin above the meadow was White Mountain, with Sundown Mountain in the distance. You could see the rocks intertwined with the new growth of spring travelling up the mountain. The little log cabin in the spruce forest was just like one I had seen on a calendar, the picture I had ripped off and kept from my youth. This was it: we had found it, the place of our dreams.

The waterfront property included the cabin, a foundation for a garage and four beautiful acres. He was asking $18,000 and only wanted to sell it to people who planned to make it their home—not a business or summer place, but their home, to develop and grow and love. Harvey, a small, quiet German man with a toothbrush moustache, lived nearby and was delighted to sell it to us. He hoped we would spend many years there and raise a family. Having completed the deal as soon as we could, only ten days after meeting Harvey, we turned off at the "KM 6" sign and drove into the driveway again, this time knowing that the treasure at the end of the road was ours. It was. We now owned property and a log cabin in the Yukon. Alaska would have to wait.

Our snug, seven-by-seven-metre cabin was built in one of the most popular and traditional log building styles, "Butt-and-Pass," using two-sided logs milled by Harvey himself. It consisted of two small bedrooms, an open living area and a bathroom-size room that extended outward next to the covered front porch. A big window that both drew light into the room, particularly important in the winter months, and provided a glorious view of the shimmering lake beyond dominated the living area that contained the kitchen and dining area. The kitchen had an apartment-size four-burner propane stove, a small counter with a sink below a window that offered

The author's cabin and first home on Little Atlin Lake in the Yukon Territory.

peeks through the forest, and a few cupboards to hold my staples and my yet-to-be-filled canning jars. There was no bathroom, but there was an outhouse down the trail behind the cabin.

Heat was provided by a sturdy, oval-shaped black airtight wood stove. A large blue old-fashioned enamel water pot stood on top of the lid to ensure it could not blow up in a strong wind; as well, the steam added humidity to the dry northern air, and there was always hot water for tea! An additional damper on the stovepipe controlled the amount of heat that escaped up the chimney. Trial and error taught us how to effectively use our stove. We learned that it is important to often let it burn very hot so creosote does not build up in the stovepipe, possibly causing a fire.

The exquisite joy of moving in and decorating our new home was bliss. I drifted in and out of the few rooms, fussing and fretting over where to put our few things, what to hang up to adorn the log walls, thinking about what kind of curtains were needed or even if we needed them and what we should purchase the next time we were in Whitehorse. A friend in California had given us a prized slab of walnut to use as a dining table and fortunately there were a couple of wonderful old captain's chairs left at the cabin for us to use with our table. Stan made a bed out of plywood and log ends and we threw our foamie down on top.

My antique treadle sewing machine, along with my loom and spinning wheel that I'd been so desperate to bring with us, became the central features in our living room, along with an old comfy couch I bought a cover for. As I fixed up the cabin, I kept pausing to glance out the windows, looking at the lake and mountains behind with disbelief. Did we really own this place? Was I dreaming? Meanwhile, Stan was busy outside clearing brush, attempting to hand-dig some of the stumps left from cut trees and gathering firewood that was readily available in the yard.

Living beside this magnificent lake was like nirvana to me. Standing on shore with the wind in my hair, my bare feet touching smooth damp stones with the water gently lapping the shore, I felt a connection to nature incomparable to anything I had ever felt before. The scent of the lake water blending with the ever-changing bouquets in the air was spellbinding. As the wind increased and the waves began to crash on shore, I could close my eyes and see myself next to the ocean. Water runs in my veins; it had always been a huge part of my life, and I couldn't live without being near it. How lucky I was to have found a home on such a magnificent body of water.

Little Atlin Lake is a relatively shallow lake, approximately twenty-one kilometres long, located in the Yukon River basin. Its shallowness makes the lake much warmer than the surrounding larger lakes. Straight out from our foreshore the lake bottom becomes increasingly sandy and at about sixty-one metres or so out, it drops off abruptly. In the heat of the day, we would take a break and head for the lake to play in the shallow waters before the dropoff, which created our own private swimming pool. Wet with perspiration from working, I would start down the path to the lake half-walking, half-running, removing my shirt and undershirt, then kicking my shoes off the closer I got to the water. Reaching the shore, and without stopping, I'd jerk one leg out of my jeans, hop to the other foot and yank the other leg out, barely wiggling out of my underwear before I'd race into the water, flopping down to feel the instant temperature transformation.

Stan and I swam for hours that summer, naked, a few metres out from shore, half leaping through the water, splashing and laughing down the lake one way, then back the other, floating, our chests to the sun. My hair was suspended around my head as I moved my legs like a mermaid might, the feeling of being one with the water surrounding my naked body was ethereal. Testing the depth, we would try and step-leap through the water out to the dropoff, seeing how far we could get, the water rising up to our necks and then our chins, just over our mouths and then the last step into oblivion, sinking completely underwater. Rising to the surface, splashing, we would swim back to where we could stand. We never tired of this on a hot summer's day.

Little Atlin Lake contains an abundance of Arctic grayling, lake trout, northern pike, and lake whitefish. But it was famous for its northern pike. More people fish northern pike at Little Atlin than at any other lake in Yukon. Our first taste of pike was when a neighbour who had just pulled several out of the lake dropped one by as a gift. It was so big we couldn't begin to eat it all and we didn't have a refrigerator or freezer. That is when I learned how to make pickled pike. We ate it on crackers and sometimes made sandwiches out of it. It was a staple for appetizers at get-togethers.

As summer progressed, we continued cleaning up the property and discussed where the gardens would go, the fire pit, and of course, a horseshoe pit. We dug a new hole and moved the outhouse from its old location, visible as soon as you drove into the driveway, to a new one down an existing trail behind the cabin. This gave us much more privacy. We oriented it toward the lake, giving us a great view, and didn't even bother with a door—it wasn't needed. The most important improvement was the addition of Styrofoam on the seat. We cut a hole the proper size and covered the entire seat area with the Styrofoam, ensuring a warm place to sit no matter how low the temperature.

We were very happy with our outhouse until one day when I was glancing out of the window and saw a small black bear walking near it down the path. It suddenly dawned on me why there was a natural path in front of the outhouse; it was a game trail. From that day on, every time I went to the outhouse I worried about a bear sauntering by in front of me when I was sitting in it. What would I do? There was no door to close, nowhere to climb up to, and I certainly wasn't going to climb down! I solved the problem by keeping an extra big "shit stick" or "poop pusher" in easy reach. In the winter your waste forms a pyramid, which freezes and doesn't collapse, so the "poop pusher" is a very important tool to knock over the pyramid before it reaches the hole. I armed the outhouse with a very big one to serve the dual purpose of "poop pusher" and "bear scarer." Every branch that cracked, every noise that startled me, I would start banging on the side of the outhouse with the stick like crazy just in case it was a bear. Stan would often yell, "What the hell are you doing in there?" Then I would finish my business, dump a scoop of wood ashes down the hole and scurry back to the house. I didn't have to worry in the winter months, but never wanted to linger during bear season.

Little Atlin Lake looking south as seen from White Mountain. The small clearing on the lake's edge, to the right of the treed knoll mid-photo, is the author's homestead. Photo courtesy of Christian Bucher.

We were in bliss in our new home, and it would have been easy to carry on as we were, in our own personal paradise, but the reality of having to earn money was inescapable. It was essential to find work. We had used almost our entire savings to purchase our dream. Stan needed to get word out that he was available to do carpentry work or other odd jobs and I planned to apply for a teaching position in the Yukon school district. When the news of a fire burning south of Atlin and a need for firefighters reached us, we jumped in the truck and drove the eighty-eight kilometres to Atlin to inquire about the possibility of working on the fire.

Blown Away

The fire in Atlin Provincial Park, the park we saw the film about that had led us to move to Atlin in the first place, was huge and burning out of control. Firefighting and the support jobs associated with it were a source of income for many of the local folks and an economic boost for the town, especially the grocery stores and local pilots.

Stan had his firefighting card and when we got to Atlin, he immediately signed up for a job. The headman in charge was a friend of ours whom we had met when we first moved to Atlin, and Stan got hired on right away as a foreman of a crew. Luckily he had packed some gear, as he was flown out right away. There was an opening for a cook, so I applied too. Though I didn't have any camp-cooking experience, I had camped a lot and cooked a lot and I was sure I was up to the task. But they weren't sure I was right for this particular crew of about twenty-five Indigenous men who had been conscripted, or pressed into service, forced to fight fire and who were not happy about it. The headman called my husband by radio when I was in the office to see if it was okay with him and asked him if he thought I could handle it. He replied with, "My wife can handle anything," so off I went. I had not been hired on as a teacher yet and the pay was good—$14.00 an hour for a cook. It would also be an opportunity to see new country—some of the most spectacular and unspoiled on the continent.

I raced home to gather together a few items I would need. My pack contained a small pup tent, sleeping bag, one change of clothes, several pairs of panties and a few toiletry items. Upon returning to Atlin, I was immediately flown to the main base camp on Pike Lake and then a helicopter took me up to my first camp. I was given no indication of how long I would be in camp or when I would be returning to Atlin or to my home. I was told if I had any questions or problems I'd have to speak to the fire marshal, our friend Bruce Johnson, or the foreman of my crew. But what I didn't realize was that, once in camp, there would be no communications with the fire marshal or, for that matter, anyone back at base camp either. The previous cook had quit and they had taken him out that morning. His helper went back to firefighting. Anxious to replace the cook, they hastily flew me in, expecting me to prepare the evening meal.

When I arrived, nobody was around. The camp consisted of a wall tent where the cooking supplies, food supplies and other items were kept, a decent size "lean-to" where the stove was set up and another large wall tent, which was where the sleeping quarters were. Plastic buckets served as chairs, and a piece of plywood over several of them served as a table. There was a small creek where an area had been dug out to serve as a cooling spot for perishable food items; there were no coolers and no ice. I wandered around checking out all of the supplies, taking stock and trying to mentally put together meals.

I knew the men had left early in the morning and that they'd return late after a long day of firefighting. There was time, and I was determined to have a good meal waiting when they got back, so I busied myself with cooking. Now, you have to understand that my camp stove was one of those small collapsible metal stoves with a very meagre oven and no burners to speak of. Wood was fed into a firebox located next to the oven. You cooked on the top of the stove, putting as many pots or pans on as would fit. It required feeding kindling into it constantly and turning or moving pots and pans around so that nothing would burn. Cooking on it at all was a bit of a feat, but cooking for twenty-five was a downright challenge. However, I didn't mind. I had all day.

I prepared a feast, including fresh biscuits, marinated cooked meat, rice, potatoes and gravy, cabbage and carrot slaw, veggies and two big deep dishes of plum crisp using the granola I had found. I wandered around and found some fresh berries to sprinkle here and there, picked some flowers for the table and waited, keeping the cooked items warm.

Eventually, I heard the men trekking back through the woods. Dirty and haggard after a very long, hard day fighting the fire, they walked one by one into camp straight to the table. They didn't sit, though, they just walked around staring at it, stealing occasional quick glances at me, then staring at the table again. I was getting a little concerned. What was wrong? Certainly it was nothing I had said. Was it the food?

Finally the boss, an older man, came and said to them, "Well, what are you looking at? Go ahead and eat," and he got his food. Still no one had said anything to me, so I just stood there perplexed. Eventually the boss came over to me, introduced himself and said how happy they were to have me cooking.

Then I learned the story…

They had started out with a cook who'd only lasted a couple of days before quitting. One of the young men on the crew decided that he'd take over (as he really didn't like fighting fire). He was not, however, a cook; in fact, he didn't know how to cook anything. So what he did was boil *everything*. The morning meal consisted of eggs and bacon, boiled in one big pot. For dinner they had been eating boiled meat, potatoes and veggies—all from one pot. That was it. Period. They had been living on this for a few days and were going crazy. When they came back and saw the spread they just couldn't believe it. They were dumbstruck.

After the men had eaten that first night they all went to their tent. The foreman of the crew and another fellow had their own separate tents and I was on my own. I didn't know where I was supposed to sleep and nobody said anything to me, so I put up my little one-man pup tent under a spruce tree. Not wanting to use the same "facilities" the men did—a hole in the ground with a board balanced between two trees to sit on and no privacy screen except a few trees—I practised no-trace wilderness camping in the woods behind my tent.

The first night after I crawled into my sleeping bag was pretty quiet compared to many of the other nights. The men were all very shy and only a bit older than myself. A few talked to me directly, but most waited until they'd crawled into their sleeping bags before yelling, "Hey, you wanna come sleep with us?" and other things like that, teasing and having fun, until their boss told them to go to sleep.

The young men, I soon came to realize, were totally harmless. Some nights after dinner they would go to the creek and have a sauna that they had made with poles and plastic by the creek. They heated rocks, took them inside and poured water on them. It was the only way to get clean as there were no other washing facilities set up. I could hear them trying to outdo each other with their stories, laughing until they were practically rolling on the ground.

The daytime was different. It seemed long, as the crew left around 6:00 in the morning and didn't return until around 8:00 at night. In the morning after breakfast, the men went into the cook tent where the food was and took what they wanted for their lunches, which worked for me. I then had all day to fuss and make dinner, and I now had a cook's helper to make it easier.

My chores completed, I had time to roam, except that roaming and exploring here was not the best thing to do as the bears, both grizzly and

The author's first firefighting camp, in Atlin Provincial Park.

black, had been displaced by the fire and posed a danger. In fact, there were so many bears around that the fire marshal had someone bring a radio to my camp, making me the only camp cook with communication to base camp. It definitely gave me a sense of security, though it was a false one because if a bear had come into camp, it would have taken a while for anyone to get there, by which time I could already have been attacked. When it comes to grizzly bears, you are supposed to climb a tree... so I had my tree picked out! I just wasn't sure how I was going to climb a tree with a radio. The radios then weren't like cell phones now: they were large, cumbersome, heavy pieces of equipment that would be very difficult to hold on to while climbing.

One day while preparing food, I was startled when the radio sounded out frantic shouts from a crew in another spot. At first I couldn't make it out, as it wasn't just one person but rather several people yelling. Then I recognized Julian's voice, an Atlinite we knew, coming through loud and clear yelling about a grizzly bear that had his whole crew treed. His men were frantic, screaming and hanging on to the tree for their lives. The bear was at the base trying to get them, swinging his massive paws, roaring, grunting and shaking the tree. In no time there was a chopper on the scene. The bear was shot and all of the men were safely down from the tree but one man, one very lucky man, had claw marks on his hard hat from this very narrow miss. He quit that day and flew home. I imagine he still has that hard hat and still tells the story. This bear incident completely unnerved me, since I was basically alone in a camp with only my cook's helper (who stayed in his tent after his early hour chores were done) and mounds of fresh meat and produce only a few metres away. We had no rifle and were a long way from anywhere.

Occasionally my long days would be broken up by a visitor, usually a foreman I knew from another crew nearby, who would wander in to see how I was doing and catch me up on what was happening in other places. One day a chopper pilot on a return flight from delivering supplies to a nearby camp picked me up and flew me to base camp on Pike Lake so I could spend some time with my girlfriend Sarah, who had just been hired. At base camp they had a real sauna for all to use. I spent a lovely day getting clean, visiting and watching a moose lazily grazing in the shallow waters of Pike Lake eating water plants. As special as it was to see this grandiose, magnificent animal mere yards from me, I was feeling a bit down because, in my haste to gather my belonging to fly into camp, I had forgotten to grab my camera. I wanted so badly to capture this moose in front of me and the beauty of this place on film. I mentioned this to Bruce, the fire marshal, and he instantly offered a solution. The plane that had just dropped off some men was getting ready to return to Atlin empty. He said I could jump on with him and come back later in the afternoon with a supply plane. He made the arrangements and off I went.

After landing in Atlin at the float plane dock, I jumped out of the plane, got into my car and drove to Little Atlin. I hurriedly said hello to my cabin and the lake and grabbed my camera before turning around and racing back to Atlin. I met the supply plane as it was still loading and said hello to the pilot, Dick, who I knew from Atlin. In addition to flying fuel in to base camp, he was making a side trip to a little lake and dropping off another man. The supplies loaded, Dick motioned for us to jump aboard. I climbed up on the floats and hoisted myself into the back of the plane, ready to take a seat… that didn't exist. The seats had been removed to make room for barrels of fuel and some other miscellaneous supplies. The pilot hopped in, turned to me and said, "Sorry about that—you'll just have to sit on a barrel. I wasn't expecting a third passenger." So hanging on to whatever I could, we took off. After circling a small lake I was unfamiliar with a short while later, we landed and the passenger grabbed his pack and lowered himself down onto the float then hopped ashore. Once again we took off, with me hanging on to whatever I could, as there were too many things in the way for me to jump into the front seat. Landing a second time at Pike Lake was a relief. It hadn't been a comfortable flight, but I had my camera and that was all that mattered. From there, I was flown back to camp in a small helicopter in time to prepare for the evening meal.

The next time I heard a helicopter, I hustled over to the landing area to greet my visitors. It was our friend Bruce, the pilot, and another man I didn't know. Bruce jumped out of the chopper with a frown on his face. I immediately thought something was wrong. As soon as he got within shouting distance of me he started yelling, "Do you know how close you are to the blades of the helicopter? Don't you know you could get your head chopped off? In fact, you almost did! NEVER ever get that close to a helicopter that is landing again, especially when you are slightly uphill!" He walked towards camp shaking his head. I was so embarrassed I thought I would die; ironically, I could have been killed, but that didn't bother me as much at the moment as being yelled at in front of the other men.

Walking sheepishly back to camp behind them, I invited the men for coffee and freshly baked pie. That was the beginning of many visitors. People started stopping by for a "coffee break" whenever possible, knowing they would get fresh baked goods with their coffee. Someone came up with the idea that maybe I could bake pies and distribute them to the other camps that weren't lucky enough to have a baker as their cook. I took full advantage on three conditions. Firstly, they would make sure I had the ingredients. Secondly, I wanted them to fly my girlfriend Sarah in to help, as it would mean many more pies. And thirdly, I wanted a ride on the helicopter to get a close-up view of the park, Atlin Lake, and the mountain goats I had only briefly seen through my binoculars on the cliffs of a mountain nearby. To my delight, they agreed on all counts.

My helicopter trip allowed me an incredible bird's-eye view of the nearly 300,000 hectare Atlin Provincial Park, the jewel being Atlin Lake, the largest natural body of fresh water in BC. Scattered all around were countless smaller lakes, some lying at the base of the enormous icefields. The Llewellyn and Willison Glaciers together cover almost one-third of the park, and the Juneau Icefield crosses the Canadian-US border, extending into Alaska. The park's vast waters and dramatic mountains are exceptional in beauty, and a playground for outdoor enthusiasts. Grizzly and black bears, mountain goats, moose, caribou, sheep and wolves, all were on the move now, disturbed by the smell of smoke and the sounds of human activity. As we circled above camp, gaining altitude, a brown streak caught my eye and then disappeared in the brush. Unsure of its identity, I couldn't help think how frightened the creature must have been.

We climbed towards the cliffs, and the massive glaciers spread out before my eyes in the distance, masses of frozen white with twisting black streaks of rock and earth running through them. We flew to the face of the craggy mountain looking for the goats. White specks appeared in front of me on the massive rock cliffs, quickly changing into the recognizable shapes of mountain goats. Perched precariously on ledges was a small herd, frozen, transfixed by the whirling helicopter hovering so near. I hastily snapped several photos to allow the chopper to retreat so as not to traumatize them. As we took another wide sweep of the area, Atlin Lake appeared below, displaying a multitude of colour variation from deep marine blue to aquamarine to cream where glacial silt entered its body. How lucky I was to get this opportunity to see this remote park, as it is not accessible by road—those wanting to visit this giant playground must boat in or fly in. One of the photos hangs on my wall today, reminding me of this treasured experience—my own personal sightseeing tour, paid for with pies not yet baked.

Sarah arrived early the next day. We spent the entire day making and baking more than twenty pies with all different types of fruit, chatting and laughing while we worked. In between, she played her fiddle. Oh, to hear the fiddle being played in the wilderness with the natural acoustics of the mountains! It was magic.

There was only one problem, and it didn't become obvious until we were done. There were too many pies to send on the small helicopter that returned to pick her up. A quick call to base camp was put in and a new plan was formed. The Sikorski , a nineteen-seater, was going to stop by and we were to give each man on board a pie to take to his respective camp. Well, I'll tell you, that day I learned a thing or two about helicopters—big helicopters, the kind that blow you away, and I mean literally! When they land, if you are not prepared and hanging onto a tree, then away you go. The chopper's rotor wash blew so hard I swear my feet lifted from the ground. Thank goodness we had the pies in a safe place.

Once the helicopter landed, Sarah and I started carrying pies into the chopper for the men to carry on their laps. The men were dirty, tired, trying to snooze if they could, and had no idea what was going on or why two young women were approaching them with pies in their arms. Clearly they thought we were crazy. "What do you mean, hold a pie?" they said. But once they found out the pies were for them and their buddies, they were quite pleased to help out.

As the chopper lifted off, the turbulence it created was absolutely astonishing. I grabbed hold of a nearby spruce tree and held on for dear life (or so it felt), briefly letting go of one hand just long enough to wave to my friend. Word quickly spread, even reaching Stan, who was working in a camp many kilometres away—everybody talked about the crazy women that baked the pies.

The work schedule was difficult for the crews with the long days, smoke and heat and the stress-inducing unpredictability of the fire. Most crews allowed the men fighting fires a couple of days off, returning to their firefighting jobs on rotation. My crew had not had any time off. Having completed their firefighting duties and mopping up in our area, we were told they were moving the camp to another location on Sloko Mountain, above Sloko Lake. So we packed up and were flown to another campsite.

By this time the crew was feeling more comfortable with me. Recently they had even been requesting that I make certain foods for them and telling me how much they liked what I had cooked. Having actual, though brief, conversations was a vast improvement and changed the tone in the camp to a friendlier one. I began feeling more like a sister and even, occasionally, like a mother to them, getting after them to move more quickly in the morning, suggesting they wash their hands before dinner, telling them to scrape off their plates before putting them in the dishwater—it was all in fun and the guys were not offended by my "mothering" of them.

It was now getting colder as the end of August approached. Our new camp, which was perched high on a mountain and had incredible views of Paradise Peak and the surrounding mountains, was at a higher elevation. Ice formed on the water buckets each night, wind blew and it rained, which was helpful for ending the forest fire, but left us cold most days. On one of these days I was graced with the most spectacular rainbow—it had me taking pictures from every angle. The moon was full at night and the smell of fall was in the air. This particular camp was not on any of the flight routes, but it was closer to my husband's camp. He was down towards the valley of the mountain.

One sunny morning after the crew left, I took a chance and headed down the mountain to see if I could meet with Stan. I knew the guys were working close to camp and I had found an old road or trail that seemed to head down. Walking was surprisingly easy, as there were many alpine meadows and the trail was visible all the way. As I was approaching the camp, I saw a man in the bushes "taking care of business" so I skirted him and walked on. I mean, who wants a woman appearing out of nowhere when you least expect it? As I walked ahead I heard my name called from behind. It was Stan. We had a quick chat and, unable to stop ourselves, a quick roll in the hay (well, actually it was moss, which is so much easier on bare skin) and then I headed back up the mountain. We did this a couple of times while I was at the Sloko camp.

As it was cooler and damper with the rainy weather, my little pup tent didn't quite cut it. It wasn't waterproof and didn't have a fly, so I decided, against my better judgment, to sleep in the cook tent. I knew you weren't supposed to sleep near food with bears in the area, and I was extremely nervous, but I had little choice. It really was the only place I could stay, as I certainly wasn't staying in a tent with the eighteen men left on the crew.

One night, not long after I'd made my move, I heard screaming at the top of someone's lungs, "BEAR! BEAR!" I froze for what must have been only a moment but seemed longer. I literally couldn't move, then with a burst of energy unequalled to any I had ever had, I ran outside into the bush nearby. I tried to find a tree to climb, but at that altitude there are no tall trees, only low shrubs, grasses, mosses, lichens and scattered dwarf trees. I crouched down as far as I could, frozen in place. I heard more noises, a yell, people talking, then silence. Not another sound. I was perplexed—what was going on? Had there really been a bear? Did I really want to go back to my tent where the meat was stored? How could I possibly stay out here in the cold all night? Eventually, exhaustion took over and I went back to my bed and had a very fretful night, feeling utterly fatigued in the morning.

That was it—the last straw. I refused to sleep in the cook tent any more. That episode set me and everyone on edge. I learned that one of the guys had dreamed about an enormous evil bear and it had created a ripple effect. Now the men were leery, feeling bad spirits were around and that the dream was both powerful and a message. The men wanted to quit. For my sake, the foreman and his second man made a lean-to next to their tent and I slept there, but not for long. Soon the camp disbanded and the crew went back to their homes. My job was finished too, as the fire was almost completely mopped up. I truly felt blessed to be able to see the exceptional beauty of the Atlin Provincial Park and surrounding area, but Stan and I were happy to return to our new home with money in our pockets!

Classroom Chaos

Living at Little Atlin Lake made it harder to get teaching jobs. After the fire, I applied to the Yukon Department of Education for long-term teaching assignments anywhere in the Yukon. These would take me away from home, but at least not for an entire year. When a substitute teaching position in historic Dawson City became available for the fall term, I applied and was hired, glad for the opportunity to both pursue my career and earn some serious money.

A historic gold rush town, Dawson is accessed by the Klondike Highway, which in those days, and still today, traverses virtually 480 kilometres of unbroken wilderness. Dawson was founded in the late 1890s by the gold seekers who made the grind up the Chilkoot Trail over the Chilkoot Pass.

I moved into an apartment complex with many of the teachers also employed at the school and formed instant relationships, joining them frequently to eat, drink and socialize. My roommate and I became friends and travelled by snow machine to another teacher's home several times, having to manoeuvre across the frozen Yukon River with huge jagged ice pieces of monumental size littering the trail.

In the summer, a free ferry service crosses the Yukon River connecting the North Klondike Highway with the Top of the World Highway. As freeze-up begins, the ferry service is suspended and access across the river is halted until a man-made ice path or ice bridge can be built across the frozen river. Ice jams during freeze-up had created the jagged ice shards, which had prevented the ice bridge from being completed when I was there. Once again in spring, access is halted until the river is free of ice and the ferry can begin service.

As the temperatures dropped in late December, hovering at forty-below, the cold weather burned our throat and lungs. We all juggled from apartment to apartment in the evenings with a myriad of excuses to share a glass of wine and the latest student calamity or happening in the lifeless winter community of Dawson. When we heard the news of Jim Jones' followers committing suicide in Jonestown, Guyana, we sat frozen in front of

The Yukon Hotel was constructed in 1898 and used as offices until 1909, when it became a hotel. The building has changed hands many times and was completely renovated in 2005–2006. It remains a hotel today.

the TV pondering this horrific event, so foreign to where we were and what we were doing.

On my days off, I roamed the streets of Dawson, marvelling at the old buildings with their faded exteriors and crazy tilts, photographing as many as I could. I imagined figures in the windows and the stories they could tell me. I was fascinated by the history of the town: the discovery of gold on Bonanza Creek in August of 1896 and the fact that Dawson grew so quickly from thirty to fifty thousand miners, prospectors, storekeepers, bankers, gamblers, saloon keeps, prostitutes and adventure-seekers. In 1904 it was the largest gold producer in the Canada and fourth largest in the world. A gold nugget was unearthed in the Klondike that weighed an unbelievable seventy-two ounces. Many of the wooden sidewalks I was walking down and buildings I was standing before were once filled with the sounds of rowdy, drunken prospectors, pianos playing, shouts from the gambling halls, dresses ruffling, sawmills buzzing, along with horses prancing down the street, their hooves making sucking noises as they struggled to pull their wagons in muck up to their axles. The frantic frenzy of the past faded as I struggled to keep my camera and myself warm. At those temperatures the film in my camera could freeze and tear if left out in the cold too long.

I went to the cabin of Robert Service, who was one of Canada's best-known poets and was inspired by the Yukon to write ballads that gave him worldwide literary fame. His first book, *Songs of a Sourdough*, contained his best-known poems, "The Shooting of Dan McGrew" and "The Cremation of Sam McGee." A bank clerk on Vancouver Island, he'd roamed penniless for years before taking a bank job in Dawson and becoming famous from his vivid descriptions of the Yukon and its people.

I also visited a replica of the former cabins of Jack London, an American author and journalist who made his way to the Yukon in 1897 as a twenty-one-year-old prospector looking for gold. He built a cabin on Henderson Creek near Dawson, hoping to strike it rich. He did not find gold after working in the Klondike so returned to his home in San Francisco, California, and began publishing stories inspired by his time in the Yukon. His novels and short stories, particularly *The Call of the Wild*, *White Fang* and "To Build a Fire," made him one of the most popular writers of all time. The replica cabin was made from half of the original logs of his cabin discovered in 1936 by two trappers on Henderson Creek. I'd read Jack London's books but will never forget the spell I fell under watching the movie *To Build a Fire*, which portrayed a man's struggle for survival before he died of hypothermia, the possibility of which seemed so very real to me at these numbing temperatures.

Before I knew it, it was mid-December and I was just finishing up my subbing stint in Dawson City, anxiously waiting my last day so I could head home and see Stan again. The art classes I was teaching to students of all ages were not the "textbook" demonstrations by teacher, complete with samples and material ready to go, as I had been trained. Instead, there was general chaos amongst the students, with the materials going everywhere and most often not on the paper or required medium. In the student's minds, substitute teachers were fair game, and it appeared to be their goal to talk more, fool around even more, and generally not complete projects, as it was just too much fun trying to drive me crazy. Classroom behaviour was not my area of expertise, and this school had some particularly difficult students. Their inappropriate antics made for some very long days at school.

In addition, I was hesitant to remove anyone from the classroom or send misbehaving students to the principal's office due to a very unpleasant experience I'd had. I sent a particularly disruptive teenaged student to the office after he ripped out a page in the science book and made lewd gestures towards me. The principal then called me in to the office at break, handed me a strap and told me to strap the student's wrist. I had no idea that corporal punishment still existed. When I refused, he then made me watch as he completed the task. I never sent another student to the office, and, for a week or so, suffered the wrath of this young fellow and his friends.

I felt huge relief as the last day of school before the Christmas break finally arrived. Walking into my classroom, I found I had a surprise visitor—the assistant superintendent of the school district. He was visiting and had come to offer me another assignment. After the Christmas break, he wanted me to cover for an Old Crow teacher going on maternity leave. Old Crow was, and still is, a fly-in community even farther north. My mind screamed, "Old Crow, oh my god. If it's forty-below here, what will it be there?" Since I had signed up for long-term subbing positions (or challenges, as I thought of them) and we needed the income, I agreed to this new assignment teaching grades one to three.

The historic post office in Dawson City, built in the early 1900s, is a prominent landmark distinguished by its three-storey octagonal corner entrance.

A week later I was on a plane circling the town of Old Crow. Beginning our approach, I could see ant-like figures moving towards the airport. As the wheels touched the ground, groups of people stood in front of the now-stopped plane, and even more folks were making their way to the plane from town. I learned later that what seems like the entire town usually turns out for the bi-weekly plane arrival. Kids and adults alike flocked to the plane to see who was visiting their town, and what the residents were bringing back from the big city of Whitehorse. Much to my surprise, everyone knew that the "new teacher" was on the plane. As I stepped out of the plane, I felt a blast of cold that immediately stung my face. I then noticed people pointing at me, whispering in each other's ears and staring at me. "You new teacher?" one of the children asked.

I replied with a big smile, "Yes." Suddenly people were tentatively shaking my hand and welcoming me in between hugging friends and relatives returning home and trying to look in the bags they carried. Standing outside the crowd, I noticed a non-Indigenous man with a big smile. I knew at once he was the principal of the school. He introduced himself as Ralph and helped me with my bags, loading them in a toboggan. Off we went, Ralph pushing the toboggan with my gear, to the teacherage down the road.

Old Crow is the most northerly community in the Yukon and the only community that can't be reached by road. The town sits on the bank of the Porcupine River, where it joins the Crow. Its name is derived from an Indigenous chief, "Deetru' K'avihdik," which means "Crow May I Walk." Following his death in the 1870s, the people named the river, mountain and area in his honour. Old Crow is north of the Arctic Circle and about 800 kilometres north of Whitehorse, Yukon. It is the home of the Vuntut Gwitch'in First Nation, which means "People of the Lakes," relating to the many large and small lakes in Crow Flats in an area north of Old Crow where they trap muskrats annually. According to archaeological evidence, the Old Crow area might be the site of the earliest human occupation in North America, which can be traced back about 15,000 years. The community of Old Crow became a year-round settlement in the 1950s with the building of a school and store. Before this, the site was a gathering spot for hunting and trading along the Porcupine River. The people throughout the generations relied heavily on the Porcupine caribou herd for their food, shelter, clothing and medicines. They still do to this day, making boots, moccasins, mitts, traditional clothing and other decorative beaded items.

When I was there, the population of Old Crow was about 300 people, all living in small log homes. There was a Royal Canadian Mounted Police detachment, a nursing station, a grocery-hardware store, an Anglican church, the band office, a community centre where potlatches, dances and entertainment for the community were held, and the Chief Zzeh Gittlit School, where I would be teaching. Behind the town lies the airport runway, which appears as a knife cut across the edge of a half circle, severing the town from the wilderness beyond.

The first six weeks I began teaching, the temperature was between forty-below and fifty-eight below or colder. The air bit my skin each time I went out. The hood of my parka was trimmed with fur, which created a cave of warmth that was invaded with each step I took. My breath was like a solid white cloud, creating the moisture that froze on my face and made my eyelashes immediately stick together. My nose would run and turn solid on my upper lip in seconds. Not wanting to remove a mitt to wipe it off, I would try to suck it in or blow it out in a very unladylike manner, holding one nostril and then the other, blowing hard. The many layers of my clothes were cumbersome and I felt like a giant walking down the road.

At such low temperatures, it is nearly impossible to work outside. Most of the community members spent their time gathering firewood and lingering by the wood stove. On top of that, there was only light for about two hours a day with a bit of dawn and dusk on either side. At school, when the bell rang for recess at 10:00 am, it was virtually pitch-black outside. At these temperatures, a wet hand would stick to metal (I once had a student who got his tongue stuck to a swing post), frostbite was easy to develop if body parts were exposed for too long, and your lungs hurt when you breathed. None of these facts stopped the students. They ran outside and jumped on sleds, sliding down the slope to the frozen Porcupine River, played tag, made snow angels and fought for the swings, all without complaining about the cold! The fact that the school was heated to more than 26°C did not help either, as the extreme temperature change only accentuated the cold. The school was heated by wood, and in order to maintain the proper pressure in the boiler system, the temperatures had to be kept high. In fact, they were kept even higher in the night and lowered some when the school day began. The teacherages were heated the same way. The winter I was there, it took up to three cords (a stack of cut and split logs measuring 1.2 by 1.2 by 2.4 metres)—that's right, *cords*—of wood a day to heat the school and a three-unit teacherage at these severe temperatures. There was an unbelievable stockpile of wood, especially with hardly a tree in sight anywhere. I wondered about this and learned that the nearest trees for cutting were about twenty-two kilometres away. Everyone just kept harvesting the small trees and each year they got farther and farther from town. In fact, many of the Indigenous families went out each day on their snowmobiles for a day's worth of firewood. When unable to do this because of some unforeseen circumstance such as a sickness, they would beg and borrow some wood from the school district. I never really did figure out how it all worked, but there was smoke coming out of everyone's chimneys.

The children in my class were absolutely wonderful. They were attentive, co-operative, respectful, eager to learn, loved to laugh and they were also the cutest kids you ever saw in your whole life. They would look at me

The author with her grade one–three class in Old Crow, Yukon Territory.

with their round little faces, cheeks frostbitten, eyes wide, big smiles, and it would instantly bring joy to my heart—truly a great reward. I would often tease them and they would tease me back. Once they learned some of my slang, they would delight in using it, always with a grin. I remember one little boy in grade two saying to me, "Teacher, you pull wool over eye?"

These children, isolated from the rest of the world and living without TV, had been raised in a unique way. I was privileged to go to a feast in the community hall while I was there. The entire town was in attendance and mounds of food were sitting on a long table. There was plenty of caribou prepared in a variety of ways, some moose, potatoes, bannocks and pies. People were gathered together waiting for everyone to arrive and for the signal to begin. And then the Elders began to be served. Every Elder in the entire place was served first. The children all sat quietly waiting their turn; from toddlers to teens, there was no whining or fooling around, just kids sitting, watching wide-eyed and waiting for their turn to eat. Next, the adults were served and finally the children. This would never happen in my culture. The young children would be pulling at their mom's or dad's shirt-tails, telling them how hungry they were or asking when the food was going to be ready. We would feed them to keep them happy and quiet and then move on to feeding everyone else. I noted the difference with admiration. There was a huge respect for the Elders.

I savoured the flavours of the wild meats and the different ways they were cooked. Equally good were the bannocks and many desserts. As people were chatting happily and finishing their meal, a man stood and addressed the group. He gave thanks for the food and proceeded to talk about the winter they had had, the many gifts they had received, their abundance in hunting, friends visiting, long evenings spent with friends and family. Then, one by one, other men got up and expounded on their good fortune and other events that had happened. I closed my eyes and thought back to movies I had seen of gatherings in a teepee with the Elders recounting their feats. It was very similar—a night to remember.

Many of the Elders did not speak English, but that did not stop them from acknowledging and interacting with us teachers. A get-together at the school brought many of them out. All of the women had very brightly coloured kerchiefs on their heads, beautiful parkas with colourful designs and appliqués and exquisitely beaded mukluks. Each woman took a turn coming up and shaking my hand, smiling and saying, "Thank you for teaching children," in their broken English. Each face was lined and wrinkled from the many years of harsh living in the north, but their smiles were warm, and their eyes sparkled while their hands shook mine. From that moment on, each time I passed one of these women in town, they always smiled and nodded their head to acknowledge me. I smiled and nodded back; it was a special connection that I've valued to this day.

SOLUTIONS OF A DIFFERENT KIND

A handsome young man appeared in the doorway of the teacherage in Old Crow late one afternoon. He didn't knock and I was totally taken by surprise, not only because the locals had never come to my door before, but also because I was stunned at how handsome he was.

I smiled and asked him if I could help him. He said, rather than asked, in a matter-of-fact sort of way, "You lonely. You need someone sleep with." I was astounded, in shock, and I didn't know if he was kidding or not, so I just didn't say anything for what seemed like a very long few seconds. Then he spoke again, this time asking a question, "You need somebody sleep with?"

I knew instinctively that he was not kidding. I smiled and said, "No, thank you." He smiled back, turned around and walked back down the steps. I have to admit I was taken aback by how extraordinarily good-looking he was. Had I been single, I believe I might have wanted to take him up on the offer!

Soon after this young man appeared at my door, Stan showed up for a visit looking forward to seeing Old Crow for himself. He met many of the locals and spent time with some of them. Stan loved the bush and took every opportunity to learn more about the area around Old Crow and the people who lived off the land there. One fellow, Dick, invited him to go to "Goose Camp." I don't recall if it was a trapline cabin or hunting cabin, but it sounded like an opportunity to see some of the country and get to know a couple of the men better. However, it was between forty-five below and fifty below and they were going by snowmobile. The thought of it made me freeze to the core. It was unfathomable to me that the human body could withstand such bitingly cold temperatures, made all the worse when going into the wind generated by a moving snow machine.

Stan, not wanting to appear like a wimp, agreed to go. He dressed in his absolute warmest clothes, pulled on his full-face wool toque and hoped for the best. Later he told me that the men headed out, Dick driving, Stan on the back of the snow machine and a third fellow jogging along behind. After a short distance they stopped and the man that had been jogging gestured for Stan to get off, which he did. Then the jogger took his place, and the snow machine started up again, leaving him behind, so Stan started jogging. After a while they stopped to trade places again, and so began the cycle began of jogging and riding and driving, which is how they stayed warm, because even the extra layer of clothing and long johns could not protect against the bitter cold. Their bodies stayed warm, but being unused to such extreme temperatures, my husband told me his lungs pounded with each almost painful breath.

I noticed that frozen long johns often hung on people's clotheslines in the middle of winter and this always puzzled me. Why would you put newly washed, wet clothes outside on the clothesline? And they looked so funny—arms and legs frozen solid, sticking out, moving stiffly in the breeze like planks. I finally watched someone take these cookie-cutter figures off the line and go in the house. I was intrigued, so I asked a local woman. She said that the clothes actually "freeze dry." The moisture is sucked out of them because it is so dry that far north. When you take them off of the line and bring them in, they thaw and are only moist or slightly damp. They dry very quickly inside by a fire as opposed to hanging them inside after wringing them out.

Yes, I learned a lot about the cold and about these people living in it. A while back, before I arrived, a government employee, probably from the health department, had told the people of Old Crow that outhouses were unsanitary. The solution was to have a chemical toilet inside the house and all of the waste collected in some very strong plastic bags that were to be taken to a special place at the dump. Toilets and plastic bags were given to the people and after that the residents didn't have to go outside to go to the bathroom. It seemed reasonable, so many people in town set up their new "indoor" toilets. When the human waste bags were full, they popped them outside and bam... they froze quickly (ready for the dump). Well, more bags were thrown on top of the ones already out in the backyard, and caribou scraps got thrown on top of them along with some rusty parts from a snowmobile. Ravens would dig for food goodies, and critters would gnaw at the bags, and eventually holes were scratched into the strong black plastic bags. So by the time spring came, it was pretty difficult to find the frozen bags that were now beginning to thaw to dispose of them properly.

As I walked around in the spring, at first I was puzzled when I kept seeing brown water running down the streets, gathering momentum and eventually flowing into the Porcupine River. Usually snowmelt was clear, there was still a lot of snow left, and it wasn't as if the ground was exposed. I asked my principal about this and he said, "Now you know why we cut ice blocks all winter." The school had an icehouse that was filled with ice blocks just waiting for the spring thaw so the school and teacherages had clean water for drinking as well as for showers that the townsfolk could use. Needless to say, it was worrisome to think about the sanitary implications of raw sewage flowing down the streets. I pondered the intelligence of the decision to provide chemical toilets to the Indigenous people, as they were so used to living in harmony with nature for so many years. I imagined people working in an office somewhere, having never spent time in a community such as this, unfamiliar with these northern latitudes and living needs, thinking about what a good idea this would be. I still shake my head.

I loved hearing stories of days past from the locals. While visiting, I once heard the story of "the phone." Almost every home had a phone, but it was not connected to anything. Then I found out why. According to the locals, the government gave them the phone. Many of the families in Old Crow are related to individuals in Fort McPherson, NWT, so there were numerous calls made to this town. Most often, someone would call and talk to someone in the other community, leave the phone off the hook on the table, and then someone else would pick it up whenever they felt like it to see if someone was on the line. This would go on and on and the phone got passed from one person to another, putting it down when they were finished speaking, and often leaving it off the hook all night. When the phone company wanted the bills paid, the people were perplexed, saying the government gave them the phone and they didn't have to pay. Hence there were phones in many of the houses but they were not connected. As far as I remember, when I was there, there were only phones at the school, RCMP station, Red Cross outpost, and general store.

The people of Old Crow loved to tease new teachers. I can remember one Saturday when I was taking a walk on one of the trails behind the village and Dick came up to me and warned me about a big grizzly bear he had just seen nearby. He used his arms to show me how tall and big it was. His eyes widened as he told me about this most incredible bear and how I had better head for home. Of course my first reaction was to head back ASAP. As I turned and started hurrying towards town, I heard Dick start laughing and laughing. I stopped and it hit me. There was no bear. Bears hibernate in the winter, especially at these temperatures. He was kidding me! Dick caught up to me and apologized for scaring me, still laughing. There is no doubt in my mind that I was the brunt of many jokes that evening around the wood stove.

North of the Arctic Circle, daylight returns quickly once you're past the winter solstice and the dark, dark days of December. By April, daylight increases at an astounding rate, anywhere from five to ten minutes a day— by June, it's up to seven or more minutes and in one week you can gain almost an hour. By June 21, the summer solstice, it is the "land of the midnight sun," which refers to the phenomenon of twenty-four consecutive hours of sunlight.

Spring is also the time of year that many of the residents of Old Crow go to the Old Crow Flats for their annual muskrat-trapping season. This area is located north of Old Crow and is approximately a hundred kilometres south of the Beaufort Sea. The flats are almost completely surrounded by mountains and comprise about 6,100 square kilometres, dotted with more than 2,000 small lakes, ponds and marshes. The northern portion of Old Crow Flats is located in the Vuntut National Park. Each family group in Old Crow has their own trapping area in Old Crow Flats. This area is referred to by each family as "their" or "my country" and is passed down from generation to generation.

More recently, Old Crow has been the Department of Education's only school community to operate on a different school year to accommodate the local lifestyle and seasonal activities. School began earlier in the summer and ended the middle of March, as entire families usually went to the flats after Easter break. But when I taught there, Old Crow shared the same school year with the other schools in the territory. Hence, when mid-April came, half of the school population left with their families to go trapping. As was the custom, the parents asked for schoolwork for their children to take with them out on the flats. The teachers spent hours putting together binders of work hoping that some of it would be completed while their students were hunting.

As the days grew longer and longer, Stan grew bored and was itching to go home, as spring had now sprung in southern Yukon. Working mostly on a seasonal basis, he needed to search for work as soon as things warmed up and building season began. He flew home a month ahead of me. On the bright and sunny day he was boarding the plane, enjoying the last breaths of the pure arctic air, the rest of the nation was reeling from the news of the nuclear power plant accident at Three Mile Island in Pennsylvania. I did not learn of it until days later until I was told by someone.

My class, now consisting of only ten children, enabled me to provide more hands-on learning experiences in the environment the students were familiar with. They were fun days. We became more like a family, participating in whole group activities. Cross-country skiing was a popular activity and trails of different lengths were groomed behind the town. As the days lengthened and warmed, I skied more, as many of the residents did, on the immaculately groomed trails. Some of the residents were training for future cross-country ski events in other provinces. Others, including many of the students, were out to just have fun.

I also got out into the community and visited some of the residents. The kindergarten teacher, Linda, was a local from Old Crow and had introduced me to her mother, Hannah Netro, a very kindly, soft-spoken Elder. I enjoyed visiting with Hannah and having tea and fresh bannock, a staple in all the households. Bannock is a biscuit-type bread that is a favourite of the Vuntut Gwitch'in people and is also used for special occasions and gatherings. Hannah's bannock was made in a cast iron frying pan in one piece, browned on both sides, and tasted delicious with butter. I asked for the recipe, which her daughter wrote down for me.

Hannah was usually busily working on a beading project during our visits, executing the endless task of sewing one bead at a time onto home-tanned moose or caribou hide. Like most of the Elders I had met, she spoke only occasionally, with pauses between. She spoke fairly good English, but since it was her second language, she had a bit of an accent. When complimented, her face lit up, a big grin completely transforming her appearance. I asked if she would make me a pair of beaded mukluks, a soft boot made of hide and lined with fur or a wool material, and mitts. She was delighted that I had admired her work so much and would want something she'd created to display her skills to other people. I wanted the beadwork to adorn the upper part of the mukluk as well as the lower. It was decided that she would bead directly onto the leather of both items to accomplish this instead of beading on a felt piece to be attached later. This process was harder to accomplish. When completed, the mitts were the most unique and magnificent I have ever laid eyes on. Hannah also beaded designs on my parka to match my mukluks and mitts. I still have these items and I treasure the quality and skills handed down by her ancestors. I cannot imagine the countless hours she spent creating these exquisite pieces. In addition, I bought a pair of hand-tanned beaded moccasins that were made to be wedding moccasins. The beading covers a larger area on wedding moccasins, more than

Hannah Netro.
Photo courtesy of Kathie Nukon.

on moccasins for utilitarian wear. Mine have pink flowers with a white background. They are all of museum quality. Years later, Hannah came to visit me at our cabin at Little Atlin. She had a friend drive her all the way out and I felt honoured by her visit and in her presence.

I returned to my home at Little Atlin Lake before the end of the school year because Denise, the teacher on maternity leave, returned to her job. Denise kept her baby in a hammock fashioned for her by a parent and was able to nurse her baby when needed. It was a wonderful experience for the few children to have a baby in the classroom and they naturally helped her enthusiastically. She and her husband, Ralph, the principal, became dear friends of ours, and we continued our friendship for many years after I left Old Crow.

To this day, teaching in Old Crow remains my most exceptional and rewarding teaching experience. I feel privileged to have had the opportunity to live in this remote community, interact with the people and teach their children, even if it was only for a short while.

BAD TIMING

Our first full summer at home was glorious. We cleared a space for two gardens, about fifteen by fifteen metres each. One was to be for growing vegetables and the other potatoes. It was not an easy task, as the stumps had to be dealt with, the ground broken up and rocks and sod removed in order to be able to use the new gas-operated Troy-Bilt rototiller that we had purchased in California. It was state-of-the-art, with rear tine tillers ideal for creating large gardens. In addition, we bought a furrower to make planting potatoes easier.

The first garden was ready to be planted by early June, which was perfect timing as there are only approximately eighty-seven frost-free days in our area. During the winter, I had pored over seed catalogues and read everything I could find about growing in northern climates—the hardiest vegetables, companion plants, soil ph, anything and everything I could get my hands on. We planned the rows to be wide enough for the rototiller to go in between to make controlling the weeds easier. I painstakingly planted all my seeds, lovingly covering them with soil to what I hoped was the correct depth, worrying about large clumps of dirt preventing a seedling from sprouting. Then I waited impatiently, checking two or three times a day to see if I could detect the tiniest hint of growth. Radishes poked through first, then one by one, each row showed a faint line of green or slightly red, as in the case of the beets. The broccoli, cauliflower, Brussels sprouts and cabbage seedlings I bought from a grower, having neither the time nor space to start them from seeds.

The second garden was not prepared as well as the first, but the seed potatoes I bought were poking their long white sprouts out of the burlap bag, begging to be put in the ground. Dumping them out and removing the longest sprouts, I cut the larger potatoes into medium-sized pieces, each of which included several eyes. These were put on cookie sheets or plywood to heal over. Healing over is a process of curing the seed potatoes after they are cut so they develop a protective covering over their exposed surfaces. This helps the "seed" to retain moisture and energy and discourage rotting or attack by organisms. White sprouts develop if the potatoes are left in the dark. Small green sprouts are good to get a head start on growing. Using the furrower, we made small ditches to plant the potatoes in. The dirt wedged out of the ditches clumped and had roots and sod tangled in it. I wasn't sure if any of the potatoes would grow in the mess we created, but in they went, eyes up, covered by a small amount of dirt.

As the days lengthened and the rain remained in the clouds, everything needed water. That was an issue, as we had no water system as yet. Buckets would have to suffice, so I began the arduous task of hauling water from the lake, two five-gallon buckets at a time. My arms were screaming and my back ached. Each bucket had to be poured into a watering can before I watered each row. The first big day of watering, I made twenty trips from the lake, a distance of at least thirty metres or more, with an almost-full five-gallon bucket in each hand. I am sure the tendonitis I have today is due to all the water I hauled for so many years, not only for the gardens but for the house too. Later we purchased a hundred-gallon tank that we pumped water up into, allowing it to warm before watering the plants, prompting faster growth, but I still had to water by hand with a watering can most of the time.

Another project on the go was the guest cabin we were constructing on the slab Harvey had poured for a garage. It was in a perfect location near the main cabin and not requiring any trees to be cut down. Stan had hoped to build a larger structure later to serve as a garage-workshop. We ordered a load of two-sided logs and my job was to peel them in preparation for building. Peeling the logs increases the longevity of the wood because the bark often provides a home for insects and a place for moisture to collect. Green logs are fairly easy to peel but it is difficult to peel logs that have been left to dry out. I spent endless hours bending over our very dry logs and stripping them until my arms and back ached so much I had to stop for the day.

Working long and hard days on the house, we were glad of a diversion when our friend Robbie invited us and our friends Dick and Holly on a trip down Tagish Lake. It was a rather chilly morning, as Yukon summer mornings often are, when the six of us headed down the lake. There is a joke about never really shedding your down coat or long johns due to the cool northern weather, especially when the breezes flow from the glaciers. Well, today we all had our down jackets on and were bundled up. We were in Robbie's freighter canoe, a large sturdy boat with an outboard, able to hold a substantial amount of weight and great for hunting and moving supplies

Looking southwest towards Ben-My-Chree from Engineer Mine. Photo courtesy of Darren O'Brian.

around. Our destination was an abandoned mine site, Engineer Mine, on the shore of Taku Arm, and we would be stopping overnight on the way. I had never been this far down the lake and was excited to see the country. I was hoping we could even get all the way to Ben-My-Chree at the end of Taku Arm.

Our first day's destination was a little cabin north of the mine near Wann River. It belonged to a couple who lived in Juneau, but usually they only stayed there one week each summer (if that) and left it open for visitors to use respectfully. This is the way of the North; hardly any cabins in the bush are locked. If someone really wants to get in, they could break in easily, so why not just leave it open in case there is an emergency or someone needs shelter for the night? Almost all cabins have a few basic supplies left in them for just these reasons.

Approaching the main cabin, I noticed that it was painted green and white, quite unlike the typical rundown trap cabin or squatter's cabin. As we glided onto shore I could see that someone had spent a lot of time maintaining the grounds and buildings. It was in a perfectly protected location with a glorious view of the lake and mountains. Dusk was nearing and everything had a wonderful orange glow. Upon entering the house, I was pleasantly surprised. It was a quaint little cabin with simple, purposeful furnishings, a wood cooking stove and heating stove, and a bedroom off to one side. It looked clean, tidy and very inviting. We were hesitant about staying there, as it seemed we were intruding on someone's home, not just an old cabin. Robbie said he had stayed there many times and that as long as we made sure we cleaned up and left it even better than we found it, it would be no problem.

We unloaded all our gear from the boat, each found a sleeping space, and we women went about readying things for dinner. I noticed a large rhubarb plant in the garden area outside the kitchen when we arrived and thought it would be a great treat to cook some for dessert. I had the ingredients for bannock, which meant I had flour, sugar and butter, so after rummaging around to see which pots and pans were available and finding pie pans, I decided to make a pie for dessert. Two pies, in fact, as there was plenty of rhubarb and we were a hungry crew.

After a fabulous dinner, complete with wine, everybody was feeling warm and tired, so we decided to get to bed early. I was just finishing up the dishes when we heard a plane. Planes are not uncommon; float planes come and go all the time in this vast land of lakes. It was almost dark, so it seemed to be right on the edge of flying time. When it started getting louder and closer, we peered outside and saw that it was circling… circling… landing… it just couldn't be the owners, could it? What were the chances of that? Maybe something had happened, and someone was trying to get in touch with us. We waited with anticipation while Robbie went out to see who was landing. It *was* the owners! We panicked and started madly throwing our stuff together, trying to clean up, not knowing what to do. Fortunately, Robbie had warned them, but we felt pretty sheepish! They walked in, looked around, forced a smile and said, "Oh, I see you've made yourselves right at home." We were all speaking at once, apologizing, thanking them, telling them how wonderful their place was, defending our need to stop and saying anything we thought would help the situation.

The lady of the house had the perfect solution. There was an old bunkhouse of sorts down a trail along the back of the property in the next bay where we could all sleep. In fact, her husband would be glad to show us. So there we were, walking in the dark with all of our sleeping gear, following a man of few words to a funky old cabin nearby. We thanked him, he left and we looked inside. There were rusty iron bed frames with springs and no coverings or anything of the sort—simply four legs and springs. We lay down our sleeping pads and bags by flashlight and tested them out. They were horrendous, noisy, uncomfortable, too small—a real nightmare, but what were our choices? It was too late and too dark to go outside and find a good campsite. We could hear the mice running around on the floor, so each couple squeezed in a single bed and tried to sleep. Every time somebody turned they woke everybody else up. We bantered back and forth for a while but finally exhaustion took over. As I lay trying to go to sleep, I wondered about the second pie… I left it, of course; it was in *her* pie dish, after all. But we had eaten one piece out of it. Would they eat it or feel disdain for me, since I'd picked some of their rhubarb, and throw it away? I'll never know. Needless to say, we did not sleep well that night. We got up early, went back and moved the boat, and gathered the rest of our gear before the owners woke up. We will never forgive Robbie for taking us there and assuring us the owners were never home mid-week!

We continued on that day to explore the Old Engineer Mine, which was once a thriving mine producing both gold and silver. Apparently, at one time, many of the original owner's claims lapsed, and a Mr. Brown from Atlin restaked them, giving him control of the mine—until, that is, a group of men from Atlin acquired the claims from him under suspicious circumstances and work began again. The mine changed hands a few more times, and it is said that in 1926 at the height of production, as many as 7,757 ounces of gold were produced from the milled ore. During this peak period, additional buildings were constructed and a power plant was installed on Wann River. It turned into more of a town than a mine site, but not for long. Most of the ore was soon depleted and the mine closed again. But until that time, the sternwheeler S. S. *Tutshi* even made regular stops there on its way to Ben-My-Chree, a popular tourist destination. When we were there, the main mine building and many of the other buildings in the small mining community were still intact. It was truly a step back in time to explore this area.

Unfortunately, we didn't have time to continue down the lake to Ben-My-Chree, which sits at the southeast end of the Taku Arm, tucked up against towering mountains capped by a deep blue glacier. An English couple, Otto and Kate Partridge, moved north during the Klondike gold rush, but never made it to Dawson. Instead they started a mining operation on this site. Otto, a Manxman from the Isle of Man, was thinking of his wife when he named the place *Ben My Chree*—"girl of my heart." Two other couples invested in the mine with them. After a mining accident, the owners

Historical Engineer Mine (once a thriving mine producing both gold and silver) on the banks of Taku Arm, Tagish Lake, Yukon Territory. Photo courtesy of Darren O'Brian.

decided to stop mining and instead planted flowers and vegetables in the valley wilderness.

As early as 1916, even before the peak mining years, tourists started coming down the lake from Carcross to visit the impressive gardens. It was considered an extraordinary place to visit for politicians, movie stars and entertainers, and the British aristocracy. Wealthy and important people such as President Roosevelt, the Prince of Wales, and the Governor General made the long trip to visit the flower gardens that were grown in this unique microclimate. Kate's gardens, said to have contained forty varieties of flowers that grew to amazing heights, were arranged around well-kept lawns.

Today, Ben-My-Cree is a private residence and the gardens have been left on their own to be reclaimed by the wilderness, but the history of this magical place lives on.

THE CRYSTAL PALACE

The bar at Jake's Corner, officially named the Crystal Palace, was a hopping place when we moved to Little Atlin. In fact, hopping over the railing from the bar on the second story into the swimming pool on the ground floor was a common occurrence. Located at Mile 866 of the Alaska Highway, at the junction of the Tagish-Carcross and Atlin roads, Jake's Corner featured a gas station, bar and café with a few motel rooms and cabins. Originally it was the site of a construction base for the Alaska Highway and was later taken over by a Ukrainian immigrant, Roy Chaykowsky.

When Roy took ownership of the Jake's Corner location, he rebuilt his business there, after the original Crystal Palace located about six kilometres north burned down. But not only had the Jake's Corner name stuck, people persisted in calling him Jake. A peculiar man, and not very friendly, he developed a reputation as an eccentric throughout the territory, in contrast to his wife, who was extremely cordial. He had goats that ran around the place and were very curious. So curious in fact, they would often surround a car getting gas and sometimes had the audacity to actually jump up on the hood. Many a gas station patron would go nearly berserk trying to get a goat off their car, not to mention being irate about the dents that had resulted. Running to the café, they would find Jake sitting with a cup of coffee. His only response to their yelling would be, "Goats? What goats? I don't see any goats." And so the reputation began; who knows if it was really true? It never happened to us personally, but the goats were always roaming around when we purchased gas and when they came near the car, we made sure to shoosh them away.

One summer we were getting gas at Jake's Corner on our way to Whitehorse when we noticed some pennies on the ground. As we looked around we found even more; they were everywhere. The rumour was that Jake had a load of gravel put down and mixed in coins so he could watch the tourists go crazy over them. We weren't sure what the truth was, but there sure were a lot of pennies there. Years later when I talked to Roy's son Ray, he confirmed that his dad had put four five-gallon buckets of pennies in the

One of the many party-goers jumping into the pool below at the Crystal Palace. Photo courtesy of Sandy Magnuson.

gravel just to mess with everybody's head. So, it turns out the rumour was right!

As odd as Jake was, we became friends of the family and developed respect for the man, as he was an incredibly hard worker. His wife, Helen, was a gem, and they were both very kind to us, taking messages and allowing us to use their phone for important calls. With my lettuce growing in abundance at Little Atlin, I often took large black plastic bags full of a variety of lettuces to Helen for use in the restaurant. We frequented the café for a coffee or bite to eat, knew his daughters, Sandy and Joann, and became friends with their son, Ray.

As wonderful as the fresh-baked goodies in the café were, the bar was where it was really happening. It was the most incredible place. The bar was on the second story open to an indoor swimming pool below. A band platform and dance floor hung suspended over half of the swimming pool. Drinks were ordered from an intercom system located at the tables, which were located under huge picture windows with a gorgeous view of the mountains. This unique bar was basically out in the middle of nowhere, about an hour from Carcross, two hours from Atlin, and an hour-and-a-half from Whitehorse, but folks drove the long distances to attend the famous parties held there. The regulars, mostly from Marsh Lake or Tagish, often wondered if the dance floor would hold the band plus all of the people energetically dancing on it. As daylight faded and the evening darkness took over, the more alcohol was consumed, the more people ended up in the pool below from the bar. They hopped in, jumped in, were thrown in and went in with a fight, still holding on to their chairs, from over the railing or off the dance floor. Some chose to take their clothes off; others did not. The exhibitionists usually did, often striding over a series of tables to the railing, then plunging dramatically over the side.

In those days, before most of us had kids, we would stay at the bar at Jake's with all of our friends until closing time. When almost everybody had left… that was when the real party started. Ray would lock up, and a chosen group of friends would fill a big table and continue on. We'd all dip into our pockets and purses for whatever money we had left and Ray would start mixing up pitchers of Caesars. It seemed like no time before dawn would appear and we would gather our belongings and either head home or have a bite at the café if it was open.

One morning at dawn I looked out the big window and saw a snowy owl sitting on the fluorescent sign right outside the window. Evidently he was a regular. It wasn't clear whether the lights attracted him or not, but I was told he would appear often, sometimes late at night before closing, sitting stoically for long periods of time.

Another evening that summer, some friends of ours came to visit so we took them up to Jake's Corner for a drink, not aware that a wedding party was in full swing there. When we realized what was going on, we respect-fully took our places on the opposite side of the bar so as not to interfere with the festivities. It was clear the wedding party had started quite a while before we got there. Drinks were being poured freely, dresses were hiked high for dancing, people were shouting across the lounge to each other and crazy staged photographs were evidence of this. All of a sudden, the bride and groom—in their bridal clothes—got up from their seats, walked over to the edge of the barrier, climbed over the railing and jumped from the second floor into the pool on the first floor, holding hands. The majority of the wedding guests followed, with their tuxes and bridesmaids' dresses. It was outrageously entertaining, and the screams told just how cold the unheated water was. Returning to the bar upstairs, many of the wedding guests jumped in again, all the while laughing and taunting their friends to join them. Yes, Jake's was hopping in those days, and Stan and I met many people from the Southern Lakes area.

BERRIES, BEAR AND MOOSE

New communities and subdivisions were springing up everywhere in southern Yukon, especially around the lakes. Many of our friends from the area, as well as people living in Whitehorse, applied for recreational lots at Marsh Lake through a government lottery. Marsh Lake was stunningly beautiful, with countless outdoor activity possibilities. Stan and I put our names into this lottery in hopes of securing some land for relatively cheap to build a "spec" vacation cabin on. It cost $100.00 to enter the lottery, and there were 117 lots and approximately 600 applicants. The winners that were lucky enough to have their names drawn first got to pick the best lots. The land was free: the $100.00 covered the lease for a lot. A few years later, title could be obtained with the completion of certain requirements that cost somewhere between $9,000 and $13,000. We weren't as lucky as many of our friends who obtained land at the lake, but we had our extraordinary piece of property already.

In the summer we joined our new friends down at the beach near the Marsh Lake Marina to watch those brave enough to water-ski in the freezing-cold water while we stayed on shore. The real test was to see if you could slide off the sandy shore on your skis onto the water and keep afloat without getting wet. Next, the trick was to let go of the rope at the proper time as the boat swung wide to the shore and end up on the beach still dry. We witnessed many a skier sink, letting out cries from the burning-cold water before not quite arriving at their destination, or overshooting it and rolling head over heels onto the beach itself, sending people fleeing in all directions.

Softball games were common too. There was an old sawmill nearby with a cleared area and we often met on Sunday afternoons, coolers in hand, ready to play ball. I was pitcher until I was unceremoniously thrown out of this position for pitching the balls too softly. Beer and food kept the crowd maintained, and if it got chilly, we lit a fire and roasted hot dogs and marshmallows.

These lazy days of summer moved into the busy days of fall where our exploring took us to berry picking areas... where the bears were abundant

as they love berries as much as people do (or more). The berries were
incredibly plentiful. Raspberries
were prolific and high-bush cranberries were everywhere. There
were bunch berries, currants, gooseberries, high and low bush blueberries, strawberries, moss berries, bear
berries, juniper berries and more.
Some of these berries grew only at
higher elevations. Driving up old
roads above the mines to pick them
was a favourite pastime. We stuffed
our mouths and filled our pails, always with an alert eye out for bears.
After a good day's picking, the work
began for me. I cleaned, cooked and
experimented with canning, making
jams, jellies, chutney, syrups and pie
fillings—anything I could think of.
The most fun was combining fruit
and discovering new jams. I think

Stan picking blueberries from the
heavily laden berry bushes.

my very favourite was a raspberry, blackcurrant and rhubarb combo.

Blueberries, both low and high bush, were profuse at the higher elevation of the Skagway Road, the road connecting Yukon and BC with Skagway, Alaska. We would pack up our camping gear, take five-gallon buckets,
small pails, our coffee-can berry picker (custom made with a baffle by our
friend Dixon) and head up the road. There was a wonderful camping spot
near a lake on the Skagway Road where the berries grew. They were so thick
we could stand in one spot and fill a bucket. Here you had to be more vigi-
lant when watching for the bears, both grizzly and black. They were just as
bound and determined to get their berries as we were. We sang and talked
and stomped around, keeping our rifle nearby. I would hear a sound and
drop everything in fear, only to see our friends making their way towards
us—most of the time, that is.

One day a group of us travelled together to our favourite berry patch.
Gathering our buckets and picking cans, Stan and I spread out to find the
best patch. I was concentrating on gathering the biggest, juiciest berries on

the bush when I heard a noise. I assumed it was our friends trying to find my private stash of berries, as they had been picking near me. I glanced over my shoulder and noticed their dog, a black German shepherd, behind the bushes a few yards away with his nose down, appearing to be sniffing the ground. Turning back to my picking, I called him and he ignored me. Finally I stood up and turned, expecting to see my friends, and right in front of me, merely a few blueberry bushes away, was a black bear busily eating berries off a bush, filling his whole mouth in a single big gulp. Well, I don't know who scared whom the most. I froze for a quick second and then started yelling hysterically and waving my arms, forcing myself not to run, but to remain stationary and look big. The bear literally jumped up and did a turn-in-the-air leap, no longer interested in the berry-laden bushes. Immediately everyone started yelling, "Bear, bear," and waving their arms too. The dog started barking frantically and my friends began screaming at the dog to "get the bear" so he would chase it away. The last I saw of the bear he was running full bore though the bushes uphill with the dog closing in. We regrouped and decided to no longer seek our own best berry patch but stay together instead. I was still shaking and had difficulty focusing on my task, as every little sound I heard startled me. I stuck like glue to Stan after that!

In those days, we were easily able to fill a five-gallon pail of high-bush blueberries each, and a few smaller buckets of low bush and moss berries. After a long day of picking berries and bear-watching, we would relax around the fire at night and pop a few blueberries in our wine. I also put some in fresh-made bannock. Then we'd have blueberries with sugar and milk for dessert, and in the morning, we would have them on our granola or in pancakes.

The truly spectacular thing about our berry-picking camping trips in the fall was not the huge amount of berries we were able to pick in a short time, but the spectacular northern light shows in the evenings. We were never cheated; they were always dancing in the sky at this time of the year. I sometimes felt they were a special gift to us as we sat looking up from our sleeping bags in the silent wilderness. The colours were breathtaking, never the usual greens, but all shades of green, purple and pink, undulating, moving to a rhythm of their own. We were mesmerized and tried to stay up as long as we could but were gently soothed by their presence and asleep in no time after a day of picking.

This grizzly bear was spotted on the side of the Atlin Road, distinguishable from its smaller black bear relatives by its prominent shoulder hump (a mass of muscles that gives the bear additional strength for digging).

It was rewarding to have picked so many blueberries, but they were difficult to clean. If you washed them, all the little leaves would stick to them. After much experimentation and asking around, I devised the best method for me. I got the woolliest blanket I could find and laid it on the floor. At the top end, I put a few cups of berries and gently let them roll down the blanket to the bottom end, allowing the fibres in the wool to collect any of the leaves and little stems. Then I put the cleaned ones into a bucket and went outside and shook the blanket. It worked like a charm but it often took a couple of days to complete the task. This process took as long as all the cooking and canning or picking, but was well worth it! When all the jars of blueberry pie filling were sitting on the shelf and the rest were in a friend's freezer, I felt extremely satisfied.

That task complete, we now needed to get our meat in for the winter, so Stan was going to go moose-hunting with Robbie, our friend from Tagish. Moose provided a lot of meat. The first moose I ever saw close up was in the back of someone's pickup truck. It was huge—bigger than any horse I had ever seen. It was not quite as tall, but had longer legs and a more massive body.

Leaving from Robbie's home on an August morning by boat, Stan and Robbie travelled through the Six-Mile River and south down Tagish Lake, retracing some of the same route we had taken that summer. Tagish Lake lies both in the Yukon Territory and BC. This was an advantage to the hunters, as Stan had a BC hunting licence and Robbie had a Yukon licence, making it possible to shoot a moose on either side of the border. Moose-hunting by boat is the hunting method preferred by many. Moose typically graze near the shore at dusk and dawn, so they are easy to spot. Most are not frightened by the whirr of a motor unless you are too close to shore. Once you are lucky enough to get a good shot and kill an animal, it is easier to pack it into a boat than carry it a long distance to a vehicle.

Stan and Robbie were lucky and shot a fairly young bull moose on their second day out. Making sure to keep the meat free of debris, dirt, hair and blood, they field dressed (gutted) it on the spot, as handling of the meat properly helps to make sure it does not get a gamy taste. If you want to keep the hide intact, you must skin it. Stan and Robbie did not want the hide, so didn't have to skin the moose. Instead, they removed the head first, then cut the body into quarters. This allows the carcass to cool and makes it easier to handle. Hide-covered quarters also help protect the meat. Some hunters wrap the carcass in cheesecloth or commercial game bags. Robbie and Stan hauled the quarters to the boat and wrapped them loosely in tarps for the trip home.

Back at Robbie's, the hide was removed and the moose quarters were hung from a cross pole in a small screened enclosure built in the shade especially for this purpose. The temperature usually stayed from just above freezing to ten degrees Celsius at this time of the year, and the best temperature range for aging meat is between four and ten degrees. Moose can be hung between three to five days or longer, depending upon the temperature and size of the moose.

Some folks take their catch to a butcher in town and pay to have it cut and wrapped. Robbie knew how to butcher a moose, so we were all on hand to help when he felt it had hung long enough. About ten days after shooting the moose, Robbie, his girlfriend, Marg, Stan and I were on hand to double wrap meat and label the packages. Once the moose was butchered and the main cuts were packaged, there was still more work to be done. All the leftover bits and pieces had to be ground. Stan and I had one of those large hand grinders you bolt down to a table; it often took two hands to turn, but it did the job. The whole process was a first-time experience for me. We designated some of the meat for regular ground meat and the rest for sausage and salami, which I planned to learn how to make. I wanted to make breakfast sausages, which were in patty form seasoned with sage, and link sausages made with different flavours.

After only two days of hunting , we had all the meat we would need for the winter. I never did find out who shot the moose or which side of the border they were on, as Stan and Robbie wouldn't say.

A few days later, Stan and I got together with Dick and Holly, who had recently shot a moose too. We had all the makings for sausages and we were going to grind the mix directly into the pig-intestine casings we had bought and then smoke the whole batch. I seem to remember a lot of beer-drinking by the guys and very little help with the grinding. It was my first experience making link sausages, and I had never even seen pig intestines before. We also had to buy a bit of pig fat to go into the concoction, since moose meat is extremely lean; there might be a thin layer of moose fat between skin and meat, but it is not enough to use for all the ground meat products. Most people purchased pig fat to supplement lean meat in their sausages. The other fat, "bum guts," was literally the fat around the bum or anus, and this was considered a delicacy, often being the first thing fried up and eaten after butchering, or offered to Elders first at Indigenous feasts. We did not save the bum guts. We passed, thank you very much.

Moose are common in the Atlin area. This one was photographed near the author's cabin in the spring, when both sexes are antler-less. The hair standing straight up on his back indicates agitation.

That day Holly and I managed to grind and stuff and twist an incredible number of sausages. All of them went directly to the smokehouse where the guys were feeding the slow, smoky fire. When we finished cleaning up inside and emerged to check on the smoking process, Stan and Dick were off somewhere and the fire was burning way too hot. We were panicked, thinking that our efforts might have been ruined. We raced to the smokehouse with a jug of water and put the flames out. Luckily we were able to salvage all the sausages, but the guys were in the doghouse for quite a while, even though they stood diligently by the smokehouse the rest of the afternoon.

HEAD OVER HEELS

I had never taught grade one before, so I was a bit apprehensive when I travelled to Carmacks before school began on several occasions to look at materials and plan for my year.

The village of Carmacks sits on the banks of the Yukon River about 180 kilometres along the Klondike Highway that runs from Skagway to Dawson City. Home to the Little Salmon-Carmacks people, originally it was an important trading area for the Indigenous peoples. An early prospector, George Washington Carmack, discovered seams of coal and tried to start a coal mine there. The cabin he built grew into a trading post and eventually it evolved into an important riverboat stop known as Carmack's Landing during the gold rush. Large wood camps provided fuel for the sternwheelers. The settlement continued to grow when the Overland Trail was routed through in 1901. Carmack went on to discover gold on Bonanza Creek in the Dawson region a few years later with Skookum Jim and Tagish Charlie, which started the Klondike gold rush. During the year I taught there, the town was made up of about 500 people, both white and Indigenous.

I learned a very valuable lesson my first week of teaching there: if a young student is trying repeatedly to get your attention, even if you are doing something you perceive to be very important, pay attention. If you don't, you might end up with "throw up" all over you, your papers and the floor. Immediately following this incident, I had a nice little chat with my grade one students, explaining that if you feel sick or have any other kind of emergency, it is okay to leave the classroom to go to the bathroom as fast as you can. It's too bad I didn't think of imparting this knowledge earlier.

I was given a teacherage to live in, which was furnished very sparsely. Stan wasn't interested in moving there with me. He wanted to stay at Little Atlin where he was set up to work on his ivory carvings, so I was bound and determined to commute to our cabin every weekend. However, this posed a problem as we only had one vehicle. I was able to use the truck when Stan stayed home, but as fall turned into winter, he kept the truck. Securing a ride to Whitehorse wasn't too hard on a Friday afternoon, but returning Sunday evening or very early Monday was difficult. I remember making dentist and doctor appointments on Monday mornings so I could catch the later bus back to Carmacks or catch a ride with one of the trucks from the local trucking company.

One Friday after school I was waiting for a ride to Whitehorse from some folks, but it kept getting later and later. I decided to hitchhike and got a ride immediately, but was terrified by the icy condition of the road and the poor condition of the truck I was riding in. I was very uncomfortable, so I asked to get out. There I was on the highway in the middle of nowhere, in winter, once again trying to get a ride. Fortunately, someone came along shortly and was not only going to Whitehorse, but was continuing down the highway to Teslin. This meant he was driving right by Jake's Corner, my turnoff to Little Atlin. As we approached the turnoff, dusk was upon the land, with shimmering light on Sundown Mountain. It was eight kilometres from Jake's Corner to my cabin. I began walking at a rapid pace to try and beat the dark. Not one car drove by during this time. Soon after making the second turn onto the Atlin Road, I came to the boat launch. It was then that I made the decision to continue walking home on the frozen lake instead of the road.

Conditions on the ice were good, and I was drawn to the last signs of daylight as it lingered on the surrounding mountains. Skirting the swamp and the many muskrat lodges in the ice, I looked south to see familiar Mount Minto on Atlin Lake in BC—its recognizable silhouette had pink tips dancing upon it. I continued walking in silence over the frozen, wind-blown snow, breathing in the silence, when I noticed a figure on the lake. It was my husband hauling water from our ice hole before dark. He had just replaced the Styrofoam cover over the hole and lifted the bucket when he turned in my direction. Imagine his astonishment when he saw me. In those days, we did not have telephones or cell phones or any means of communication, just messages from the kind folks at Jake's Corner. Stan often did not know if I would make it home or be able to get a ride. Since only a glimmer of light remained, he assumed I would not make it that Friday, so he was utterly surprised at my arrival. I could see a grin expand on his face each step I took closer. We embraced, exchanging few words. We were both just happy to see each other. The snow reflected the light glowing brightly from the kerosene lamps in the cabin, welcoming us as we walked up from the lake. It was warm and cozy inside, worth every mile of riding and walking to get home.

Christmas break arrived and I was happy to go home and visit with friends and attend some holiday gatherings. Stan and I, along with another couple who were good friends of ours living nearby, were invited to Jake's Corner for Christmas dinner. We were very moved by this invitation, as it was a family gathering. We all sat at one long table made up of several smaller tables donned with tablecloths. There was wine and champagne assembled down the centre, and the food was astonishing, both in amounts and in flavour. We gorged ourselves on the many dishes that were so lovingly prepared. Helen Chaykowski was an amazing cook and produced not only classic Ukrainian dishes but traditional North American Christmas dishes too. Warmth infused me as we shared a meal with this family, but I was also missing my own family. Returning home to our cabin, Stan and I climbed into bed feeling blessed to have the relationships we did with so many people.

After Christmas I transported gallons of rhubarb wine I had started making to Carmacks, as I would have the advantage of maintaining a constant temperature in the forced-air environment of my government housing. The previous year, Harvey had split his rhubarb plants and given me about ten roots to start in my berry garden. They were old roots and yielded a good crop the first year. In fact, I had so much I didn't know what to do with all of it, so someone suggested making rhubarb wine. Being a wine drinker, I immediately began asking people for advice about how to make it. I cannot remember the exact recipe or the time frames, but it involved a large amount of rhubarb chopped and put into a sterilized forty-five-gallon garbage can. A big bag of sugar was added, boiling water was poured over it and then a couple of packages of yeast were sprinkled on a piece of rye bread that was left to float on the top. After a period of fermentation, the liquid was strained off into five-gallon buckets for transporting to Carmacks. With the lids tightly secured, I loaded the buckets into our truck along with boxes of gallon jugs I had collected. Once I was at home in Carmacks, I strained the wine into the gallon bottles. Since I didn't have any fermentation locks (devices to allow carbon dioxide gas to escape from the jugs without letting in air), I used coloured balloons placed over the mouth of the bottles.

I then racked, or filtered, the gallon jugs of wine several more times during the winter. Hearing a whoosh sound in the basement indicated that another balloon had been ejected from the top of the bottle and needed replacing. I continued racking and ballooning all winter until the rich amber liquid was crystal clear, and then I corked it.

I am not sure how, but my rhubarb wine became famous—everybody that tasted it wanted more and people begged to know how I made it and how to split the roots of their rhubarb so they could increase their productivity. As evidenced by the antics of those who drank it prematurely, the wine had a substantial amount of alcohol in it. The wine's good reputation must have continued to get around, as I was contacted by a friend of a friend who knew a CBC host that apparently wanted me to come in and talk about my wine-making on a daytime show she hosted. The use of the balloons fascinated her. A meeting was arranged at the CBC studio in Whitehorse and very nervously I answered questions and talked about making my homemade rhubarb wine. During my visit to the studio and in a personal interview before going on air, it came out that I was a textile artist, and the host said they might be interested in doing another segment about my artwork at a later date.

During spring break from school that year, Stan and I travelled to visit our friends, Dick and Holly, at their trapline cabin. They shared the trapline with our other friends, Bonnie and Huey. Dick and Holly's cabin was a historic cabin located on the site of an old fox farm on Moose Arm on Tagish Lake. It is accessible only by boat, or snow machine in the winter. We travelled by snow machine north across Atlin Lake, past Logger Bay (where we had spent New Year's in 1976 on our trek down Atlin Lake), to Fox Bay, then continued overland past Bonnie and Huey's cabin on Jones Lake, about six-and-a-half kilometres south of the base of Mount Minto. Dick and Holly lived in a cabin right on the shore of the lake at Moose Arm. The trapline these friends shared covered a huge area, hundreds of square kilometres. Both cabins were part of the historic mail run route from Carcross to Atlin in the gold rush days. Bonnie and Huey bought the lease from an individual that entitled them to trap the land and build cabins, but all of the property itself remained public. It was still a viable option for earning an income. They were all serious trappers, trapping muskrat, mink, otter, beaver, coyotes, wolves, weasel and lynx. In those years, lynx were running anywhere from $500 to $1,500 a pelt, depending upon quality and size. Several other people we knew owned trapline leases too, some more serious about it than others; a few used the leases as a means to live in the bush legally without having to buy a place outright.

Dick and Holly had their herd of horses there as well as Holly's sled dogs and were settled in for the winter. This had been a particularly harsh winter for the horses, as wolves had attacked several of them. Our first night there, we heard wolves howling in the distance during the night, which made our friends very nervous. The next afternoon, I joined Holly in walking to where the horses had been grazing, or more accurately, where they had been pawing through the snow to find grass. We were going to herd them in towards the cabin and feed them grains so we could keep an eye on them. There was no corral to speak of, but the temptation of food would do a good job of keeping them around for a few days.

We could see the horses in the distance as we headed out to round them up. Holly had halters and rope with her in hopes of leading one of them while the others followed. One of Holly's horses was extremely happy to see her, snuggling up, rubbing his head up and down on her chest and easily letting her put on the halter. We were also able to put a halter on another one that I was going to lead back. Holly decided to ride her horse back, anxious to just sit on him and leisurely walk to the barn. I asked Holly if I could ride the horse I was going to lead. She figured it would be okay since he was a gentle horse and was used to being ridden. What she didn't tell me was that he hadn't been ridden in a long, long time.

I jumped on with Holly's help, as he was a big horse, and was settling on his bare back when he suddenly jolted forward and started running. All I had was a halter rope and nothing else to hold on to. He started going faster and faster until he was at a full gallop. I was terrified. I did everything humanly possible to try and stay on his bare back. Holly kept yelling at me, "Jump, jump!" I looked down and all I could see were legs all jumbled together with hoofs kicking up snow and the ground seemed like such a long ways away. I was afraid to jump—I envisioned getting trampled. I hung on for dear life. Just as I thought I was doomed to fall and be caught beneath this beast, he stopped. I don't mean he slowed down; he came to a roaring stop, just like you see in the cartoons, all four legs together in a screeching halt. I went head over heels in a complete flip over his head and landed on my back on frozen horse manure in a fenced enclosure. I lay there stunned; I wasn't even sure if I could move! I looked up and this horse was just standing on the other side of the fence looking at me like not a thing in the world had happened. While I was moving around trying to get up, Holly arrived to help me. I had landed in a fenced-in area with old cages that had been used to raise foxes for their fur. It was next to the old barn, which is where my horse ran to before putting on the brakes.

I stood up slowly and began walking to the cabin, carefully placing one foot in front of the other, becoming increasingly aware of sore body parts.

Inside, the guys were sitting at a table, beers in hand, chatting away, with no clue about what had just happened and how I had just been traumatized. I sat down slowly and let Holly tell the story. I just couldn't speak—I think I was still in shock.

The rest of the week was fairly uneventful compared to that experience. I basked in the beauty of the area. We went snowshoeing through the bush to Bonnie's cabin and drank tea, and ate homemade meals lovingly cooked over the wood cook stove, served with a variety of home-canned goodies. For breakfast we ate fresh-caught grayling with bannock. We played cards, told stories and laughed a lot about my horse escapade. In the meantime, I nursed a very sore body over the next while—thankfully nothing was broken.

Dick and Holly loaned me a truck for the rest of the winter. Driving it was like driving an amusement-park ride, as I had to hang on to a very stiff, unresponsive steering wheel. This made me nervous, especially on icy roads, but it got me back and forth to Little Atlin for the rest of the winter. I often had piles of schoolwork and had to remain in Carmacks for the weekend, though. The teacherage was actually a very nice structure, fairly new with two levels, three bedrooms, a modern kitchen and a large picture window in the living room. But it was very sparsely furnished and I had not moved any personal items in, so it did not feel like anything like home. Another teacher, Cathy, and I had become quite close and visited often, which gave me something to do other than sitting at home. I didn't make a lot of connections with the community, partly because of my focus on school and home, and partly because I chose not to do much socializing. The town itself did not feel quaint and friendly. It was more of a highway town, catering to those driving the Klondike Highway. When taking a walk on a beautiful day, I tended to take the roads leading away from the town centre, enjoying the bush surrounding the town.

Shortly after spring break, I found out I was pregnant. My pregnancy was not planned, but Stan and I had been together eight years, and as time went on, my maternal instincts had kicked in and I wanted a baby. Because Stan was twelve years older than me and had a child from a previous marriage that had ended poorly, he really didn't want children. I had told Stan when we were married that I was okay with not having children, so he was surprised when I announced I was pregnant. Fortunately, a good friend he spoke with about my situation conveyed to Stan that he might lose me if he didn't allow me to have a child. He explained to him that most women at one time or another want a child; it is in their hormones, a maternal instinct they can't ignore. I did not know they had this conversation at the time, but found out later and was truly grateful; I'm sure that is one reason why Stan was not too upset that I was pregnant after eight years of marriage. He accepted it and we moved forward.

I finished my teaching stint in Carmacks at the end of the school year in June and went on a maternity leave. I was ecstatic to be living back at Little Atlin. With a baby due that fall, we undertook major renovations to our cabin and water supply that summer of 1980. Stan wanted to have access to water from the cabin to make things easier for me, so two small rooms were added, one for a hand pump, sink and pantry and the other a bedroom for Stan and me. The small, bathroom-size room became the baby's room, the front porch was closed in for my weaving space and the two small bedrooms were transformed into a kitchen and a dining room. A well was dug by hand to feed the new hand pump, and it was fortunate that it only took a few lengths of pipe and the brute strength of Stan and a friend to hit water about six metres below the surface of the ground.

We bought a wood cook stove with warming ovens that I loved more than anything, and exchanged our airtight stove for a different style that allowed you to open the doors—with a screen in front, it acted as a fireplace. Together, these made for a huge, much-welcomed change. My Puritan cook stove also served as a heating source, taking the chill off the house in the cool summer mornings. Its cast-iron body stood on four nickel-plated legs, and the main unit was a large box shape with an oven occupying two-thirds of one side. The other side was the wood box with cleanout below. The top had two cast-iron lids that could be lifted easily with a lid lifter.

To operate it, I opened the damper on the side of the firebox and the one in the stovepipe, placed kindling on some paper in the firebox and simply lit it. I loved the roar of the fire taking off with dampers wide open, the stove emitting heat instantly. Cooking on the stovetop was a matter of constantly rearranging pots and pans until the desired heat was achieved, those directly over the firebox being hottest, the area above the oven less hot. Using damper control helped to maintain an even heat, which was crucial for baking. Some oven doors have a temperature gauge installed directly on them, but mine didn't so I used a small store-bought one. When baking bread, or almost anything, I needed to turn the item around in the oven, as the back was hotter than the front. Often I needed to place baked goods on the top of the stove for a bit more browning on the bottom. With practice, I became a pro.

One of the marvellous things about this stove was the ability to grill meat directly above the wood box. I could easily remove the two lids and stove piece between them with the lid lifter, and then replace them with a cast-iron grill with a handle that fit perfectly into the space. It worked better than a George Foreman grill and had the authentic taste of charcoal-grilled food. This was a treat in the winter when we were not barbequing outside.

I had a large window screen hanging horizontally above my stove. I used it to dry everything from mittens and socks to mushrooms and jerky. The continual heat from cooking made it perfect for this. Although I still had my propane apartment-sized stove in the kitchen, I tended to use the wood cook stove most of the time. It was situated on the side of the living room near the kitchen to provide heat in the central living area. My Puritan baked countless loaves of bread and pies and fed many people over the years.

The Jolles, Alan and Maureen, were our closest neighbours; their homestead was located only about 150 metres away by trail through the bush, but longer by road. Deathly afraid of bears, Maureen gardened with a powerful Colt 45 gun strapped to her hip. Bending over pulling weeds one day, she looked up to her surprise to see a big black bear just on the other side of the fence of her vegetable garden. It had been hanging around for days, but never this close. Screaming bloody hell, she tried to get her pistol out and take a shot but was too shaky to aim properly. Her husband, hearing the commotion and knowing exactly what was happening by the uncontrollable screaming, grabbed his rifle and quickly put an end to the pesky bear's life.

Having shot the bear, Alan drove over to our place to see if we wanted any meat and to see if Stan could help dispose of the carcass. Most people usually shun bear meat, but if the bear has had a diet of mostly plants, roots and berries, not fish, the meat can be very tasty. The most important thing is making certain it is well cooked to prevent trichinosis, a disease characterized by digestive disturbances, fever and muscular rigidity. We had eaten a bear roast at a friend's and found it to be quite flavourful, much like pork. The decision was made to keep the top of the hindquarter, which could be cut out without field dressing the bear.

This necessitated learning how to prepare and cook bear meat. As one of our favourites was corned moose, I decided to use a variation of this recipe to process the bear meat. I knew it would be hard work, but imagined it would be well worth it, if the corned moose was any indication. I took chunks of the meat (about two-and-a-half kilograms a chunk), weighted it down and cured it in brine for three weeks, then I simmered it slowly for four hours. Next, to ensure that it was absolutely cooked and there was no chance of contracting trichinosis, I pressure-canned the corned meat to be used for sandwiches and snacks later. I think this bear made better corned meat than the moose. So did our dog Jubilee, who was never forgiven for dragging a chunk of it from the brine pot across the floor and consuming half of it before we caught her!

Earlier that summer, Jubilee had given birth to five of the most adorable puppies I had ever seen. They had Kodi's long hair, Jubilee's beautiful markings and were just a bundle of energetic fur. They raced around the property and were curious and underfoot all the time. They stuck together so closely they looked like a herd of fleecy sheep bunched together zig zagging this way and that, following one another's lead. I wanted to keep them all. I grew increasingly attached and thought maybe I should create my own dog team, but I remembered the trials I had with training Jubilee and abruptly stifled that idea.

One day, while still nursing, Jubilee ran off with her puppies to the swamp nearby. Since she had given birth she had never run off like she used to until this day. We noticed the silence and missed the furry little bodies rubbing against our legs. We called frantically for Jubilee and heard cries from the bush. Donning our rubber boots, we spent countless hours wandering through the swamp trying to follow the cries, but to no avail. At dusk she appeared, with only four puppies in tow. I was devastated. Too dark to continue our search, we chained Jubilee and made a strategy for the next day's search. We searched for three days. I felt physically ill knowing that a little puppy was alone and scared and without food somewhere in the swamp nearby. I was angry with Jubilee, even knowing her instinct to run was a part of who she was.

And then a miracle happened. A full six weeks later, almost to the day, Stan and I were sitting outside with visiting friends when I noticed movement in the bush behind the meadow. Too small to be a bear, whatever it was wasn't frightened by my actions as I cautiously crept towards it. Before I reached the edge of the meadow, a little puppy walked into the yard. Leaning down to pick it up, it leapt into my arms. I sat cross-legged right there in the meadow with tears streaming down my cheeks (as they are now as I write this), looking at Jubilee's lost puppy and stroking her. She refused to leave my lap, sitting in my arms like a contented little baby. She was a scrawny little thing, and her joints were swollen. I yelled for Stan to get some milk and food, not wanting to release this marvel. Suddenly this pup snapped so

Kodi and Jubilee's first litter of puppies at about six weeks old.

incredibly quickly at a bug nearby that I was stunned. She did it again and again, even catching the mosquitoes flying in the air nearby. So this was how she survived—by eating bugs.

It was a joyous reunion. I coddled this little one for days. I didn't have to worry about letting her out of my sight, as she stuck to me like glue. She filled out and her coat developed a lustre, but her joints remained deformed from rickets. Of course I wanted to keep her, but we had kept one pup from the litter and the others had been sold, and we really didn't want a fourth dog. As hard as it was, I put an ad in the paper for her to go to a good family. It seemed like I was interviewing for a child's placement the way I questioned those who responded. This puppy was going not only to a good home, but to the very best one I could find. The family she ended up going to had five children and lived on an acreage near a community down the Alaska Highway. The kids loved her and she loved them. Watching them romp and play together in the meadow, I reluctantly turned her over to her new family. My mixed feelings of happiness about her new family and sadness at giving her up followed me for days.

My belly was getting big and I found myself getting exhausted easily so I decided not to do any more (what I called) hard physical labour. Stan counted on my help, but I worried I might do something accidentally to injure my baby. This was disappointing to Stan, as I had always been his "right hand man," but he understood and accepted my decision. Instead, I spent a lot of time wandering around the property picking high-bush cranberries and made jams and jellies from my rhubarb, currants and gooseberry bushes.

High-bush cranberries, which are actually not a cranberry at all but are related to the honeysuckle family, have an unmistakable scent that I associate with fall. They grow on a deciduous shrub a couple of metres high in very small clumps of (usually) two, with three-lobed leaves looking similar to a maple leaf. The berry itself is very tart and has a single heart-shaped seed in it. It takes a lot of picking to fill a container, but it's worth it. The unique flavour goes a long way. I often mixed the puree with rosehip, which is very bland, to make jams and syrup. Low-bush cranberries look and taste like the cultivated cranberries but are much smaller and a bit sweeter, I think. They grow on a very small shrub in the heath family, with leathery oval-shaped leaves, and are mostly found at higher elevations in the cool mountain air. The low-bush cranberry can be mixed into muffins and sauces and used for juices and in jams, like the cranberries bought in the store. Blueberries and low-bush cranberries are often found growing near each other.

The blowing wind carried distinct aromas in my direction as I gathered berries in the fall. To me, it was a very satisfying activity. But even more enjoyable was when I was spreading the fruits of my labour on fresh baked bread in a warm cabin with a cup of tea in hand, watching the varicoloured leaves floating to the ground and feeling my unborn baby moving inside me.

A TRUE TREASURE

My visions of wanting to give birth to my firstborn in our log cabin in the bush with a midwife with kerosene lighting and a fire blazing in the background had been abandoned as I got close to the due date and worried that we were so far from the hospital. This feeling grew when I started getting my first labour pains. We hopped in the truck and drove the ninety-six kilometres to Whitehorse. I was glad I had made the decision to have my baby in the hospital instead.

Travis Stanley Milos was born by natural childbirth on November 27, 1980, at 9:25 pm, after eight hours of labour. While in the hospital, I met two other women, Marilyn and Alice, having babies the same time I had Travis. I ended up teaching one of these children in Atlin School and I am still in contact with both of their mothers today.

It was a delight to spend the winter in our warm and cozy cabin with our new baby. My sister Cheryl and her husband came for Christmas less than a month after Travis was born, bringing with her all the news of friends and family, upcoming events and what people thought of the newly elected ex-movie star president of the United States, Ronald Reagan. The weather plummeted to forty-below, but we had plenty of food and firewood and didn't really need to go anywhere. We were content to stay in the warmth of our cabin and visit with family.

The entire winter was a gift. As a first-time mom, I was content to spend these days at home. I kept the cabin very warm, much to my husband's discomfort, but I loved it that way and it made getting up in the middle of the night two and three times to nurse Travis so much easier. I never brought him to bed with us, but always got up and took him into the living room, sat in the willow Amish rocking chair I had purchased by mail order from Ontario and nursed him until he fell asleep.

There were incredible moonlit nights when I could hear the wolves howling in the distance as I sat nursing. Our dogs would howl back, their howls more urgent each time.

There were days when there were so many rabbits in the yard it looked

Proud parents showing off their son Travis, at five months old.

like a video game with bouncing rabbits everywhere. They have seven-year cycles, and it was the year of the highest population.

We kept a box of frozen suet on the porch to feed the birds and we used to chop it up for the dogs occasionally. A pure white ermine would sneak onto the porch to steal little pieces. He became almost tame, just like the little mink that had eaten out of our hands the summer before. All of these things were fascinating to me. I so enjoyed seeing the animals, watching the seasons change, living in the bush. My life seemed complete with the addition of our son.

Being at home full-time that winter, there was time for me to once again concentrate on my artwork. I spun hair gathered from our dogs and friends' dog teams in front of the fire in the evenings and my loom was warped with a project as was my tapestry loom.

When Travis was only five months old, my girlfriend Holly and I were invited for tea at our friend Jenielle's house to see her newborn baby. Judy, another friend going with us, was very pregnant. Jenielle and her partner Bruce, the fire marshal, lived in a cabin on the Atlin River where I had collapsed exhausted following Stan's infamous bet that we could hike over Atlin Mountain in one day.

Instead of snow machines, we went by dog sled. Judy had a team of dogs and Holly ran her team. Travis and I rode with Holly in her basket. It was an incredibly beautiful winter day; you could see the ice crystals in the air. Travis was tucked into a snugly inside my parka and I got to enjoy the ride. I had mushed my own dogs before, but had never spent much time in the basket of a sleigh while someone else was in control. I learned quickly that the person in the sleigh gets all of the smells from the dogs! When sled dogs are tied up for long periods of time they are unbelievably excited to run. You can hardly control them, they are so anxious to get going. Once they start, they go flat out. Their systems get a good workout and gas is often expelled. The person in the basket seems to get the worst of it. But on a beautiful day such as the one we went on, nothing could have dampened the mood. It was exhilarating! I loved watching Judy flying across the lake at the "helm" of her sled with her huge baby bump and a smile on her face. After an afternoon spent drinking tea and enjoying the newborns, we returned home.

That weekend, there happened to be a woman in town from *Alaska* magazine. When she heard about our little adventure, she contacted me and asked if we could write up an article and submit some pictures for possible publication. Although I never did submit anything, it was still fun to be asked.

Late that spring, CBC contacted me about my artwork, having learned about it when I was in the studio the year before doing the interview on rhubarb wine. They were interested in highlighting me in a half-hour program airing on TV, a personal interest program featuring people living in the Yukon, many of them artists. I was thrilled, but apprehensive. I'd had a hard enough time talking into a microphone in the studio, and I didn't know if I could pull off talking into a TV camera. Connections were made with the studio and a day was chosen for a woman to come out to do the interview and the filming. I was a nervous wreck as the time approached. I cleaned the house so it was immaculate and fussed with all of my weaving supplies, moving them around a ridiculous number of times. I went over and over in my head what I was going to say in response to the list of possible questions I'd been given. I worried about what to do with Travis, since Stan had been hired on a renovations contract and could not be at home. My neighbour Maureen was the only one close, and I did not have a phone to make other arrangements, so I asked her to watch Travis for a short while. Maureen was uncertain and worried about how long I would be, as I didn't use bottles or soothers so there wouldn't be much she could do to comfort him.

I jogged home for the interview, which began with the camera filming the cabin and gardens with the mountains in the background. Inside the house, the host concentrated on my weaving area and the completed projects I had on hand. A question and answer period ended the interview. The interviewer was extremely kind and she stopped the filming often to tell me what was coming next. We said our goodbyes and I literally ran through the woods to see how Travis and Maureen were doing. Travis was screaming bloody murder, but magically stopped as soon as I arrived. Evidently he had screamed from the time I left until I came back. I never asked her to babysit again—and she never offered.

The program aired several months later. Not having a TV, we arranged to go into Whitehorse to the CBC studio to watch the show. I was surprised to see myself so relaxed since I had felt so nervous. The experience of seeing myself and my life through somebody else's eyes felt surreal. Leaving the studio, I reflected on my accomplishments and how I had arrived at this point in my life and felt content.

The following year, which went by quickly, my brother Matt, his wife DJ and their son Matthew came to visit from California. During their stay, I suggested we go to Alaska to visit my friend Sarah and her two boys. She had obtained a subsistence fishing licence, allowing her to legally net fish in the rivers, with certain restrictions, and offered me the use of the licence for twenty-four hours. Whatever I caught, I would get to keep.

Unfortunately, Stan had a job and couldn't go, so the five of us drove to Haines, Alaska, in my brother's VW bus, met with Sarah and set up camp on the edge of the Chilkat River, which flows southward through the Coast Mountains to the Haines area, where it empties in to the ocean. This river is home to the Alaska Chilkat Bald Eagle Preserve, which, due to the availability of spawned-out salmon and open waters in the late fall and winter, is thought to be the world's largest concentration of bald eagles. They are an awesome sight to see.

A few days before we arrived, Sarah and a friend had set a stake net— best for catching salmon—in a gentle curve upriver from where we made camp. It consisted of a net stretched between stakes fixed into the riverbed, secured by rope to the shore. Swimming upriver, the fish get tangled in the net, where they remain until they can be extricated. Sarah and I paddled out into the river in her canoe and she showed me how to release the salmon caught in the net. It took both of us to keep the canoe steady in the current while we worked the net. The fish were challenging to remove since they were extremely slimy and tried frantically to escape, thrashing about and slapping their tails on our arms, but we didn't lose a single one. Securing them in the boat, we paddled back to shore. This procedure had to be repeated about every hour or so to ensure the salmon were not trapped in the net for too long. We all took turns and netted late into the night, as it stayed light for almost twenty-four hours.

The next morning the real work began. Up until that time, I had not gutted a lot of fish, but I became an expert that day. I was flipping fish onto the cutting board, making incisions, pulling out guts, scraping the fish clean and washing them in no time. After gutting the salmon, I filleted them, improving with each fish, then cut them into pieces that would fit into a pint canning jar. Next, we put all the fish meat in the smoker. Normally it takes only twenty-four to forty-eight hours to complete the smoking process, but because of the excessive amount of humidity, it took a lot longer. After almost four days, the smoking process was complete, and I was able to dry can (canning with no water) all of the fish. Packing the fish into jars, I processed them in a pressure canner because I had heard there were regulations about taking fish across the border—any amount of canned fish was allowed. When the fish had cooled, we all piled into my brother's van and drove home. Travis was too young to remember this adventure, but years later he and his brother would return to the Chilkat River near to the place we had fished to view the immense numbers of bald eagles.

The author in Haines, Alaska, with her girlfriend's son, gathering her first catch of salmon from the stake net on the Chilkat River.

A multitude of weeds in my gardens needed removing when we returned to Little Atlin. It is amazing how fast things grow in the long days of summer, weeds as well as the vegetables. To help combat this, I laid clear plastic down, thinking this would be ideal to keep the weeds away and allow the sun to warm the ground. I chose this over black plastic which, although it heats the ground, also traps the cold. After securing the plastic on the ground, I cut slits for all my seedlings. The weeds loved it; they grew twice as big as the ones in between the rows. The plastic began sticking up, in some places growing as high as the seedlings almost overnight. I would squat down and run my hand under the plastic, ripping out as many weeds as I could, in the process missing a lot of the roots, which resulted in them growing back even more vigorously. That was the first and last time I used clear plastic, or any kind of plastic, in my garden.

A better solution seemed to be an improved water system—one with warmer water to promote better growth. My brother, who was still visiting, went to work putting together a system with sprinklers. We had bought a water pump to pump water from the lake into a large tank to allow it to warm, but I still had to water by hand. We could also pump water directly to the sprinklers, but it was very cold. Often the lake doesn't thaw until the end of May and the garden is planted when there is still ice in the lake. A twelve-volt pump became an easy solution and was able to pump the water from the tank to the sprinklers. I just had to keep moving the sprinklers around.

While teaching in Carmacks, I had seen a dirty old bathtub in a field outside of town. On one of my weekend trips home, I had stopped and asked the owner of the ranch if I could buy it. He could not really fathom why I wanted to buy a dirty tub he used for a water trough. He sold it to me for $50.00, and I was ecstatic. Hauling it home was the problem: it was cast iron and weighed a ton. Earlier in my brother's visit, he and Stan had gone to pick it up. I cleaned and scrubbed it until it shone. It didn't have all of the legs, but I didn't care—it was a big tub to bathe in. Previous to this, I had been bathing in the round tin washtub we kept hanging on the wall outside. I would fire up the wood cook stove, fill up as many containers as I could to heat, usually using half the water in the forty-five-gallon barrel. Setting the tub in the middle of the living room, I would fill it at least halfway and slowly sit in it, basking in the luxury of the hot water surrounding my body (or more correctly, the parts of my body that fit in). A reserved pot of hot water remained nearby to top up the bath water when it cooled down. There I would sit, peering out the multi-paned windows, sun filtering in through the trees, praying no one would break the silence.

My new tub sat under a big fir tree near the fire pit. Hauling buckets of water from the garden water tank, my brother would heat it over the fire and continue pouring it into the tub until the cast iron tub was heated up and there was enough water for me to get in. A makeshift curtain created privacy. Matt continued to heat water and would yell, "Ready?" That was the cue for me to jump up and move to the far end of the tub as he poured the next batch of water in. After I had lain in the wonderfully hot water a while, I would jump out and the next person would jump in. The guys always went last; we women, naturally, were cleaner than they were.

As Travis began to eat solid foods, I had choices to make. I could buy baby food or I could make my own using a grinder. I did neither, choosing to do what the Inuit women did for their children—chew their food for them first. I would chew up whatever we were eating, fill his baby spoon with the masticated puree and feed it to him. I know it may sound disgusting to some, but in reality it is one of the best ways to feed a child, as the mother's saliva mixes with the food making digestion easier for the baby learning how to eat solid food. I was a bit of a purist in those days. I didn't use formula—Travis was only breast-fed. However, I did break down and buy a baby food grinder, as some people were put off by my baby food preparation and I did not want to offend anyone, especially when I was in their home.

One of Travis's favourite foods was strawberries and my berry garden had oodles of good-sized, juicy, flavourful strawberries. My red and black currant bushes and gooseberries were growing well too, but it took a lot of bushes to yield a reasonable amount of these berries. So I enlarged the strawberry patch and continued nurturing the rhubarb patch for future batches of wine.

The addition of a propane refrigerator we bought that summer was a godsend. Cranking the thermostat all the way up, it became a freezer. We could now keep our moose meat at home and I was able to freeze vegetables from the garden. While Travis sat in the garden crumbling dirt in his little hands, half of it going into his mouth, I harvested the remainder of my crops.

I froze broccoli, cauliflower, Brussels sprouts and green beans picked in peak condition. I washed all the vegetables thoroughly and then blanched them, which is lightly steaming or boiling them to stop continued growth, destroy any bacteria and allow for easier packing into plastic bags or containers. After blanching, I submerged the veggies in ice-cold water, about the same amount of time they are blanched, which cools them down and helps maintain their colour and texture. Finally, I packaged them in Ziploc freezer bags.

The root crops I grew were stored in the in-ground wellhead box, a cool, dark, humid space that didn't freeze. I experimented with growing carrots, beets, turnips, kohlrabi and parsnips. The beet and turnip greens, as well as spinach and mustard greens that we didn't eat raw, I blanched and froze and the carrot greens I dried for soups and stews. I also grew a small amount of summer squash like zucchini, and I tried acorn squash, a winter squash, but without a greenhouse it did not produce well. Most of the winter squashes are vine-type plants whose fruits take longer to mature than the summer squashes that usually take three months or more. We ate all the summer squash, green and yellow zucchini and scallop squash. It was deeply satisfying to have so many organically grown vegetables processed and ready for my family to eat at any time.

Excited to show our beautiful son to my family, we made plans to travel to California after we harvested the garden and the days shortened significantly. My maternity leave was over, but I made a decision not to return to work, allowing me to raise our son full-time and giving us more options for travelling. We decided to take the Alaska State Ferry from Skagway to Prince Rupert to give Travis more space to run around, as only one month earlier he had been walking around the couch and coffee table holding on with one or two hands. All of a sudden he let go and took a few steps, then a few more, then he literally ran around the couch three times clapping his hands, shouting with glee. He was only nine-and-a-half months old. At ten-and-a-half months he was running around like crazy, and the ferry seemed like the answer.

I had little time to take in the extraordinary magnificent views of the inland passageway along the Alaska Panhandle to Prince Rupert, as Travis kept me busy chasing around after him almost the entire time. He never stopped; we went in circles around the boat and I managed to get him to sit down only when it was time to eat. He still did not nap and his curiosity could not be curbed in any way—he wanted to see and touch everything. Fortunately, many of the other passengers enjoyed watching our little guy run around and often tried to talk to him or distract him. Bedtime was worse. We did not purchase a stateroom because of the expense, so we were sleeping in the lounge along with an abundance of other people. There were four seats in a row and most people were lying down in front of the seats with blankets. I was the crib, trying to form sides with luggage and blankets to keep Travis confined to one place. We hoped that having easy access to my breast would settle him. But there was so much going on that his head popped up every few minutes and he peeked under the seats in front and tried to grab things on the floor. He screamed when I wouldn't let him touch something. Not wanting to wake others, I scooped him up and began walking. The next time I tried to put him to sleep the same thing happened. Needless to say, it was a very long two nights and three days as the ferry made its way south down the Alaska Panhandle from Skagway to Juneau, Petersburg, Wrangell and Ketchikan with stops at each port before finally arriving in Prince Rupert.

We broke up the California portion of our trip by stopping in Sawyers Bar to visit friends first before carrying on to Monterey-Carmel. We had been the recipients of the first collective quilt made by our friends from the Salmon River area. A good friend who headed the project distributed a quilt square to everyone we knew and they each embroidered, painted and decorated the square, returning it to organizers who sewed it all together and quilted it. When the package arrived in the mail and I opened it, I was stunned, tears flowing from my face. I was overwhelmed with gratitude for such a loving and incredible gift. It touched my heart more than I can express. We wanted to stop in and thank the wonderful friends we'd made in such a short time when we'd lived there for bestowing such a precious gift on us.

In Carmel, we moved in with my brother and his family. While there, I read about a woman from the UK who was teaching local infants to swim. The program, Water Babies, took advantage of the gag reflex that, when it kicks in, enables a baby to instinctively hold its breath and avoid inhaling water when feeling the sensation of water on its face. It also taught babies to control their breathing before they went underwater, helping them to become independent swimmers sooner.

I immediately enrolled Travis in the program and attended lessons twice a week. It was absolutely amazing how comfortable the babies were in the water, especially the youngest ones. The infants in our group ranged from six months to two years. Travis progressed extremely well, and in a couple of months, he was swimming without any help across the width of the entire pool (with me close by, of course). It was a wonderful experience and even though Travis didn't spend a lot of time in the water in the next couple of years, I feel this contributed to the ease and confidence with which he learned to swim so effortlessly when he took swimming lessons at an older age.

My mom and dad arrived from Florida and rented a house in Carmel for the month of December, and Stan, Travis and I moved in with them. What a joy to be able to surround my son with my family. On Christmas morning, Travis delighted in ripping the paper off all his gifts more than seeing his presents or playing with them. It took him hours and he played with each piece of paper, sitting on the floor clapping it in his hands, wadding it up and throwing it, then getting up stumbling over ribbons and toys, picking it up and throwing it again, and finally chewing whatever he could stuff in his mouth before we made him spit it out. We had fun with the family, and Travis and his cousin Matthew became best play buddies.

Uncertain of our plans at the end of December, we were pleasantly surprised when a friend of my brother's offered us her home to stay in since she was going away for the winter. We accepted the offer, moved in, and stayed until early spring when we returned to the Yukon so Stan could find work, as we were running out of money. As beautiful and expertly executed as his carvings were, they were not generating enough money to support our family with my time off from teaching.

That winter I had become pregnant with our second child, and Stan was not happy. I wanted another child, a sibling for Travis, especially since we lived isolated in the bush, but he didn't. Given our sketchy financial picture, it seemed overwhelming to him to have another child to raise. But luck was with us. Soon after our return to the North, Stan was hired by the Yukon government to stabilize historic sites. His first job was the Robinson Roadhouse Historical Site, once a stop on the White Pass & Yukon Route. It was one of many roadhouses between Skagway and Whitehorse, consisting of a main building and several smaller log cabins with mud roofs. It was named after William Robinson or "Stikine Bill," as he was known. At one time there was talk of it becoming a townsite but the town never really materialized into any size and it remained a base camp for miners. This job was a real bonus for us, as the Robinson Roadhouse was located only thirty-eight kilometres from Carcross—driving distance from our home—so Stan could be home every night.

Chasing Travis around the property and ensuring he didn't wander down to the lake unsupervised while planting and maintaining my gardens took most of my time that summer. My unborn baby was sitting in a "birth position," putting terrible stress on my legs. I was advised to wear special stockings, and put my feet up ten minutes of every hour and one full hour in the morning and in the afternoon. I'm sure that if my doctor had had a child as active as mine he'd have understood the absurdity of advising me to do this—it was nearly impossible, especially since Travis still refused to nap.

I was alone with Travis most of the summer during the day, and I savoured this time with my son. I knew that soon I would be busy with another little one and was grateful for every second Travis and I had. I made learning books for him by cutting out pictures of northern animals from *National Geographic* magazine, putting them all in a binder and saying the names of each one. He astounded me by easily being able to name any animal in no time and finding the photos on request. I cut swaths of fabric and sponges and sandpaper, anything I could find, for him to have a binder of things to touch and describe the feeling. I cut clothes up with zippers, buttons and snaps and put them in a binder too, to support his learning about fasteners. Today you can buy all these types of books, but back then I was isolated and had the time to make anything I thought would benefit my child. We read and listened to songs and rhymes during my rest breaks, which were short but cherished. On occasion, someone would stop by, but often not for a week or two at a time. My isolation didn't bother me, especially as I was sharing my days with my unborn growing in my body and my precious human dynamo lighting my days, plus Stan was home in the evenings.

Once again my belly was getting big and it became harder to do all the chores, especially when harvest time arrived. But with my little helper we managed to pick and freeze the vegetables, pull the root crops and dig the potatoes. This was Travis's favourite chore—first he pulled the plant from the ground as hard as he could to see how many potatoes remained attached to it, then, digging like a puppy to find the rest still hidden, he would squeal with delight when he yanked a big one out of the ground. After allowing the potatoes to sit in the sun for a day or two to toughen their skins we would then sort them by size, put them in burlap bags and bring them down into our root cellar.

Harvest complete, I was content to spend the cool days of September taking walks, picking some berries, baking cinnamon rolls and bread with Travis and crocheting booties and hats for our new baby, as well as new socks and mitts for Travis. Now all I had to do was wait for the birth of our child.

HOME ALONE

Brett Matthew Milos was born twenty-three months after his brother, on October 25, 1982. I was warned that he would come quickly and he did, popping out and almost landing on the delivery room floor. The attending nurse literally caught him as the doctor and Stan were scrubbing up to enter the room. Several days before his due date, Stan and I had travelled into Whitehorse to stay at the home of Brian and Sharon, friends who had a cabin on Little Atlin Lake. We raced to the hospital minutes after I started feeling contractions, which increased exponentially, leaving little time for me to be prepped for delivery and no time for the doctor or Stan to even be in the room to witness the birth. The nurse and doctor told me how lucky I was it was a fast and easy birth, but as I hadn't had contractions so continually and so severe with Travis, I wasn't so sure I agreed with them. But happily, my second son was born healthy, although I panicked for a moment when he didn't cry, and instead lay his head on me quietly. I hadn't realized he was blissfully sleeping. This was quite the opposite from Travis's loud arrival into the world, but I soon learned this dear child of mine was a mellow, sweet little baby.

That winter I was alone with Travis and Brett at the cabin with no vehicle or means of communication, their dad having been offered another contract restoring heritage sites under the Heritage Branch of the government. Stan had proved that he could work well with small parties of unskilled workers. This job was at Fort Selkirk, a former trading post on the Yukon River at the confluence of the Pelly River and home to the Selkirk First Nation. Fort Selkirk is accessible by boat only and is therefore isolated, so Stan worked in for ten days straight, and then came home for three or four days, leaving me alone for longer periods of time than his previous jobs had.

Before leaving, Stan would stack firewood in the porch, fill our forty-five-gallon barrel with water and complete any chores that needed to be done. I was normally very good at not wasting any water and had established routines to conserve. With the boys, however, I used more, so I needed to haul water again. It was a very special time of my life with my beautiful

119

The author's family with its new addition, son Brett.

boys, but also a scary time for me. I worried about something happening while on my own with the children, like falling while hauling water, cutting myself chopping kindling or needing to contact a doctor for one of the kids. But my biggest fear was about a man who had recently been let out of jail and was once again living somewhere in the area.

The previous year while driving, Stan and I had seen a very strange man walking along Atlin Road near our home. We assumed he was squatting somewhere nearby and wanted to keep the location a secret, but we weren't sure. Neighbours expressed similar concerns to ours, having caught glimpses of him walking down the road and ducking into the bushes whenever a car went by. We later found out that people called him Sheslay Mike because he had been living in the remote Sheslay River area south of Teslin, Yukon. Then we found out he was living in the bush near a man we knew from Atlin named Gunter Lishy. When Gunter mysteriously disappeared, Sheslay Mike was rumoured to have been involved in the disappearance.

Just about everyone knew Gunter, a single, quiet German man who owned a log cabin in Atlin and trapped in the area south of Teslin Lake. He liked things neat and tidy and kept his cabin meticulously clean—once a year he even used a toothbrush to scrub the caulking between the logs. He had an old yellow truck he drove to town to get supplies and was friendly to those he met on the street.

In late June 1981, a pilot flying for Taku Air dropped Gunter off at Hutsigola Lake, one of the first lakes in a chain lying at the southern end of the Teslin Valley beyond Teslin Lake. Gunter had building materials and provisions to last him until September. Mike Oros was already living on the lake in a rough-hewn octagonal cabin, but was believed to be down in the Sheslay area when Gunter was dropped off.

On September 10, Dave, the pilot, returned to pick Gunter up as they had prearranged, but instead was met by Sheslay Mike, wearing some of what appeared to be Gunter's clothes. He said he had never seen or heard of Gunter and that perhaps Dave was mistaken and had dropped him off elsewhere. The pilot returned to Atlin and contacted the RCMP. Speculation in town was that something bad had happened to Gunter. The locals suspected Shesley Mike. On September 17, the RCMP searched the area but could find no sign of Gunter.

An investigation into Gunter's disappearance showed that Sheslay Mike was Mike Oros, a landed immigrant in Canada, who had a criminal record for possession of narcotics and fraud. A recluse who lived off the land, his threats, break-ins and harassment of trappers and fishermen gained him notoriety that spread across the area. He was also obsessed with the "Mad Trapper of Rat River," Albert Johnson, who, in the early 1930s, fatally shot an RCMP officer investigating alleged tampering with Indigenous traplines. In the manhunt that ensued, he killed another Mountie and eventually himself.

Mike Oros was a very troubled man. He claimed he had been in Vietnam and that the CIA was after him. He refused to eat food made by strangers, thinking they were poisoning him. Notes were found in an abandoned cabin he was staying in, warning about "red power" and the "wrath of God," and a letter that said "You did this to me, you fed me drugs, you tried to put me away. My revenge will be something to behold." Many felt that something should have been done about him years ago… what, I don't know.

In 1981, like Johnson, Oros evaded seven RCMP officers and two tracking dogs for a week when they hunted him down following Gunter's disappearance. A year later, in March of 1982, Oros was eventually arrested at a remote cabin. He was wearing Gunter's clothes, and when his cabin was searched, Gunter's 44-magnum pistol was found in a box beside his bed and his belongings and building materials were found cached in the area. Oros was placed in a cell at the RCMP detachment in Atlin but released in late summer of the same year and was seen back in the Atlin area. In fact, a former student of mine, Brad, and his buddy picked him up and gave him a ride along the Atlin Road in September.

As a young woman alone in the bush with little means of self-defence, I felt vulnerable. On occasion, strangers had made their way to our cabin looking for someone, needing to borrow a tool to fix their rig broken down on the road or wanting a bit of gas. I hadn't worried about these things much, but now it wasn't just me I had to worry about, but my two treasured children as well. Memories of "peeping toms" from long ago when I was an adolescent crept in—we once had one looking into my sister's and my windows at our home in Florida. I thought I had gotten over these fears, but Sheslay Mike being in the neighbourhood made me terribly uneasy and revived these feelings from my past. I took small comfort in the fact that there was a rifle in the cabin, but it wasn't loaded and I did not know how to use it well.

A friend from Jake's Corner checked in once in a while, but that was all the contact I had with the "outside world" that winter. My entertainment in any quiet time I had was listening to the radio. The news kept me updated about what was happening in the world. I celebrated by myself when I heard that San Francisco had won the Superbowl. I was an old football fan from way back, having had a dad who'd been a football star. So, besides having a sometimes overactive mind at times and being riddled with worry, I really didn't mind the isolation; it was my time with my precious little ones.

Spring brought melting snow and new buds pushing through the ground. It also brought a moose to our property. This huge creature decided to hang out for four days in the yard, eating new shoots off the willows, nibbling greens at the lake and generally ignoring our three barking dogs, who gave up after the second day of this animal stalking around near them. The boys were intrigued, especially Travis, who glued his nose to the window watching this great animal for what seemed like hours. I snuck out one day when the boys were having a rest to snap a photo of our moose friend. I silently crept up behind a tree mere feet from where he was standing a few feet from shore in very shallow water, the lake ice "rotten" and floating behind him. He was drinking from the lake when he suddenly noticed me and looked up. I snapped a couple of shots and quickly retreated to the cabin. I was excited about getting so close to such a magnificent animal. Well, when we had the film developed, Stan was quick to point out emphatically, "For God's sakes, the hair on the back of his neck was sticking darn well straight up and you were damn lucky he didn't charge you! You had better be more careful. You have no idea how close you came to getting maimed or killed." Hmmm, this hadn't been on my worry list before, but it was now!

Break-up was gentle that year. The rotten ice, mixed with snow that was melting and disintegrating, floated around in patches, moving from one end of the lake to the other. It slowly melted away, rather than all at once, as was usually the case. This was partly due to the sunshine and windless air lasting for so many days at break-up with the honeycombed ice not getting a chance to blow onto shore to melt on the banks of the lake.

The boys delighted in being outside once again. Travis entertained Brett with all of his antics and brought him pieces of wood he was hauling for the wood cook stove to bang and play with. I had been working on my artwork over the winter, exploring felting as a new medium to use with my weaving and on its own for wall hangings.

First I dyed large batches of wool and then carded my dyed wool by hand or with my hand-cranked carding machine. On a piece of fibreglass screen, I laid a layer of wool all in one direction. Then a second layer went down at a 90° angle to the first, and so on until it reached the desired thickness for my piece. This was my base layer. Another piece of fibreglass screen went on top and the two were sewed together with a large needle and thread. This is where Travis came in to help with my big pieces. I wanted him to perform the agitation segment. With a tarp on the ground, I laid the enclosed fibres down, poured boiling water over them, added soap, and had Travis stomp up and down on it with rubber boots long enough to complete a partial matting of the fibres. Giggling loudly as he jumped up and down, he couldn't get enough of it. Brett was thoroughly amused. After bubbles coated the wool and almost every spot on Travis, it was time to rinse. Using a cold-water rinse created additional shock to the fibres to assist in matting them.

Trav also joined in on helping me with the smaller pieces I felted, which were mostly northern themed—Peregrine falcons, a great horned owl, the northern lights, ptarmigan and whales.

Stan was shipped around to several sites that summer, including Hootalinqua Island, where a forty-eight kilometre section of the Yukon River is a narrow channel beginning at the northern end of Lake Labarge and ending at the Teslin River at Hootalinqua. This island was a shipping hub and

"Winter Ptarmigan," felted with natural and dyed wools, with hand-stitching added.

"Big Horned Owl," woven with hand-spun dog hair with felted background of wool, dog hair and muskox qiviut, (soft underwool).

historical site with several old buildings and boats. Stan was home off and on during the summer. The gardens were tilled and planted and the boys and I kept busy at the homestead. Although I'd planned to stay close to home, I'd kept the truck so I had transportation if I wanted or needed to get out. And one evening, I did need to.

I was feeding Brett in his high chair, which was pulled up to the dining room table, when Travis walked over, wooden toy hammer with a metal head in hand, to show Brett something. And then it happened—Brett grabbed the hammer and hit Travis in the head. Travis reacted by pushing the high chair, causing it to topple over. Travis's head started spurting blood, because Brett had hit an artery. Scooping Brett off the floor, I raced to get a cloth to hold over Travis's head.

Trying to calm both screaming kids, I noticed blood was running from Brett's mouth. He had put his tooth through his lip when he fell. I needed to get Travis to a doctor, so I jumped in the truck, strapped both shrieking children into their seats and started driving to Whitehorse, one hand on the wheel, one hand holding the cloth firmly on Travis's head, while blood still ran out of Brett's mouth. Stan was due home that day, but I had no way of notifying him. Rounding a corner of

Marsh Lake, about twenty minutes from Whitehorse, Stan passed by going the other way. He recognized the truck and had his ride turn around and catch up to us. I pulled over and he went into momentary shock at the scene before his eyes. Jumping in and taking over the driving, Stan got us to the hospital and we went straight to emergency. A half-hour later, Travis was butterflied together and Brett had two stitches. We drove home and all fell into bed exhausted, the crisis over.

As summer inched by, I began to get out more and visit friends. Several of my girlfriends had newborn babies or young children and we had begun to feel almost an urgency to get together. We needed to share joys and fears, discuss issues with our kids, explore discipline strategies for the older children and confer about our absent men. I relished this time, not realizing how much I had missed female companionship. We vowed to organize more time together and renew our lives of adventure.

I also applied for a job cleaning the two Yukon government campgrounds, Snafu and Tarfu, farther down the Atlin Road, to give me an opportunity to get out and make some money too. These campgrounds were named when the Northwest Highway System built the road in 1949. Their names were obviously influenced by World War II, as SNAFU means "Situation Normal, All Fu… Up" and TARFU meant "Things are Really Fu… Up." Both campgrounds sit on lakes with their respective names and each has campsites with picnic tables, pit toilets, water, firewood, boat launches and they provide opportunities or camping, hiking, boating, canoeing and fishing.

Snafu was located only about ten kilometres south of our home and had great grayling fishing. Tarfu was located about seven kilometres farther on, south of Snafu. The larger of the two lakes, it had grayling, lake trout and pike in it. I was hired, and my duties including removing the garbage, cleaning the outhouses and campsites and supplying the firewood to each site. I was also responsible for collecting the fees. It was a great job, as I could go any time, any day, as long as I made an appearance at each campground twice a week, and the boys could come too. Travis was a big help, often raking the campsites and picking up pieces of garbage. We enjoyed meeting many wonderful tourists as well as locals, and I often sat and chatted with them while the boys played nearby.

As the end of summer neared, my girlfriends and I were left alone again while our men were all away working. Stan was working at another historical site, one of my girlfriends' husbands was big-game guiding, and my girlfriend Carmen's husband was working as marine engineer on a freighter in the Arctic. So in mid-August, the three of us—Carmen, Bonnie and I, with eight kids between us—decided to go moose hunting. Hunting season had just opened and since none of our men were around to hunt, we decided we would give it a shot. The plan was to go by boat to Carmen's summer cabin across Windy Arm on Tagish Lake. Windy Arm is one of the two main arms of Tagish Lake, which is mostly in the Yukon. Carmen and her husband, Arne, bought the cabin and a third of an acre in 1978 and got title to the land, originally staked when the Yukon government had a staking program in the late sixties. It was home until they moved to Atlin when their oldest son was school aged, but they still enjoyed spending time at their cabin in the warm days of summer when they could, where they could garden, fish, hike and relax in such a splendid, peaceful environment. It was also a good place to go hunting from, so it seemed perfect for us to try our hand at getting a moose.

Bonnie was the only one that had her hunting licence, but we all knew how to shoot a rifle. I had recently taken my hunter safety course, had become more comfortable with a rifle and was ready to try for a moose. Since Bonnie was the most experienced and the only one who knew how to dress a moose properly, we decided we would take turns going out with her while the third person stayed with the kids. On the day of our trip, we all met at the boat dock on Tagish River where Carmen had their boat *Iota*. It was a wonderful 5.5-metre single-cylinder diesel crab trawler originally from Vancouver Island. She and her husband had bought it from a woman in Atlin. The wooden wheelhouse had a forward "V" bunk, and behind this was a small cockpit with a steering wheel and sink, a back deck as well as a small auxiliary motor for emergencies. A large rudder in the rear of the boat allowed steering from outside, which was most favourable in the summer. We had enough food and supplies for a few days in the bush. Carmen's son was the oldest, at eight years old, and the rest of the eight children were all under five years old, with three of them under a year and breast-feeding. It was quite a group.

After loading the supplies on Carmen's boat and making sure all of the children had life jackets on, we put the three youngest in the cabin. We were not taking any chances, as the water in Tagish Lake, like most of the large lakes in the north, never warmed much over four or five degrees Celsius. Plus, the wind can come up in a flash and the waves increase in size quickly. Windy Arm is named appropriately for the strong winds that channel through the area, but on this day it was relatively calm and perfect for boating to the cabin.

The two-hour trip to the cabin was enthralling—the motion of the boat was rhythmic and the scene changed every few minutes with each island or bay we peeked into. As soon as we angled into the bay where Carmen's cabin was and neared the dock, the older kids came alive, fighting to jump off the boat. They scampered up the dock with their younger brothers and sisters trailing behind trying to catch up. They ran along the shore, splashed in the cold water and inspected the workshop and toys in the sandbox before being coerced to help unload the boat.

We opened up the cabin to air it out, gave it a sweep and organized the supplies and sleeping gear. Carmen got the sauna going and we lazed around most of the afternoon watching the kids and enjoying being in such an isolated, magnificently beautiful place. Dinner was early that night, as the first hunting crew was heading out in the boat right after eating, hoping to spot a moose nibbling on fresh greens or drinking from the cool waters around dusk.

Bonnie and Carmen were selected to be the first hunting party, so I was left to care for all eight kids. They had played hard and the hope was that they would all fall asleep early. Since the youngest were still nursing, Bonnie and Carmen fed their little ones before leaving and they headed out with the rest of us waving and yelling encouraging words for the big moose hunt.

Getting the kids to bed easily and all at once did not happen. Even Shawn, Carmen's oldest, tried to help me, but between giggling, crying, diaper changing, going to the bathroom, needing water and wanting more food, it was a long process of quieting everyone down, let alone getting them to sleep.

As darkness fell, there was no sign of the boat. I surmised this was a good thing, as maybe, just maybe, they'd shot a moose and were dressing it out, which was keeping them from returning at dark. Silence was short-lived in the cabin; first one child started crying, then another. Some of the kids fell asleep, and I took Bonnie's little boy and put him to my breast to feed him and comfort him, but he did not want any part of me. I was not his mom, and he knew it. Carmen's little girl was the same way. She fussed and carried on, but would not suck more than a few seconds before crying even harder. Only my Brett was content to suck. None of the kids had ever had a bottle.

The wailing got worse and woke the others up. I tried repeatedly to soothe and comfort the babies. The little bit of sucking they all did made my milk come in even more and now I had huge breasts needing to be emptied. The bawling wouldn't stop and I kept trading babies around trying to get them to nurse. Then one by one the older kids all woke up needing to pee. Travis refused to go outside, as he wasn't familiar with the surroundings and wanted to pee in a bucket, so I had to go and find something to pee in. Carmen's second son ran outside, and her oldest son was yelling for everybody to be quiet. All the while my boobs were getting bigger and hurting more and more, with no relief. Poor Brett was filled to the brim with milk. When I finally got them all settled down again and just about to fall asleep, another would wake. All the while I was thinking to myself, *they better have a moose to make all this worth it.*

Morning comes early in August, and all the kids were up with the light, the youngest still cranky and wanting their moms. I assumed that it got too dark for Bonnie and Carmen to return the night before, especially if they were busy skinning a moose and dissecting it into parts to put into the boat. I fed the kids and scooted them out to play, staying right behind them to keep an eye on the brood. We talked about the probability of their moms getting a moose. The kids were so excited, they all watched for the boat, making a game out of it. I was exhausted, but when the boat rounded the corner everyone jumped for joy. We all headed for the dock, the older kids screaming, "Did you get a moose, did you get a moose?"

Bonnie threw the rope to Shawn and jumped out with Carmen following. The youngest ones, shrieking when they saw their moms, were half-running, half-crawling down the dock. There was a bit of a smile on the women's faces and they were blushing slightly. "No, no we didn't get a moose," they said. Disappointed only for a moment, the older kids all ran back to shore.

"Well," I asked, "why were you gone all night? The kids really missed you and I was getting a bit worried. I was sure you had shot a moose and that's why you didn't come home."

"Well, actually," Carmen replied sheepishly, "we met some folks at one of the trapline cabins down the lake and partied with them. We lost track of time and waited until morning to head back."

I thought I was going to scream. I was so upset. They were partying all night and I was trying to manage eight kids, breast-feeding three of them. Didn't they understand how difficult that was? How tired I was? How could they forget about me? Just look at my boobs! Needless to say, I got the day

Some of the kids playing outside on a hot summer's day at Carmen's cabin on Tagish Lake.

off from watching the kids. We all laughed about it later in the day while lying in the sun.

It was a noble thought to try and get the meat for the winter since the men were working, but that was the end of moose hunting. Instead, we took saunas and hikes, made pizza on the old Finley wood cook stove and had a marvellous time. The kids ran around mostly naked, jumping in and out of a little pool and building things in the workshop, but supplies were running low and we had to get back. We had already stayed longer than planned due to the fact that Windy Arm was living up to its name—it was way too windy to get out on the lake.

The wind kept blowing and blowing, day and night, blasting everything in sight with its force. We were now down to staples and of course no communication to the mainland. We stayed another day... then another. On the third night of waiting for the wind to die, Carmen woke Bonnie and me up at about 4:00 in the morning. "It is just getting light," she said, "It's calmer now than it has been for days. It is now or never. Get up, get everything to the boat." We packed all of our gear in an 5.5-metre canoe that we pulled behind *Iota*, leaving plenty of space in the boat for all of the kids. We woke the children gently and carried them to the boat, putting them all on the bed in the boat's cabin, and headed out across the arm.

The wind began to pick up. Thank goodness the children all stayed asleep. It got rougher and rougher. I have never been seasick, but both Bonnie and I were feeling a bit green. We huddled in the back, plugging our ears and trying to keep from throwing up. Carmen was a trooper, sitting at the helm on the back of the boat steering. The waves rolled the little boat around almost violently at times. It was when the weather was at its worst that the tie line to the canoe broke, unleashing it from *Iota*. The canoe had all of our sleeping bags, purses, clothes, everything. Carmen, an experienced boat person, yelled at the top of her lungs above the wind: "I am going to turn this boat around and you have one chance, one chance *only* to grab that canoe." Carmen doesn't normally use profanity, but I believe there was definitely a couple of swear words in her sentence. We got the message loud and clear.

The right moment arrived to turn the boat in between the waves. She turned and moved towards the canoe, bobbing up and down in a frenzy. Carmen brought us broadside to the canoe and Bonnie and I frantically grabbed at it. We hung on for dear life while trying to secure it to the boat with another line. To this day I cannot believe the amount of wave action that it took to cause a half-inch nylon rope to break.

As we neared the shore and entrance to the river, the waves subsided and the wind lessened, the land acting as a windbreak. We sighed with relief—we were across and safe. We hailed our captain. It was at this point that one of the kids stuck his head out of the cabin door and said, "Where are we?" It was another adventure I will never forget! To celebrate the success of our crossing, we decided to reward ourselves with a snack at Jake's Corner. Perched upon the Jake's Corner sign sat the snowy owl, a good omen, we all agreed, as it was not quite noon!

Midnight Madness

My girlfriends and I may not have gotten a moose, but we harvested an abundance of vegetables from our gardens and prepared a huge collection of home-canned goodies to savour in the winter. A good friend of ours very generously gave us a hindquarter of some moose meat, which we butchered ourselves following a book. We ground up all of the leftover tidbits of moose meat and I made salami. It was delicious!

The skies began to fill with V's as flocks of Canadian geese, swans and other ducks migrated south. Often a flock would land in the lake near the swamp and we could hear them call to each other as loud as if they were right in front of our property. But the real treat was when we heard the unmistakable hollow nasal honking sound of the appropriately named trumpeter swan.

Stan finished his contract with the government and was home for the winter. When the first snow covered the ground, it was an incredibly satisfying feeling to have your food and firewood in, to know you will be able to make it through a winter no matter how harsh. We burned approximately six cords of wood a year, most of it cut from the nearby forest, some purchased if Stan was unable to gather a sufficient amount, but we never began a winter without enough firewood. We snuggled in and spent most of our time at home with the boys.

We were all sleeping peacefully late one night when a group of friends who'd been partying decided it would be fun to come to our place to continue their party on the ice skating rink we'd made out on the lake. They were not deterred when they drove down the long driveway and saw that it was pitch black in the cabin and that we were sleeping. Hooting and hollering and banging on the door as loud as they could, they gave us little choice but to get up. So up we got, stoked the fire, got dressed and headed down to the lake to join in the party on our mini rink.

Wanting a bonfire to warm up by, the guys busied themselves getting it going. Having a bonfire on ice was an interesting experience. Once you get it burning, the heat warming everyone, it also begins to melt the ice. We had to watch our feet so they didn't get wet. When it is really cold and the fire is blazing, like it was this night, the metre or so thick layer of ice begins to melt and the water quickly starts to re-freeze as it seeps away from the fire. If you are caught in the wrong place, your boots can get frozen into the ice. Then there is the drinking of your beer… when it is very cold, your beer actually begins freezing in your hand, so it is imperative to get near the fire and keep turning your beer, as well as your body, to remain warm. These are the trials of partying outside on the lake ice in the middle of winter, but somehow they made it all the more enjoyable.

This particular night, I harnessed our dog Kodi to our sleigh, which had a box on it for the kids. The moon was shining brightly and the reflection on the snow made it seem almost like daylight. I was running down the lake next to Kodi pulling the boys, who were soundly sleeping, bundled in the sled box, oblivious to where they were. The fire was glowing and you could hear the voices of all our friends. The stars were out and it was a breathtaking night. Breathing in the crisp cold air I just couldn't imagine anything else I would rather be doing at that moment. I was grateful to our friends for rousing us from our warm bed for a fun-filled night! Hearing the wolves howl in the distance just topped it all off.

Festivals, parties and spontaneous visits are a part of life in the North in any season. Loving parties ourselves, we had a big celebration at our place for our tenth wedding anniversary on May 1, 1984. All of our friends and their families were invited. Someone even gave us a whole pig to roast. On the morning of the party, I was starting to prepare food and Stan was getting the open pit barbeque going and completing the finishing touches on the yard when, at 9:30, a car drove down the driveway. Our friend Doug had just left a party and was passing by on his way home. Our official first arrival, he ended up in front of the fire at the BBQ pit snoozing off and on for most of the day until the others arrived.

There must have been thirty or more people, kids, babies and adults alike. Down at the horseshoe pit cheers rang out with each clink of the shoe, people of all ages were playing soccer in the meadow and others were splashing in the lake and wandering around the property. The kids were having a ball, playing on the swing set and in the fort, grabbing their favourite snacks off the tables and stealing desserts before dinner. The older children took care of the younger kids, the young girls mothering the babies. It was a beautiful sunny May Day, perfect for the celebration.

Party-goers at our annual May 1 anniversary party.

As the evening progressed, the guitars and a variety of other instruments appeared and people began jamming. One friend even put up a drum set in the meadow (which was not popular in the morning). People sang and danced and eventually the kids got so tired they fell into the arms of their parents and had to be carried to their sleeping bags in their tents.

Stan and I were up early the next morning, by habit, I suppose. Sneaking out of the cabin so as not to wake the boys, we surveyed the situation in the yard, seeing how much of a mess there was. Another friend was up, too. As we walked around hearing heavy snores from the tents, a mischievous idea formed: what if we played a joke on some of the folks? It just so happened that our friend from Jake's Corner had a tow truck, and for some reason he had driven it to the party instead of his regular truck. The keys were in it. In no time, Stan and some guys had the tow truck started and were literally moving cars around, towing some down one of the side roads into the bush, moving others to new places. They were just having a ball when the kids started on the drum set, suddenly waking up some of the adults.

It was hysterical watching people. Most of them just wandered out of their tent over to where I was cooking breakfast. As soon as one person went to get something out of their car and their car wasn't there, the entertainment began. *What the hell happened? I know I parked next to the horseshoe*

Travis and Brett dressed up for the annual Yukon Rendezvous, a winter carnival in Whitehorse celebrating the 1890s sourdoughs.

pit. Am I going crazy? Did my wife take the car? We were laughing hysterically, but the truck hanging from the tow truck gave it away. It was a great way to start the day! The party was such a success it became an annual event and every year someone tried to outdo the practical jokes of the previous years.

Break-up was a much anticipated event, as it was different every year. Sometimes the ice would just sit there and melt slowly, and other times it would break up and be pushed from one shore to the next with the wind. This year it was late, the ice breaking up in grid-like lines, floating around the lake, settling wherever the wind took it. One day we'd see patches of ice amidst a sea of blue down by our shore, the next day it would be gone, only to reappear the following day. Each year created a different mosaic on the lake, piquing our curiosity about what the ice would do next until it finally disappeared.

Eventually spring melted into summer and the boys were anticipating the upcoming visit of their grandparents. When the day arrived they were glued to the airport's observation lounge window watching the plane arrive. So excited they could hardly contain themselves, they jumped up and down and waved, then ran into my parents' arms as they stepped through the door into the arrival area. It was great to see my mom and dad, and for them to have a chance to see our home at Little Atlin. We drove to the cabin, the boys, now two and four, talking non-stop, my mom spoiling them all the way with home-baked cookies.

My dad loved the opportunity to be in the "woods," as he called it, reminding him of his roots in West Virginia. He volunteered to wash clothes in the washtub with a toilet plunger, even though we went to the laundromat whenever we were in town, and he loved to take a bath in a tub by the wood heating stove in the guest cabin. But his main focus was on the windmill he bought us to generate power for our cabin. It arrived in Whitehorse several days before my mom and dad flew in so we had it on hand and ready to be installed. Stan and my dad worked diligently on putting it together and hooking it up. It was a small-home wind-energy system consisting of a rotor, a generator-alternator mounted on a frame, a tail, self-supporting tower and wiring. The model was designed to give us plenty of power for our new twelve-volt lights and the miscellaneous appliances we hoped to purchase.

Having observed the trees and wind patterns for some time, we picked what we felt would be the ideal location. With the boys helping, Stan and my dad poured a cement pad, dug a ditch to the house for the encased wiring, put together the wind generator system, mounted it on a fifteen-metre tower and hoisted it up with a block and tackle. It was a stand-alone system requiring batteries to store excess power generated for use when the wind was calm. We also purchased a charge controller so the deep cycle batteries would not overcharge. We would start with this kind of a system and decide later if we would install an inverter to convert the DC electricity from the batteries to AC if we felt the need. Installation complete, all we needed was wind to test it out.

It was calm for days, but on the days there was some wind, the rotors just weren't turning. I felt badly for my dad as he sat outside for hours watching the rotors standing still while trees were blowing nearby. At the end of the week, we simply had to accept the fact that the system was located in the wrong place. After much deliberation, my father concluded it should be installed closer to the lake, which of course meant moving everything. Through a series of brainstorming sessions, Stan came up with an idea. He made a quick trip to Jake's Corner and returned with the tow truck, borrowed from Ray. With a bit of effort and some good ingenuity, the entire wind generator system, cement pad and all, was literally dragged closer to its new location. Once again my father sat watching the rotors like a

The author's father, Matt Borek, washing his clothes in a bucket.

hawk, hardly noticing the boys playing by his side, and with every gust of wind he held his breath. The instant the rotor responded, he jumped up, yelling at the kids, "Look at it go!"

In its new location, the system worked like a charm. The batteries charged up and we had twelve-volt lighting in the bedrooms and kitchen to supplement our one propane lamp. Up to this point, kerosene lamps had been our main source of light. Although I loved the warm glow from the old fashioned lamps sitting on their decorative bases and hanging from the walls, I'd always worried about them in Brett and Travis's room. I was afraid that they would accidentally hit one with a ball or something else and cause a fire. We had fire extinguishers, both large and small, placed strategically in the house but the new twelve-volt lamps provided relief from this worry. They also needed less maintenance than the kerosene lamps, which required constant filling, trimming the wicks and cleaning the glass globes.

With the wind generator installed and working properly, we spent the last few days of my parents' trip sightseeing. On our way to Atlin, we showed them the campgrounds, and the boys and I did a quick cleanup. We took a trip to Whitehorse to visit the S.S. Klondike National Historic Site and toured the S.S. *Klondike II*, a sternwheeler that ran passengers and freight between Whitehorse and Dawson City. This boat was an exact replica of the S.S. *Klondike I* that was built in 1929, then tragically sank in 1936 on a section of the Yukon River known as the Thirty Mile. The S.S. *Klondike* made the downstream run from Whitehorse to Dawson City—a distance of some 740 kilometres—in approximately thirty-six hours with one or two stops for wood. The upstream journey back to Whitehorse, including a stop at Stewart Landing to take on ore, would take four or five days and six wood-stops. The high cost of operation ended her career in 1950 and she became a cruise ship for a few years before being retired in 1955. She now sat on the banks of the Yukon River, and the tour was a hit with everyone in my family that day and it was a great way to end the visit from my parents.

Earlier in the year Stan and I had submitted our art resumes and portfolios together to a Yukon government Department of Tourism and Culture program to enhance public appreciation of the arts and to assist the many talented local artists. If chosen, you were assigned to a store in downtown Whitehorse to design a display in their front window exhibiting your works of art, and would be paid a sum of $350.00.

We were thrilled when we got the news that we had been chosen as two of the artists to be represented and that the store displaying our work would be Mac's Fireweed Bookstore, one of the most popular stores in Whitehorse. Stan had a collection of completed carvings, mostly whales made of ancient mastodon tusk purchased from miners in Dawson City who were finding these tusks and other remnants of Yukon's prehistoric past while using hydraulic hoses and heavy equipment. He also used ivory teeth for his carvings, often making them into birds. For our display, we were going to highlight Stan's carvings on a felted ocean created by me.

Using all the different hues of blue and green wool, I felted, with the boys' help, an ocean that was approximately three metres by four metres. I incorporated raw carded wool, raw wool fleece pieces, wool roving, some hand-spun yarn and small pre-felted balls, serving as bubbles, into this massive piece. Brett and Travis stomped and stomped on the large encased mat off and on for days to get the desired effect. My ocean was draped over a backboard, flowing out towards the window over plastic containers of all shapes to create waves, or an undulation effect. Stan's carvings were set on the raised areas. It was a hit and generated more interest in our art—Stan sold a few pieces and I had the opportunity to show more of my work in galleries.

As summer moved into fall, the lake began to freeze almost overnight. The shallow areas at the swamp and near the lakeshore froze first, producing a thin, translucent, almost invisible layer of ice. The boys and I were driving home from Jake's one afternoon and as we neared the boat launch for Little Atlin Lake, we witnessed geese landing on what they thought was open water on their way south. Unable to see that a recently frozen layer of ice covered their landing spot, they came in feet first, hitting the ice and sliding in every direction, bumping into each other and honking like crazy. I stopped the car and we got out quietly, sneaking over to the bushes and squatting down to watch the activity. Astoundingly, more geese followed the first set and the exact thing happened to them, with only a few landing on the water a short distance out. It was a riot watching them flopping around trying to walk or swim on the frozen lake. I wish I had had my camera to catch this cartoonish sight on film. Back at our cabin, we listened to them all evening honking down at the swamp.

NEVER-ENDING PARTY

In the winter of 1984, we went "out." That is the term used by northerners when they leave the bush or isolated communities and go south to the more populated areas. The boys weren't in school yet and I wasn't working, so we wanted to take them south to see friends and family and expose them to as many experiences as possible. We didn't have very much money, but decided to head out anyway.

Our first stop was Sawyers Bar, California, to see friends. Turning off I-5 towards the coast, and then travelling through Yreka, Fort Jones and Etna, we eventually began the climb up Etna Mountain, which took us away from the masses into the California wilderness. The road twists and turns as it climbs up to the summit at almost 2,133 metres. From there we had an incredible view towards the west into the valley embracing the north fork of the rushing Salmon River and town of Sawyers Bar. Many of the folks we had become friends with lived in cabins on old mining claims scattered in and around the community, some located on steep trails near the banks of the river. Some of the cabins were so close to the road you could almost touch the tiny porches with their welcoming swinging chairs.

We had only been there for a day when I was bombarded with information about the school needing a teacher. It was late fall and they were desperate. The school had approximately thirty students in grades one through eight and they were looking for someone to teach grades four through eight. No wonder nobody had applied—five grades in one room is a very demanding situation. People were wondering if there was any chance I might apply; they would love to have me teach their kids, they said. Well, I had taught three grades in one room before and figured I could do it. And we were broke, so we could use the money. I spoke with the person doing the hiring and was told that because the school district was having so much difficulty hiring a teacher, they'd like me to start immediately, and I could quit when I needed to. They would figure something out at a later date. But I needed to figure out a few things too. If I took the job and we stayed in Sawyers Bar, the kids would not be able to spend time with my family.

Another concern was for my boys' care while I was working, but between my girlfriend Sharon and Stan, we figured it out.

The principal and I devised a plan of teaching and accommodating all of the students, which would meet all of our needs too. I was going to teach everything but math to grades four through eight, and he would teach math to my students while I taught art and science to his grade one through three students. There was also a part-time kindergarten teacher employed in the school, an aid to help support my students, and a part-time secretary.

In order to understand the atmosphere of the school and parents, you would have to know something about the people of Sawyers Bar. The once-booming gold rush town was made up of mostly sixties back-to-the-land folk living on mining claims up gulches and along the Salmon River. Some mined, others worked for the forestry industry, and many survived by growing marijuana to supplement whatever jobs they could get. It was a very laid-back community. There was no electricity in the whole town. The school, general store with gas pump and bar were the only buildings that used generators for power. The post office was a tiny building; most days when you picked up your mail, folks were walking in with a beer to chat with others.

When it was time for school to start, one of the staff would ring the big bell by pulling down on a rope. If you were busy talking to a parent or something came up, you just rang the bell when you were finished. Staff meetings were held next door at the principal's teacherage and we drank wine during these meetings—but the biggest surprise was my first school board meeting.

The head of the school board was Brenda, a woman younger than myself who lived on a mining claim just outside of town. There were a few townsfolk, about eight, who wanted to talk about an issue that had come up. The meeting was recorded so notes could be written later. At one point, the conversation got a little heated and Brenda spoke directly into the tape saying something to the effect that she "didn't care if it was on tape or not, they didn't f...ing like what was going on," referring to something in the district. I thought, "Oh well, nobody will hear the tape, it's just for notes." When the formal part of the meeting ended everybody got up, walked outside the back door, and… smoked a joint. I couldn't believe it! It was like the most natural thing to do; they passed the joint around and then went back inside and finished up. I was astounded. I knew most of the folks smoked marijuana, but at a break during a school board meeting? I had indulged in smoking marijuana when I was in high school and during my early university years but as soon as I became a teacher, that was it. I did not smoke anything anymore.

My Sawyers Bar teaching experience was an anomaly. The students were very well behaved, and we were all part of one big family. Parents were always stopping by to tell you something or bringing in goodies. On the weekends you interacted with all the kids you taught as well as their parents. Every Sunday afternoon there was a big volleyball game down at the "triangle" by the river. Folks from all over the area came to play. They brought an abundance of food and beer and it was an all-day affair with the kids running around, riding bikes and playing down at the river.

On many of these Sundays, some of the parents had a bit too much to drink. Instead of winding down and going home, they devised ways to continue partying. Since good old Terry the schoolteacher would be in school for sure on Monday morning, it made sense to see if I could take a few of the kids home. That way, the kids would be up and ready for school in case their parents partied most of the night. It started with a couple of kids and worked its way up to as many as five kids. I would take them home and they would crash in various places in the house that we were renting, which was a large older home with a wraparound veranda overlooking the Salmon River. There were several furnished rooms and a baby grand piano in the living room sitting beneath the framed photos of the ancestors of the family we rented from.

In the morning I would wander out in my flannel nightgown, get the wood stove going, wake the kids up and we would all have breakfast together. Then the group of us would walk down the road to school. In the spring, the kids would pick lilac flowers for my hair or wildflowers for my desk as we walked the narrow, winding road to school.

The highway patrol was required to drive through the town of Sawyers Bar once a month, or so I had been told. Their presence was virtually non-existent in the winter. They seemed to appear mostly at harvest time, along with the police helicopters, as the area was known to grow a great deal of marijuana. The fact that the highway patrol could drive through at any time did not stop the town's folks from having big parties in the community hall, advertising for them on the sign board with the date and the instructions to "Bring Your Own Booze and Dope."

Our first party at the cherished town hall was a memorable one. As the band was setting up, the mothers were putting up playpens in one corner for

Main street through the small community of Sawyers Bar, located on the North Fork of the Salmon River in northern California.

their youngest kids—they had learned to sleep through anything. Food and booze were abundant and the party usually continued on through the night.

Often at these affairs, the beer would run dry even though it had been in abundance earlier in the evening. A collection was taken and the guys would decide who was going to wake Bill, the owner of the general store, so they could buy more. He lived across from the hall beside the store, and the partiers would bang on the door and beg and plead. He usually opened just to keep everybody from hassling him, but we never could figure out who was louder: his wife yelling at him not to dare open the store or the begging and screaming from the crowd. Poor guy.

Another worthy experience in Sawyers Bar were the "road parties," in which you would pass someone on the road, and both of you would pull over to chat and then maybe drink a beer. Then someone else would drive by and stop. If there were kids, they would get out and run around a bit while the adults were visiting. After a couple more cars pulled over, possibly blocking the road a bit so others had to slow down, the party began to get a bit more serious. Usually someone had to go for a beer run. If it was late in the day, there might be a snack run, or even better, why not light a fire next to the road and get some hot dogs for the kids to roast? Before you know it, you'd have a road party.

Yes, life in Sawyers Bar was quite something and will always be a wonderful memory. We met many fabulous people who continue to remain friends today, and I have even kept in touch with several of my students and still visit them when I pass through California.

After the winter, my family and I left and continued on our journey south to see other family and friends. Our boys got to camp, play in the ocean, explore national parks and visit with Grandpa and Grandma.

When we arrived home at the beginning of April, we were stunned to find out that only two weeks before our arrival, Mike Oros had shot an RCMP constable after being hunted by a thirteen-member RCMP emergency response team. He was then shot dead on Teslin Lake, not far as the crow flies from Little Atlin. Mike Oros or "Shesley Mike" was the strange man that had been lurking in the woods off the Atlin Road near our cabin years ago.

On Monday, March 18, 1985, two weeks before we came home, Oros was suspected of breaking into a cabin. When the owners, a family from Whitehorse, went to check on their place at the southern end of Teslin Lake, they found it had been occupied and several things stolen. Using binoculars, they recognized Oros walking up the trail but instead of confronting him, they returned to Teslin and called the police. On Tuesday the RCMP chartered a plane and spotted Oros at the lake. He shot at the aircraft but missed, and the police returned to Teslin to recruit more officers to confront him. Oros was spotted again walking on Teslin Lake, but in the officers' attempts to contain him he managed to duck into the bush near the shoreline. Evidently Oros circled behind the RCMP team and killed Constable Buday. When the shot rang out, officers turned and saw Oros reloading so they shot him to death.

In August, Gunter's body was found at the south end of Hutsigola Lake when Teslin RCMP returned to search. He was identified through dental records obtained from a Whitehorse dentist. He had been shot in the back with a .303 British Enfield, like one Oros had in his possession when arrested in March 1982—the same gun used to shoot Constable Buday.

We were lucky he had not broken into our cabin and stolen from us or worse when he lived by us, like he did to many others. We felt relieved that he could no longer do harm to anyone.

LAND OF THE MIDNIGHT SUN

The following summer, Stan was once again working on a restoration project, this time as a crew chief at Herschel Island in the Bering Sea. He was to stay there until the project was complete, leaving me alone again at Little Atlin. In late summer I learned that I had an opportunity to fly to Herschel Island to visit him. As an employee of the Yukon government Parks Department, I was able to take advantage of a visit to another park when the opportunity presented itself, and it helped that we were friends with Stan's employer. The crew had all left, except the cook, and an empty plane was flying in to remove the last of the supplies. I arranged to leave the boys with Darlene so I could go.

I was so naïve the first time I ever flew in a float plane when we first moved up north. It was a glorious hot and sunny day. The windows were open and I was in the cockpit with the pilot in awe of the sights below. Without thinking, I stuck my arm out of the window like one would in a car. Well, my arm was whipped back in a split second and just about got ripped off. I immediately brought my arm back in and sheepishly looked at the pilot in hopes he hadn't seen my foolish act. He hadn't, thank goodness. I was supposed to fly up on a Navaho but it turned out that the aircraft I would be flying on this time was a de Havilland Otter, a larger and more powerful version of the de Havilland Beaver. When I drove up to Schwatka Lake and parked, the pilot was just making his way towards the dock. We smiled and said hello, and without bothering to tie up, he had me jump on. Off the two of us went for the long, nearly ten-hour flight to the Arctic.

After being seated on the plane, I was given some earplugs, as a single-engine Otter is a very loud high-wing, propeller-driven aircraft. It is too loud to talk or have any kind of conversation so the only interaction the pilot, Jim, and I had was pointing our fingers at sights, smiling and sharing food. An Otter flies much lower and slower than a Navaho so it was ideal for viewing the scenery. It was early August and fall colours had covered the hills at higher elevations, dotting the dwarf shrubs of the alpine meadows with reds, oranges and yellows. Coloured mosses and lichens covered the rocks like paint on a canvas. Occasionally I would spot a moose running through a meadow.

Our flight route took us over the Eagle Plains, which is really not a plain at all, but a large rolling section of hills nestled between the Ogilvie and Richardson mountain ranges. The area is covered mostly with stunted black spruce and is also enveloped with mosses, lichen and short shrubs. The Eagle River runs through the plains, giving it its name. I was lucky to glimpse a herd of caribou. It became a bit of a game with me and Joe to see who could spot more wildlife.

Continuing north towards the Bering Sea, we were flying farther into the Richardson Mountains. These mountains rise to an elevation of 1,239 metres. They are unglaciated and look mostly rocky and barren at the higher elevations. The lower sections show some greenery from spruce forest. It was here, as we were flying through a valley high in the mountains, that the unthinkable happened. Jim fell asleep. His head kept getting heavier and heavier and then, all of a sudden, he just closed his eyes with his head bent and he fell asleep! I was in shock. I didn't know what to do. The plane was still flying straight ahead and hadn't lost elevation, so I just kind of hung in there for a few minutes. When we hit a patch of turbulence he woke up, looked ahead, turned to me and smiled, then nodded his head and went to sleep again. I had heard that this sometimes happens, as planes are allowed to remain in the air as long as it is daylight, and in the summer in the north, it is light almost twenty-four hours a day. It was the busiest season of the year, so the pilots often had extended workdays. I was unsure what the rules were, but I knew they were often stretched. Because of my husband's job, he spent a lot of time flying around the territory and more than once he was asked to take over the controls for a few minutes so the pilot could have a catnap. I was hoping this would be a small catnap.

I was on pins and needles. The moment the plane changed its elevation or did anything unusual, I was planning to wake him up. Bush pilots are renowned for making monumental contributions to the North by opening up remote areas, making daring flights to deliver supplies and aiding those in remote places needing medical attention. These pilots were experienced and often risked their lives to help others. I hoped Jim was one of these exceptionally experienced, bold, and determined young pilots, but not so eager as to put us in danger.

Immediately after thinking this thought, I felt the plane beginning to descend. It was very gradual at first, then all of a sudden the nose began to point downward. I reached for Jim's arm as a giant scream was building in my lungs, and he suddenly jerked his head up, grabbed tightly onto the flight controls and righted the plane almost instantly. Looking straight ahead with eyes wide open, he continued flying as if nothing had happened, not even bothering to glance at me. After a few minutes, my heart began to beat more slowly and I once again looked out at the scene in front of me, praying he wouldn't fall asleep again.

Abruptly the landscape changed ahead. I could see a large river dotted with islands widening with every mile. I knew that we were nearing the Mackenzie River Delta, which covered a sizeable section of land. The Mackenzie River is the longest river in Canada and is the largest river system emptying into the Arctic Ocean. Many of Canada's wilderness rivers drain into the Mackenzie. The delta is vast—eighty kilometres across and a maze of channels, lakes and ponds. As we flew over this remarkable area, I noted pairs of swans in their own little body of water. Tundra swans mate for life and the delta is one area they come to mate and have their young. Occasionally I would see one lonely swan. I felt sad, as I assumed it was because its mate was no longer alive.

Clouds began to cover the sky above us as we continued on. We were heading to Tuktoyaktuk, an Inuvialuit hamlet located on the edge of the Mackenzie Delta on the shores of the Arctic Ocean. There we were going to make a short stop, unload a few things, get fuel and pick up a few supplies. As we neared the town, the clouds above became thicker, but we were beneath them and could see the town clearly. When we asked for permission to land, we were told the ceiling was too low. We began circling Tuk to wait for the okay. Well, we circled and circled and circled, a total of ten times. I just didn't understand, since we could clearly see the airport. Finally, the pilot radioed and said in a loud voice, "We're going to run out of fuel if we have to keep circling." We landed. First stop: the bathroom!

For years I had heard of the small, northern community of Tuktoyaktuk lying north of the Arctic Circle, accessible only by plane in the summer and ice roads in the winter. It had unique terrain, including massive pingos—ice-covered hills that rise out of the arctic tundra. The town still used sod roofs on many of their buildings as well. I never dreamed I would get a chance to go there. I would have loved to walk the streets, to see the community and do some sightseeing, but our stop was short and soon after landing we took off again for Herschel Island.

Gaining altitude after takeoff from Tuk, as it is known in the North, I suddenly sighted a pod of beluga whales, small white whales with a distinctive prominent forehead and no dorsal fin. They are hunted for food, mainly mattak or muktuk, a meal of frozen whale skin and blubber that is an important source of vitamin C in the diet of some Inuit. Whaling is still carried out by various Inuit groups in small numbers and is managed by the Department of Fisheries and Oceans.

Well, if this wasn't exciting enough, my next sight completely sent me over the top. Three narwhals were swimming just under the surface of the water, undulating as they moved in unison. I'm not sure I even realized these whales were real creatures; they were in the category of unicorns in my mind, but there they were. I could barely see the long, straight tusks, which distinguishes them from the beluga, whose bodies are similarly shaped. It was a sight I will never forget and feel privileged to have witnessed, as a sighting in the Beaufort Sea is extremely rare. I learned later that the narwhal is related to the beluga and that they were also hunted for muktuk, but mostly for their ivory to use for tools and art—the meat is often used for their sled dogs. They are an endangered species and most countries have quotas on their catches as well as an import ban on their tusks.

As we neared Herschel Island, I could see the camp and a few people moving about in the cove. I wondered if my presence would be a surprise, as I wasn't supposed to be there until later in the day. We landed uneventfully and taxied to shore. I could see Stan staring into the plane as he noticed someone beside the pilot. I jumped out and gave him a big hug. He was excited to see me and show me around.

Herschel Island is in the Beaufort Sea (part of the Arctic Ocean), off the coast of the Yukon Territory. The Inuvialuit living in the western Arctic have used the site for thousands of years and many of their old dwellings are still visible on the island. The first European to see the island was John Franklin in 1826. He named the island after his friend, an English scientist named Sir John Herschel. In the late 1800s, American whalers established a station at Pauline Cove on Herschel Island, which became a centre for commercial whaling. There was a police headquarters, an Anglican mission for the people of the area and a trading centre. In the summer, pack ice floats near the island and the shores collect driftwood of all sizes and shapes. In 1987, the Yukon government created Herschel Island Territorial Park.

In 1893, the Pacific Steam Whaling Company (PSW Co.) constructed a building called the Community House. In 1896 the company gave the house to the Anglican church, which used the building until 1906 at which point the Royal Canadian Mounted Police (RCMP) purchased all Herschel Island assets. The Community House is still there and is believed to be the oldest frame building in Yukon. It is now used as a park office and visitor centre.

There were several other buildings and a small log cabin that an Inuvialuit family lived in. It was from this family that my husband bought a seal skin and was given a baleen plate, an extremely difficult item to obtain. Baleen plates, or whalebone as they are often called, are a filter-feeder system inside the mouths of baleen whales. After the whale opens its mouth and fills it with water, it pushes the water out through the plates that are lined with hairs and the krill (their food source) remains in its mouth. Baleen plates can range from half a metre to around three metres long. I was excited about this, as I wanted to show the baleen to my kids at school when we studied whales.

With camera in hand, I wandered the old settlement. One of the most fascinating things to me was the old graveyard. Caskets were actually partially exposed due to the unstable ground and heaving permafrost. I felt uncomfortable walking around and peering into some of the caskets, but was captivated by what I saw: exposed or partial skeletons, one with a rusted old rifle. Many of the caskets were half in the ground and half out, covered with moss and lichen, the wood partially rotted. I walked carefully and did not touch anything out of respect. The thing I remember the most was the division of the buried. There were two distinct graveyards and one solitary grave up on a hill. I learned that the whites buried their dead in one section, the Inuvialuit were buried in another, and one lone black man was placed all alone on the hill.

Herschel Island is also famous as the site of the Arctic's first trial. Two Inuvialuit men were charged with murder. Jury members found the men guilty, and they were hanged from a tie beam in the Bonehouse, which was used for storing whalebone. When the RCMP left the island they removed the beam, though the building was still there when I visited.

Tundra wildflowers were everywhere. They were extraordinary, wonderful profusions of colour on small, compact plants. It looked more like late spring, even though it was summer. I snapped pictures of numerous flowers so I could to try to identify them later, but I did recognize many of them, including vetches, louseworts, arctic lupines, arnicas, and forget-me-nots. The flowers were scattered across gently sloping hills that were barren of trees.

Since the camp was shutting down, the only people left of the crew were my husband and the amazing cook, who was a friend of ours. Hans took me on a little tour and to see the food storage cave. Because of the permafrost, the cave served as a built-in fridge and all of their food was kept chilled while they were working on the island. I was hesitant to wander too far from the camp, as a grizzly bear had been sighted on several occasions, and sadly, my husband had had to shoot one earlier in the season because it continually came into camp and posed a threat to the crew.

As evening approached, the wind picked up and brought the salt air mixed with scents of the arctic environment to my nostrils. It was like a dream being there. Reflecting on my day, I felt honoured. After staying up late chatting, we finally fell asleep. Hans awakened us early in the morning with two mugs of steaming coffee. It was a busy day as the plane would be returning and everything left in camp had to be packed up to go.

Everything on shore was supposed to go, even the aluminum boat. I wasn't sure how it was all going to fit into the plane, but the guys kept loading it up. Then they strapped the boat to the floats on one side of the plane. The only thing left on shore were some barrels of sewage that were to be hauled out and disposed of later.

Stan and I jumped in the back and Hans pushed the plane off the shore and jumped up into the cockpit. We were a few yards from shore when the pilot turned to Stan and said, "She's pretty heavy, not sure if I can get her up." Well, the floats were partially submerged under the water. There was a bit of a conversation about unloading a few things.

I yelled over the engine at Stan, "Yes, unload something, we don't really need those heavy glass battery casings and…"

The pilot then said, "I'll just taxi out of the cove to get some lift." So we taxied out of Pauline Cove into the Bering Sea, and it was nasty. The wind was howling and the waves were huge. With full throttle we would hit a wave, go up in the air and then flop down hard. Then we would do it again on the next wave. This happened quite a few times before we finally lifted off. I was feeling very unsettled; it just wasn't as magical as it had been the day before.

As we moved inland from the Bering Sea and back into the Richardson Mountains, I began to feel better and was enjoying the sights. The river below meandered through the valley and the mountains were glorious. All of a sudden, it was dead quiet. I looked forward. The propeller made a few more rotations and then stopped. It went from excruciatingly loud to dead quiet in a second. Stan and I looked at each other, dumbfounded. The pilot was frantically checking gauges and throwing switches. All I could think

The Porcupine River, one of the many rivers we flew over, winding its way through the tundra to where it eventually joins the Yukon River, which drains into the Bering Sea on the west coast of Alaska.

about was the kids and how we had just completed our first will. The plane began to float gently downwards, the wind rushing over the struts making a soft hissing sound. Being on a float plane has its merits, but when the river seems like a trickle below, it is a little hard to think about landing in it. Moments seemed like hours, but all of a sudden the engine coughed, the prop kicked over, the noise resumed and we were on our way again, regaining back the elevation we had lost. The pilot turned and smiled at us. Well, smile or not, I was terrified. I didn't know what had happened to make the motor stop and I was panicked at the thought that it might happen again. My guts hurt, I had to go to the bathroom, my mind was racing, and I was simply in agony.

As we were getting close to the town of Mayo, about halfway to White-horse, we needed to make a decision. We had to either stay in Mayo over-night or continue to Whitehorse with the possibility that we might have to put the plane down on a lake for an hour or two waiting until daylight re-turned. My husband did not even need to ask me what I wanted to do—he knew I wanted off that plane! We put down near the float plane dock on the river in Mayo. As soon as the plane landed and slowed down, it also began to sink. By the time we got to the dock, the floats were almost completely submerged under the water due to the weight in the plane. The ocean salt water had provided much-needed additional buoyancy, but there was none to be found on fresh water.

I hopped out as fast as I could. That was it, I was not getting back on that plane! Stan was a bit embarrassed, but I announced that I was hitchhiking back to Whitehorse, and everybody else could do whatever they wanted. The decision was made. We would stay in Mayo overnight and leave early in the morning. Meanwhile, part of the freight had to be unloaded and stored to be retrieved another time due to the excess weight. The men were thinking that a dinner and glass of wine would change my mind, and we all went out to eat. But later in our room I continued to insist that I was not getting on the plane in the morning.

However, when morning came, I reluctantly got on the plane without having time to venture into the town itself. Mayo is about six hours from Whitehorse and off the well-travelled road to Dawson City. As much as I didn't want to get back on the plane, I realized that I really didn't want to stand out on the road and hitchhike with mosquitoes biting me, trying to catch a ride the 400 or so kilometres back to Whitehorse with who knows who.

The ride back was fairly uneventful, but I was a nervous wreck. Every time we flew into the clouds and couldn't see the ground, I silently panicked. When we could finally see Whitehorse in the distance and eventually landed, I was never so happy in my life.

When we picked up Travis and Brett at Darlene's, I jumped out of the truck and ran inside, first grabbing one child then the other, hugging them so tightly they were squirming to get out of my arms. I was in tears, so thankful to see my two precious sons, recognizing that in an instant I could have lost everything. I vowed to savour each moment with these two treasured gifts and live each day to the fullest.

For years after this incident, I was afraid of flying, whether it was in small planes or jet airliners.

CARIBOU CROSSING

I had been hired to teach in Carcross that September, and Travis, who would be turning five soon, was going to be starting kindergarten. He was quite the little helper—always trying to assist me with something, whether it was hauling firewood, helping me prepare food or getting things for his younger brother. He kept busy constantly, forever wanting to learn to do new things. When he was nearing his fifth birthday, he proved that he was finally old enough to be able to follow the path through the woods to our only neighbours, as well as walk up our long driveway to the road to flag someone down in case of an emergency. He was very adept at a young age. I trusted him, and I was now more comfortable when I was home alone with the boys.

The wild raspberries in the meadow and around our property were in season and producing berries faster than we could pick them that summer. Every three days I would give the boys each a gallon bucket and tell them to go out and pick as many as they could. Of course, Travis always complained that his little brother wasn't picking his share, and in the end they dumped their bounty together and brought me the one full pail, eagerly trying to convince me that there were no more ripe ones to pick. But I would remind them of all the goodies I planned to make for them that needed berries and shoo them out for more.

Shaggymane mushrooms were also popping up everywhere along the gravelly areas by the roadside in the late summer and fall. They are very easy to identify, as the caps are tall, pointy cylinder shapes covered with frilly, almost lacey, scales. When they are fresh their gills are an off-white, but with age they quickly turn first pink, then black, and they secrete a black ink-like liquid. They must be picked fresh and cooked immediately, not dried like other mushrooms. The boys eagerly helped me pick these. I cut them up and cooked them with garlic and butter, then popped bags into the freezer. We also collected and dried boletus mushrooms we found growing profusely under spruces. They are fairly large with a brownish-red, meaty cap and swollen stem.

Travis with our bounty of Shaggymane mushrooms cleaned and ready to process.

The long weekend in September before school started, Travis and I hiked Monarch Mountain together. Brett was too young to go with us, so he stayed with a friend. The trail takes close to three hours round-trip, but by driving up the road past the trailhead we could catch the trail a little farther up, cutting the distance down a bit. This was the same place I took my class for their field trip the first time I taught in Atlin. The elevation gain made it steep and I wasn't sure if Trav could make it, but he had no problem.

The trail goes through sub-alpine to a magnificent view of the lake. The colours were brilliant, and the higher we went the brighter they became. Reaching the flats, we passed many small rock outcroppings, ponds and saw evidence of caribou. Sitting in the sun eating our lunch, we shared a moment of silence taking in the beauty of the lake with Atlin Mountain and Birch Mountain on Teresa Island standing majestically in front of the deep blue, cloudless sky backing the Juneau Icefield. But our moment was brief as Travis jumped up continually to eat some ripe berries, watch a bug crawl along a rock or roll a boulder over to see if anything was underneath.

The community of Carcross is located on the north end of Bennett Lake in southern Yukon and is home to the Carcross Tagish First Nation. The community was originally known as Caribou Crossing, referring to the spot where the local woodland herd caribou crossed the narrows between Bennett and Nares lakes. In 1896, during the Klondike gold rush, the community began to boom, as it was the stopping-off point for prospectors going to Dawson City after making the demanding hike over the Chilkoot Pass and taking a boat trip down Bennett Lake.

I was glad to be offered the teaching job. Stan's carpentry work was seasonal, so our winters were tough financially; attaining a part-time government job gave us some monetary security and still allowed me to spend time with the boys.

Each morning the boys and I would get up early, jump into the truck and head to Carcross. Stan stayed home stoking the fires, gathering firewood and doing some carving. After dropping Brett off at a preschool, Travis and I would carry on to the school. This worked well before the snows fell and winter settled in, but not during severe cold or heavy storms when we couldn't get the truck out of our long sloped driveway, which was now impassible. On bitter cold mornings, Brett would stay in the warmth of the cabin with his dad. Travis and I, bundled to the hilt, trudged up the driveway and stood on the road waiting for the mail truck, which also acted as a bus for travel between small communities, to pick us up and carry us the ninety-six kilometres to school. The timing was perfect. We could get to school with about fifteen minutes to spare and take it home again on its route back. There were many below-zero mornings where we stood on the road freezing, waiting for the mail truck. There were also days it never came, so then we had to hitchhike—nobody would pass by without stopping. Travis was so bundled up he looked like a little stuffed comic-book character. He was tough.

I was at a school professional development day that winter when I met Ted Harrison, one of Canada's most popular and loved artists, who settled in Carcross in 1967 with his wife and son. His colourful paintings and distinctive style showing his love of the land and the people of the Yukon brought him national acclaim. The quaint and charming community of Carcross, its people and buildings, were the inspiration for many of his paintings. He was a schoolteacher who spent much of his career teaching art to children of all ages before he became an internationally recognized author and illustrator of children's books. I hung on every word spoken by this kindhearted man, who obviously held Carcross in a special place in his heart. I learned a variety of techniques to use when teaching the children art as well as hearing numerous stories about his past and present life.

The narrow gauge tracks of the White Pass & Yukon Route Railroad, dating back to 1898 and the Klondike gold rush, link the port of Skagway, Alaska, to Whitehorse, Yukon.

It is no wonder Carcross so heavily influenced Ted Harrison's art. It is one of the most picturesque villages in the Yukon, with lots of old historic buildings still remaining, many transported from Bennett City and other abandoned mining communities. The three-story Caribou Hotel is the oldest operating hotel in the Yukon. Built in 1898 at Bennett during the gold rush and known as the Yukon Hotel, it was transported across Bennett Lake on a barge by its owner in 1901. Renamed the Caribou, it then burned down in 1909. It was rebuilt on its current location in 1910 using material from a building torn down at Conrad, a mining community nearby. It is still believed to this day to be haunted by ghosts, especially by that of Bessie Gideon, who ran the hotel until she died in 1933. A figure of a woman who often stands near a third floor window and bangs on floorboards has been seen by locals and kept tourists awake. Bessie took care of Polly the Parrot for the owner of Engineer Mine, who died at sea. The parrot remained at the Caribou Hotel until 1972, when it died. I sat in the Caribou many times with locals for a beer, talking to the new Polly the Parrot and listening to ghost tales of Bessie carrying on.

The White Pass & Yukon Route Railroad Depot was built in 1910 and was used by the White Pass & Yukon Route Railroad until 1982 when mining operations collapsed. It reopened again in 1988 as a seasonal tourism operation. My class and I had purchased tickets for our trip to Skagway in this historic building.

The historical buildings and people of Carcross, along with countless other Yukoners of all ancestries, provided the vision and originality for Ted Harrison's compositions. The Caribou Hotel is in the foreground of many

The steam locomotive, "The Duchess," built in 1878, sitting in front of the sternwheeler *Tutshui*. It carried passengers and freight from Carcross, Yukon, bound for Atlin, transferring them to the world's shortest narrow gauge railway, which ran almost four kilometres between Taku Arm and the shore of Atlin Lake.

of his paintings along with whimsical renditions of the many small cabins and homes and the steeple of the Anglican church, mixed with the brilliance of the northern lights, the bright colours of the parkas, the kids, their pets and sled dogs—all creating a backdrop for his work. I feel grateful for the opportunity to have met and learned from this man. He passed away in January of 2015.

As fall turned towards winter, the leaves once again turned brilliant colours, at times floating softly to the ground, or flying violently off their branches in the strong autumn winds, which abated soon after. Little Atlin Lake began to freeze and the sun hid behind the ice fog for several weeks. Ice formed near the lake's edge and the cloud began to shrink, until one day it was gone and the sun shone again, bouncing light off the clear, glassy ice. The cold temperature and lack of wind caused the lake not only to freeze smoothly, but it was translucent—a first for us. You could actually see through the ice and because the water wasn't any deeper than a couple of metres for about ninety metres out, it was like viewing an aquarium. The boys were thrilled! We put on their ice skates, gave them a chair to push around for stability and off they went, squealing with delight at seeing the big fish swim beneath them. They chased pike and lingcod until they were about to drop. Then we headed up towards the swamp, and did we ever get a treat! The muskrats were visible under the ice. They travelled in and out of their homes, which were mounds sticking partially out of the ice. Travis and Brett whooped and hollered and watched until they got so cold they couldn't stand it. The otters sliding down an ice bank on the shore also amused them.

The ice remained in good condition for skating that winter, and the smooth surface made it easy to remove the snow. Both Brett and Travis were given a snow shovel and the chore of cleaning off the rink we had made. We had a birthday skating party on the lake for Travis's birthday; a carload of his friends arrived with skates in hand, hit the rink and chased each other around with a hockey puck, Brett trying to stand long enough on the ice to join in. After drinking a gallon of hot chocolate and eating birthday cake, they all piled in the car and I was told were asleep within the first few kilometres of the drive back to Whitehorse.

Travelling long distances for parties or to visit friends is a common occurrence in the North. It is assumed that you may or may not spend the night, and you always carry whatever you need with you, just in case. It's a good idea anyway, as you never know when you might get stuck somewhere or break down. Not all of the long distances are over road, either. The many frozen lakes turn into highways and roads of a different kind—a snowmobile or dog sled can get you almost anywhere.

One beautiful spring day in April, my friend Bonnie had a birthday party for her son at their trapline cabin across Atlin Lake. Several of us moms packed up our kids, some goodies to eat and a gift for the birthday boy and headed over on our snow machines for a day of celebration. The kids played outside the entire time, delighting in pinning the tail on the moose and other traditional birthday games. Bob Fraser, the old-timer who taught us gold panning, was staying there at the time to take a break from Atlin and his drinking. He cut wood every day and helped out with Bonnie's boys. He was amused at all the kids playing and running around, and he loved teasing them and playing jokes on them. Bonnie told me how one morning he got up from sleeping with his coat still on. As he stood up two piles of sawdust fell out of his pockets from cutting wood the day before, leaving perfect little piles on his cot.

We laughed about that and marvelled at how the children could keep going all day without seeming to get tired or cold. It was hard to tear them away to go home. Luckily, the days were longer and warmer in the spring, giving us plenty of time to get home before dusk. When Stan got home, he told me he had just heard the news of the nuclear accident at the Soviet Union's Chernobyl power station, the second world nuclear disaster since we moved to the North. We wondered if it would affect us in any way, since Russia was not that far away. It seemed preposterous that we were living such a clean and healthy life in a remote area and had to fear the possibility of the effects of such a disaster. We tried to focus on the positive and enjoy our little piece of paradise.

Crocuses are the first flower to show their beautiful colour in the spring, and we delighted in searching for them as the days warmed and only small patches of snow remained. It warmed my heart when the boys found bunches of these lovely flowers—Brett would often pick some and thrust them towards me. Mother's Day breakfast trays always had a bouquet of these purple gems.

Break-up continued to be an exciting event. This particular spring, the ice had candled, which means the rotten ice has developed columns perpendicular to the surface of the lake. It makes a clinking sound similar to a chime when it breaks apart and the columns bump into each other. We would all go down to the lake and watch and listen to this phenomenon. Huge masses of ice would move towards the shore, the force of the ice behind it creating incredible clinking sounds while piling up as much as three metres onto our shore. The boys would climb over the ice as it mounded up, pick out the pieces that looked like icicles and play sword games or suck on them like a popsicle. The pieces were quite long, as the ice can get around a metre thick in the winter. Break-up was evidence of just how thick the ice had actually gotten that winter. Each day we would return to the lake to see the changes, and each day it was a different, but always spectacular, event.

JOY AND TRAGEDY

One early June morning when I went to pick up my friend Bonnie and her kids from the Greyhound bus stop at Jake's Corner at 5:00, she was sitting with an elderly man. The man had mentioned to her that he was trying to get to Atlin, but didn't know how. Apparently he had hopped on a bus from Dawson, BC, and headed north to find his friend. He had planned to go to Whitehorse and figure it out, but being a typical northerner, Bonnie invited him to my house and offered him a ride to Atlin when I drove her and her kids home that day. We all piled into the car and headed to my cabin. I had coffee going and began to make breakfast for everyone. The old guy was a hoot. He could hardly see anything as he was legally blind, and kept talking about his wife, who was mad at him for taking this "hair-brained" trip—but he was on a mission to see his good friend Ben who he hadn't seen for over thirty years.

After breakfast we all piled back into the car and headed down the Atlin Road. Although Bonnie lived twenty-seven kilometres north of Atlin, she wanted to go to Atlin first and then be dropped off at her place on the way home. She was dying to see the expression on Ben's face when his old buddy unexpectedly showed up.

Ben was home. When he walked out of the door of his cabin and looked at the gentleman on his walkway, it took only a brief moment for him to recognize his longtime friend. He quickened his step and they warmly embraced. We felt privileged to see this special interaction and witness the first words between these men who had been separated for many years. We said our goodbyes and left them to themselves.

That summer, Stan and I invited my nephew Matthew to come and stay with us as my brother and his wife were working full-time. He was seven, a year older than Travis, and we thought it would be good for Matthew to spend the summer with us instead of remaining in California with a babysitter. It would be wonderful for the three boys to spend time together.

In midsummer we put the camper we had bought on our truck, packed up, and headed to the Kenai Peninsula in Alaska to visit Stan's relatives. Driving west from Whitehorse, we passed through the settlement of Champagne, a small Indigenous settlement on the Alaska Highway. Sitting on a hill next to the highway was the cemetery—the spirit houses and gravesites surrounded by picket fences, standing like soldiers pointing to the heavens.

Continuing west, we stopped at Silver City, a ghost town on the shores of Kluane Lake that had once been a small community and mining outpost in the early 1900s. It had consisted of a trading post, roadhouse, mining office, post office and North West Mounted Police barracks. It was a waypoint between the local goldfields and Whitehorse, and the end of the road from Whitehorse—further travels required getting on a boat on Kluane Lake and using the rivers. The town had been revived in 1942, when the Alaska Highway was built from Silver City through to Alaska, but it was now a ghost town again.

Old houses had caved-in roofs with boards looking like pick-up sticks still covering them, and other buildings were scattered amongst the trees. An old bridge over a stream remained with a sign warning it wasn't safe, and a lone small cabin sat on the shore of the lake. Rusted machine and car parts were visible through bushes growing up around them. The kids gravitated to a collage of automobile parts resembling an old flatbed truck and climbed up to play on it.

Skirting the west side of Kluane Lake on the edge of Kluane National Park, we were able to see the St. Elias Mountain Range, which includes Mount Logan, the highest peak in Canada. The park itself is 82 per cent covered in mountains and ice, having the largest non-polar icefields on the planet.

Passing by two communities sitting on the shore of Kluane Lake, Destruction Bay and Burwash Landing, which was the traditional hunting and fishing site of the Tutchone people, we continued heading northwest to the Alaska border. After crossing the Yukon-Alaska border, we drove towards Anchorage and onto the large peninsula of Kenai, which possesses a rich history of Indigenous peoples and Russian culture. Kenai, where Stan's relatives lived, is the site of the first white settlement on the peninsula. We toured the town and admired the many historical buildings, many of them Russian. After spending a few days visiting with his kind and generous relatives, we headed even farther south to Homer to give the boys the experience of gathering razor clams, a long, narrow saltwater clam resembling a closed straight razor.

The low tide and prospect of gathering the juicy, meaty clams brought hordes of people to the shores of Homer. They are found by looking for a little hole or depression in the sand. Sometimes they even expose their necks, but not often. Spotting the holes, the boys would stick their hand in the sand to pull out the three-to-six inch or sometimes larger clams, but as soon as they touched it, the clam would retreat deeper into the sand. All three of them, anxious to outdo each other, would sit on the sand, stick their arm in to grab the clam, then be forced to lie down with their arm extending below the sand all the way up to their shoulders, yelling for us to come and help them. Stan and I were like ping-pong balls bouncing back and forth between kids, slithering our arms down to their hands and grabbing the clam to pull it out. Immediately we would hand the clam to them so they could yell to the others and show their find. This went on for what seemed like hours. We were exhausted and the kids looked like sand castle statues, they had so much sand on them. Drained, and with our five-gallon bucket full, we started back towards Kenai.

Thinking we could wait until we got home to clean the clams, we began our drive back to the Yukon the next day. Crossing the border again, we drove past Kluane Lake and Haines Junction to the campground at Kathleen Lake, having heard it was a fabulous place to camp, and it was! When we arrived, the sun was shining on the turquoise-green lake and the mountains standing on the shore seemed as if they were on top of the lake. The pebbly, sandy beach drew the kids to the waterfront to splash and play in the cool, shallow waters and then with shrieks of joy they ran to the playground nearby to climb on the apparatus.

Settling in for the evening, Stan and I checked on the clams, only to find that they were on the verge of turning, which meant they might go bad in the near future. We immediately rinsed them one more time and set about de-shelling them with a sharp knife, putting the contents in a freshly drawn bucket of water from the frigid waters of Kluane Lake. Icing our catch the next morning, we arrived home, cooked up a few fresh and ground the rest up for freezing to make clam cakes and clam fritters for special occasions in the winter.

The rest of the summer was busy taking care of all the boys and tending the gardens. I also started selling clothes from Bali for my sister's business so I could generate extra income. She would send shipments from California to Skagway, the nearest pickup point place for me in the US, then I would travel to nearby locations, display them and take orders or have home shows.

The author's nephew Matthew and her son Brett showing off a razor clam they worked so hard to get on the Kenai Peninsula near Homer, Alaska.

My nephew Matthew returned home and, since Stan was not working full-time, he was able to watch the boys during my road trips.

Carcross was the first town on my list and fortunately, the Caribou Hotel was delighted to have me come on several weekends and sell my wares in the back of the restaurant, displaying a sign outside to entice more tourists to come into the building. This gave me an opportunity to get out and meet people as well as giving me the extra income.

As summer came to an end, we were worried that we might not have enough money to support our family through the winter, even though I was selling clothing and still cleaning the campgrounds and Stan had various carpentry jobs. Stan's job with the Yukon government on historical sites was complete, so he had returned to building, which can be a very seasonal occupation in the North. We needed a way to generate more income, so I applied for a teaching job with School District #87 in hopes that I could once again work at the Atlin School.

That fall, on September 27, 1986, Stan and I were in the bar at Jake's Corner enjoying our evening with a great group of people from both Atlin and Marsh Lake, when a friend walked into the bar with look of terror on her face. We repeatedly asked her what was wrong, but she couldn't answer. After taking a minute to collect herself, she leaned over to her good friend Christine and whispered in her ear. Christine looked horrified, and I began to panic. Finally, one of them spoke. There had been a horrible plane accident in which our friend Beth's husband's sister from Atlin was killed along with our other friend and the owner of the Atlin Inn, Joe Florence. Ben Able, the friend of the elderly man, had also been killed, as well as local politician Al Passarell and his pregnant wife. The pilot, Teresa Bond, was the only one to survive—all the passengers drowned. It was a bluebird day, and evidently the flight was uneventful but eyewitnesses say the float plane nosedived into Dease Lake at full cruising speed. Someone in a boat nearby raced to the accident scene and attached a line to the plane, but when it began to pull the boat under, the line had to be cut.

I was in shock, unable to speak myself. I immediately got up and went to the bar and asked to use the phone. I phoned the Atlin Inn to see if the information I had just received was really true, praying it wasn't. But it was. They were all dead. I felt similar to the way I did when I found out President Kennedy had been shot; I will never forget it. I was in my grade seven classroom and Mrs. Stonecipher was teaching and the news came over the intercom and she ran out of the room. But this was more personal. Now, when I think back to that day, I see myself at Jake's. I see the horror on everyone's faces, the silence that overtook the bar, the disbelief, the immediate grief, the overwhelming sadness that stopped time, the slow motion of movement and the tears.

It was later determined that pilot error was the cause. The phenomenon of landing a float plane on perfectly calm water where the horizon meets a reflection can cause pilots to lose the ability to accurately determine their height above the water. All too often, pilots will stall the airplane, thinking they are about to touch the water when they are still well above it, or as in this case, fly right into the water thinking they still have lots of altitude.

I remember thinking how fortunate it was that Ben and the friend he hadn't seen for thirty years were able to connect before this tragedy, and I wondered if some sort of subconscious precognition had prompted the trip.

This tragedy affected the lives of every Atlin resident and anyone who knew and loved the people that tragically lost their lives in this accident. The town was in shock and no one really knew how to deal with it. Joe Florence was an icon in town—the Atlin Inn, which he owned and ran, was the central meeting place for everyone. He was warm and welcoming and always accommodated everyone with a smile on his face, happy to listen to a sad story or laugh along with you at a funny one. Shelley was young and vibrant and enjoyed everything about life. Ben was a kind man whom everyone cared for, and I did not know Al and his wife that well but they were respected members of the community. The pain remains with us all.

DAD'S VISIT

The following fall of 1987 I was hired to teach at the Atlin School again. A new school had been built outside of town on the Warm Bay Road. It was a beautiful facility with everything necessary for grades kindergarten to ten—even a large, bright gym with a high ceiling. In the old days, we used to have to take our students to the community hall for P.E. Each classroom had big bay windows that let lots of light in, and in my room I had a view of the mountaintops poking above the trees. I felt very lucky to be back teaching in Atlin. I was offered a teacherage, a singlewide trailer located on the old school site in town, which became home during the week. I travelled back and forth with the boys, now both in school, going home to Little Atlin whenever possible on the weekends that fall.

Stan remained at home for the month of September working on the foundation for my greenhouse. I was thrilled that I was finally going to get the greenhouse I'd always dreamed about. We'd decided to construct it partially built into the bank closer to the lake where there was excellent exposure and the north bank would provide insulation. We laid out the sixteen-by-thirty-foot foundation, which allowed for six-inch walls, two-and-a-half-foot beds along the outside side, a five-foot bed in the middle, leaving ample room for us to get a wheelbarrow down the two aisles. In addition to that, we laid out a foundation for an attached ten-by-twelve-foot sunroom. The goal for this fall was to complete the footings and as much of the foundation rock and mortar walls as possible.

In December, my dad came from Florida to visit. One of his dreams was to experience the north in the winter; however, it meant the first Christmas away from my mother in fifty-five years. She had no desire to subject herself to the cold temperatures and live in a log cabin with no modern facilities. My dad was raised in West Virginia where it snows in the winter and as an adult, he fondly remembered the fun times he had in the snow and cold as a child, and he wanted to experience it anew. I was ecstatic when he wanted to come and visit with us at Christmas time.

The boys were so happy to see their grandpa as he stepped into the airport terminal. The day he arrived in Whitehorse was the coldest day of the winter yet: -26°F (-32°C), and even with the heater on full blast, our van remained frigid. We were all bundled up, but since my dad wasn't dressed for such cold temperatures, we threw a blanket over him and headed to our teacherage in Atlin, stopping at Jake's Corner for some hot chocolate to warm him up. As I still had a few days left of teaching in Atlin before the Christmas break, our stay at Little Atlin would have to wait.

My dad's first morning in Atlin, Brett took him for a walk around town. It was only -18°F (-27°C), as Atlin is almost always warmer than Whitehorse due to its proximity to the coast. My dad, a big man anyway, looked like a giant all bundled up sporting his new full-face mask. That evening he attended the annual school Christmas concert, thoroughly enjoying watching his two grandsons on stage, evidenced by his broad smiles.

Bright and early the next morning we packed up groceries and everything we would need for our stay at Little Atlin. Arriving back at the cabin, we unloaded the van and started the fire to warm up the cabin, which takes a longer time when the logs are so cold. First on the agenda was to cut a Christmas tree, which we had waited to do until my dad arrived, as he wanted to go into the bush and cut down a tree like in the "old" days. It was his first time ever on a snow machine, and he was like a little kid, hanging on for dear life and making sounds of joy as Stan and he turned and headed down the trail to the lake towards a nice stand of spruce. Travis was on the dogsled behind, attached to the snowmobile.

The whirr of the snow machine announced their arrival back and Brett and I raced out to greet them and see the tree. It was a perfect Christmas-card tree. We brought it into the cabin, let it thaw out and began trimming it with our assortment of wooden tree ornaments. There were also lots of handcrafted ones the kids had made over the years and a box of homemade decorations one of my students had given me—cookies baked with candy pieces placed in the dough. While Dad helped the boys trim the tree, I cooked spare ribs on the grate over the wood box of my stove. That evening I was delegated to stringing popcorn, and I think the boys ate more from the bowl than got onto my strand, but eventually it was long enough to drape around the tree.

Christmas Eve day, my dad installed a new twelve-volt light and hauled water with the boys. He took three trips to the lake, two for water and one for ice to make homemade ice cream with our new ice-cream maker.

Before we got it, we would often make ice cream when there was a party if, and only if, it was exceptionally cold. The women would take turns running outside, madly whisking the ingredients in a bowl until the flavoured cream would begin to freeze, first around the sides of the bowl, until eventually turning soft-solid consistency. But it took a lot of whisking and standing outside in the extreme cold. When it started to get the least bit hard, we would insist that the guys go outside and finish it off, threatening not to let them have any if they didn't. The new ice-cream maker was a delight to use, and the days of whipping ice cream in a bowl outside were finished!

Christmas morning was the best day of all. Being less than a week after the winter solstice, the shortest day of the year, the boys had an excruciating time staying in bed until it was almost light. Once up, the paper-ripping began, exposing a multitude of toys. My dad played right alongside the boys trying out each toy, laughing and carrying on just as much as they were. The next day we boxed up our leftover food and went to a Boxing Day party at Marsh Lake at the home of Ray and Christine's from Jake's Corner. It was a real mix of folks of all ages and Dad enjoyed meeting them all, but what he really got a kick out of was the local Boxing Day drink. Also known as a "yukaflux," it was a concoction of fruit, citron, cherries, vodka and ice, all mixed into a gallon jar with a wet towel wrapped around it and a dry towel around that. Everybody took turns shaking the jar for a total of twenty minutes and then they drank from the jar as it was passed around. Dad was a real trooper and gulped the goods with the rest of us!

We bounced back and forth between our cabin and the teacherage in Atlin the rest of my dad's stay, heading for Atlin when the temperature was forecasted to make a drastic drop to minus-forty or lower, as we were concerned that we might not be able to start our vehicle with no electricity to plug in our block heater, and might be stuck for an indefinite time. While in Atlin, we visited our friend Jeff's salmon plant at his home down the Warm Bay Road south of Atlin. This was a good-sized and very impressive processing plant that quick-froze, smoked and vacuum-packed the salmon flown up from the Taku River near Juneau. The boys and Dad were intrigued by all the gleaming stainless-steel equipment, filleting knives, big tables with drains, deep sinks, tall smoking racks and the vacuum packer. The smoker, with its big hopper and hot rotating plate, was located outside at the back of the building.

During Dad's stay, we ate some of Jeff's salmon, and I prepared a variety of wild game meals, including moose, mountain goat, caribou and grouse. I also spoiled him with homemade bread, jams and pies from all the berries we picked. Dad watched the boys ice skate, go sledding, and shoot rifles for target practice. We drove to the gold rush town of Discovery, where we walked around taking photos, and to the steaming warm springs and to the old graveyard outside the village in Atlin. Dad also survived several parties, including a New Year's Eve party at Marsh Lake that kept him up much, much later than usual.

It wasn't until years later when my dad was ninety-one years old and my sister and I were moving him into a senior's housing unit that I found the journal he had kept during his stay with us. It was written on a small notepad and carefully tucked away with his treasured items in a drawer. I had no idea it existed, and reading it after all those years, I was intrigued by what he had seen from his perspective. The one entry I thoroughly enjoyed described a long walk he had taken along the lake with Brett and our dog Kodi, pulling the new sled the boys had gotten for Christmas. Dad had rigged up a rope so that he could help pull some, and Brett had looked up to him, saying, "You are a clever devil, Grandpa." This little episode had clearly meant a lot to my dad then, just as it touches my heart now.

Terry and her dad celebrating the bringing in of the New Year together at a party with her friends at Marsh Lake in the Yukon.

On Sundays that winter, we women often cross-country skied at Marsh Lake. A considerable number of trails had been cut and were coded as to level of ability. We didn't really care which trails we went on; the big deal for us was getting a break and being out on our own. I am not sure how it happened, but it became an understanding that on Sunday afternoons the men had to care for the children, giving us time off. We would all arrive at someone's house, Ray and Christine's or Paulette and Dave's, with an assortment of food and drinks to keep the kids happy. The guys would build a big bonfire, drink beer and tell stories and take over all the kids. I'm not too sure how much they actually watched the kids, though, but we didn't care—we were happy to have a break, and the kids were now old enough to take care of each other and were great about keeping themselves entertained.

At some point in the spring, I started taking kids from the class home with us for the weekend. It gave the boys a chance to play and have different friends stay at the cabin. We even had a foster child, Robert, live with us for six months. He was the most adorable child, bright and always smiling. He had entered my class in grade four but could only read at a grade two level. With care and extra time, his reading skills improved about two grade levels in just the one year. When we found out he was going to be placed in foster care in Terrace, BC, the other teachers and I were terribly upset, as he was loved by all and making so much progress, so Stan and I applied to be foster parents.

Unfortunately, we were not approved as there was concern raised about Stan's involvement in an alcohol-related incident that had occurred years before at the local pub. There had been a commotion at the bar and the police were called, but no one was arrested or removed from the bar. However, this incident had resulted in the police starting a file on Stan, and this came to light with our foster child application. I was devastated. We were totally unaware that any records had been kept as Stan had never been arrested for anything. But I was furious that something my husband had done could impact us like this. I began to question my relationship. It was the first time I had to face the doubts that had been creeping into my mind about the soundness of our marriage and the direction our lives were going.

In conversations with Robert's father (who preferred that he remain in Atlin so he could see him) and a counsellor friend, we came up with a plan. It was very simple; we got around the foster child issue by having his father sign guardianship over to me temporarily so Robert could finish the school

year, giving him the opportunity to
continue with his exceptional learning progress in school and live with
us until the end of June. Robert and
our two boys became the best of
friends, building forts and rafts and
playing endlessly until exhausted. It
was a very sad day when Robert left
us for his permanent foster home at
the end of the school year, but our
agreement had been a temporary
one, and it was in Robert's best in-
terest to go to Terrace. It warms my heart that Robert, now a successful
photographer with a family of his own, is still in touch to this day.

Travis, Robert and Brett on *Iota*.

As the days grew longer, my yearning to be at our cabin instead of staying in town while teaching grew stronger. There were so many things to do,
especially planting and tending to my gardens. Instead of heading back to
town on Sunday to be ready for school on Monday morning, I woke up at
about 5:00 am on Mondays and drove the eighty-eight kilometres to Atlin.
The kids had a hard time waking up and getting into the car at that early
hour, so we solved that problem—they spent the night in the car. We put a
foam mattress in the back and they snuggled into their sleeping bags. This
made it much easier for me. I would get up, light the wood cook stove, make
a cup of coffee, jump in the car and head out.

Those mornings were magical. The sun would just begin to show,
spreading a warm glow over the land; everything began to sparkle as the
light reflected off the ice crystals that had formed after the snow that had
melted the previous day had frozen again overnight. Fresh greens began
to appear, bringing animals out to savour the young shoots. We saw more
wildlife on our drives to school on those early mornings than at any other
time. Almost every day we saw a moose, coyote or fox, and we frequently saw mountain sheep and goats too. Mountain goats lived on White
Mountain behind our cabin. You could often see their white bodies on the
rocky ledges high above. Near the Yukon-BC border, there was a turn in
the road with a high bluff that the sheep liked to hang out on. We would
drive slowly and look up at the cliffs on the mountain, and often a big ram
would be looking down at us with a halo of morning light. The first time
I yelled, "Moose!" or "Sheep!" Travis would be up, checking everything

out. Sometimes Brett would pop his head out of his sleeping bag, ask "Where?", take a look and hunker back down, but usually Travis was up for the duration.

Our biggest surprise came when we spotted something in the poplar trees near the road, but couldn't identify what animal was making the tree sway back and forth. Curiosity got the best of us and I stopped and backed up. There in a tree were two lynxes, both high in the branches. The moment we stopped, the boys and I watched as they leaped, one by one, to the next tree. It was absolutely unbelievable to see such graceful, magnificent creatures balancing on such narrow branches, the large pads on their feet seeming to grip the limbs. We got out of the car to see better, but remained a safe distance, and the cats stared over at us, ears twitching, muscles rippling, as they struggled with what appeared to be indecision about what to do. One of the lynxes began to urinate. Unsure if it was from fear or to act as a deterrent to us, we climbed back in the car to give them their space. Immediately they flew from the trees in the opposite direction and disappeared in a flash.

One morning we saw a grizzly just out of hibernation, busily digging for grubs near the side of the road. Approaching slowly, but at a distance, I rolled down the window to get a photo. After seeing the lynxes and not having a camera, I made sure to travel with one at all times now. It looked up briefly, then went right back to digging. We watched for a few minutes and I quickly snapped a few shots in case the bear bolted, all the while with my car in gear and foot ready to put "the pedal to the metal" if necessary. There have been cases reported where a grizzly has actually attacked a car, and I didn't want to be one of those cases. But the bear continued to dig and move a few metres to the left or right, seeming to not have a care in the world except food. Its coat shone in the light, quivering as it dug. It looked very healthy for a bear that had been in hibernation all winter. Having to move on, we drove by as far as possible on the other side of the road, with the window down a few inches and me taking a few more shots on the fly. For us to see these magnificent creatures in the wild was truly the most amazing experience. How lucky we were to have these treasured mornings.

You Can Lead a Horse to Water but...

After break-up, when all the ice had melted on Atlin Lake and Atlin was bustling with summer activity, a friend decided to have a big party in her new place downtown. Word got around quickly and the crowd that showed up was a bit overwhelming. In fact, at one point, the hostess was out walking the streets because it was getting too rowdy indoors. Right about that time, the men inside were betting to see who would be the first one to catch a horse and ride it into the bar. In the early days, there was open grazing and the horses and cows just wandered the streets all the time. The tourists seemed to really like this, but the locals certainly did not. The cows ate every flower in sight, the roads were dotted with droppings, and half the time the animals wouldn't move even if you honked at them.

So out went a group of the fellows, euphoric on booze, carousing through the town in search of the perfect horse that would allow them to not only catch it, but also climb on it and lead it without a bridle or halter. It was quite a sight to see—horses bolting, men trying to jump on moving animals, general chaos. Finally, someone got the idea to take off his belt or find a length of rope somewhere so that if they did manage to get on, they could at least lead the horse towards the bar.

Only one person succeeded, which, of course, was my husband Stan. "Stan the Man" rode the horse right up to the double doors of the bar, had someone open them, coaxed the horse into the room through the jumble of people, tables and chairs... and ordered a beer. Well, everybody was so stunned that for a moment they didn't know what to do or say—except the bartender who reached up and handed him a beer.

This was just another in a long string of stories, told and retold, some growing with the telling, about the antics of some of the town's more colourful characters. Since a schoolteacher was held to a higher standard of behaviour than the average person, I initially felt a bit sheepish about my husband's antics, but as long as the schoolteacher wasn't doing these things, I guess nobody really cared but me.

Back at Little Atlin, growing, gathering and preparing food for the winter was a major job. Our two gardens were flourishing, and I had strawberries, gooseberries, currants and more rhubarb than I knew what to do with. Although I canned, froze and made jams out of the rhubarb, most of it was still destined for wine. I continued making rhubarb wine by the forty-five gallon barrel the old fashioned way, as well as dandelion wine. Picking enough dandelions turned out to be an easy chore, as I delegated picking bags of dandelion flower heads to my students during our nature walks in Atlin. I gave them strict instructions that I needed clean ones, not the ones on the street corner that dogs could have lifted their leg to. I told them I was doing an experiment and making some kind of juice with the dandelions and oranges and lemons. I held my breath waiting for the day they would ask if they could taste the special juice, which eventually came, but I simply explained that the experiment failed and it really didn't taste any good, but I would happily bring some juice and cookies for a treat for them instead. So now I had a big batch of dandelion wine brewing too.

The greenhouse was finished and it was fantastic! Stan did an incredible job, completing it the way he knew I wanted. I could grow all of the vegetables in it that needed an extra bit of warmth, such as tomatoes, cucumbers, zucchini, other squashes and more. Brett and Travis had their own Sweet 100 tomato plants, from which they could pick and eat as many as they wanted. In addition, I planted some tiger lilies, flowers in pots in the sunroom and let vine nasturtiums grow freely on and round the tomatoes. I watered the greenhouse using a hose with a shut-off valve that came from a large water tank on a platform at one of the gable ends. We pumped water from the lake to the tank, allowed it to warm up and then gravity allowed me to water. It was a super set-up!

The absolutely mind-boggling thing was how fast the plants grew in the summer when influenced by so many hours of sunlight. You could literally measure a zucchini in the morning and then again in the evening and it would have grown an inch or more in the long summer days. The greenhouse provided us not only with lots of fresh food to eat, but also the basis for pickles and many other canned goodies, as well as squashes and pumpkins to store. The sitting room at the end housed a solar shower and eventually we put in a wood-heated water tank. On chilly days I could warm up and read a book, or have a glass of wine looking out at the lake.

A big addition to our homestead that summer was the purchase of a gas wringer washer machine. I could now wash all our clothes at home, at least in the summer. It was a luxury, as all I had to do was fill up the gas tank, pull on the cord and she started up. The noise didn't bother me at all, even though it penetrated the silence for a period of time, as it washed all the clothes beautifully and wrung the wet clothes almost dry after I fed them through the rollers, which flattened them like a pancake. Our friends living in the bush had invented a dog-operated washing "machine" once, utilizing their sled dogs to power it. They hooked the dog's harnesses to an overhead turnstile that created agitation in a tub when they ran in circles. As the saying goes, necessity is the mother of invention.

Summer ended and the new school year began. I continued commuting back and forth on the weekends to complete the harvest and put the garden to bed. All of our efforts would provide a winter of food gifts. Somehow, knowing you have grown and processed everything makes it taste all that much better. Adding to that your own home-baked breads and wild game, you feel like you are providing the healthiest foods possible for your family.

October arrived, the first bitter days of winter showing up sooner than expected, biting our noses and toes before we were ready. Hovering around the wood stove while at home, the boys excitedly discussed their costumes for Hallowe'en. After much deliberation, Travis decided to make a space creature costume, consuming rolls of tin foil and reams of wire. Brett opted to be a pirate, sifting through my scarves and clothing to find the proper attire and making a patch for his eye. Meanwhile, news penetrated the town about a big Hallowe'en party that would be held at the airport hangar. It was a "bring your own food and booze" event for the whole family; kids welcome early, no rules for adults.

For this particular party, my friend Carmen and I, after getting into a few glasses of wine, started trying on the velvet gowns I'd kept in my cedar chest for years. I had inherited them from a baroness of Denmark when I was eighteen. The kids were with their dads, so we had the house to ourselves. We tried every combination of clothes, put on heavy makeup while listening to our favourite songs blaring on the stereo and turned up at the hangar feeling quite good and ready to dance. It was a wild night with every creature on hand, most hiding behind their full-body costumes and refusing to expose their identity. This added to the mystique, as did the blatant touching and unexpected kisses from unidentifiable creatures, which everyone pretended to ignore.

The fact that the hangar did not have adequate bathroom facilities didn't seem to bother anybody, either. Nobody knew who anyone was when he or she dashed outside to find a bush. Taking my turn to relieve myself, I bumped into a mysterious couple, bodies entwined, hiding in the shadows. I am sure there were more, as it was a gorgeous night to be outside, and there were so many anonymous people in an alcohol-fueled euphoria. The party was such a success that everybody begged the hanger owner to make it an annual event.

This party, and the many ones held at the community hall, were cherished times, when almost the entire community forgot about its troubles and turned out to share in the fun together.

One of the best times would be Stan's surprise fiftieth birthday party. As Stan loved parties and dancing, it seemed the only reasonable thing to do was to have a private party at the community hall, hiring the local band, getting the recreation centre bar downstairs to provide the drinks, and making plenty of food to have on hand all evening. But I also wanted to do something really outstanding.

Formulating a plan, I first obtained a photo of Stan when he was fifteen, sporting a ducktail hairdo, then I had it silkscreened onto a T-shirt with "Stan the Man" written underneath, along with "50 years." Without telling him, I then sold the T-shirts at cost to all our friends invited to the party, giving them strict instructions to wear it under their party clothing and not say a word! Then I asked the band, who donated their time for the occasion, to play the striptease melody about three songs into the evening—a signal to everyone to take off their shirts to reveal their "Stan the Man" T-shirts and hopefully catch him totally off guard.

My girlfriends Rose and Marilyn and I set about making the decorations for the hall. We spent hours drinking wine and making tissue-paper flowers for floral arrangements for the tables. I secured tablecloths and vases from everyone I knew. Sheets of crepe paper of all colours adorned the various posts as well as the stage skirt. Other friends contributed food, and I cooked up a storm.

Finally the night arrived, and the recreation centre came alive with people laughing and chatting under the low lights with drinks flowing freely. As the band began to play, people wove their way to the dance floor, keeping in step with the music, twirling around and dancing to the beat. The next dance got almost everyone onto the floor and then the third dance began… stopping abruptly and changing to the striptease. Slowly everyone began to remove their shirts and blouses, exposing their T-shirts. Stan stood there with his mouth wide open, disbelief on his face. He stared at me, and then all his friends, unable to speak. The tune continued as shirts were now ripped off and thrown onto nearby tables, the women crowding

Stan with Terry and a friend wearing one of the "Stan the Man" T-shirts she had made up for his surprise fiftieth birthday party.

around Stan, dancing provocatively and smiling. The music stopped and the lights came on. The mob yelled "Happy Birthday!" Stan was stunned, repeatedly asking, "How did you do this... behind my back? I had no idea." The lights were lowered once again and the band continued playing. Everyone was dancing, loving the fact that it really had been a surprise.

The party continued late into the night. The band played "Happy Birthday" near midnight, with me producing a huge cake I had made for the occasion, decorated with his favourite, whales, and fifty candles—I had to have help lighting them. Fortified with birthday cake and generous amounts of food, the band remained playing until we got the word that we had to shut down. The party ended up continuing at our home, with a large group of folks eager to keep the night going. The basket of gifts from the dance were taken to the house and opened by Stan with another round of drinks. He was flustered by the attention and generous gifts. It was truly a night to be remembered. Exhausted, we fell into bed as the sun was threatening to rise, praying for a few hours' sleep before the kids woke up.

Stan's birthday party was one of the best parties ever by far, but I think the most terrific time we ladies had was the annual Ladies Bonspiel, a curling tournament. I didn't curl on a regular basis, nor did half of my friends, but when Atlin hosted the Ladies Bonspiel, we all participated. It was the only weekend of the whole year where our husbands took care of the kids for the entire two days, so we didn't even go home. We rented a house in town for ourselves and all our out-of-town friends. We ate and curled and partied day and night. The Ladies Bonspiel was a twenty-four-hour affair and you never knew when your team would play next—it could be 2:00 am, 6:00 am or 11:00 pm. You caught winks of sleep when you could and forced yourself to stay up all hours. The house was never quiet, with people coming and going all the time. The late-night games and early morning ones were really a hoot as we all wandered down to the curling rink in pyjamas and housecoats, sometimes with curlers in our hair and usually with a thermos of coffee flavoured with a unique blend of spirits.

We loved this weekend and looked forward to it every winter. It was a challenge not to check in at home, but we all made a pact that we wouldn't. Sometimes the dads would bring the kids to watch an afternoon game through the glass windows. We would wave and smile and blow kisses, but quickly get back to the game at hand and the good time we were having with our friends.

Like our two-day curling parties and many other events in the North, strange things can seem perfectly (or almost) normal. Once when I was driving home with the boys for a weekend, we stopped in at Jake's to fuel up and say hello to our friends living there. As we pulled up to the Alaska Highway, Brett yelled and pointed to two men pushing a small plane up to the gas pumps. Driving up to the pumps ourselves, we found out that they had almost run out of gas and knew they couldn't make it to Whitehorse so took a chance, landing on the Alaska Highway when they saw the gas station at Jake's Corner. After taxiing up the entranceway they stopped short of the pumps, then jumped out and pushed the plane the rest of the way, checking to see that the wings cleared all obstacles.

Since we were there, they wondered if we could help them with take-off, ensuring that there was no traffic coming in either direction. The boys loved this, jumping up and down in their seats saying excitedly, "Can we, Dad, can we?" So they pushed the plane out of the driveway and onto the Alaska Highway while Stan and the boys drove about a kilometre or less in their direction of take-off, and I stayed at the crossroads to stop any cars coming in their direction. They took off without a hitch, tipping their wings as they flew over the car. Travis and Brett couldn't stop talking about this incident and told everybody they saw for days.

IDLING ON *IOTA*

Iota, which means *little bit*, changed our lives in a very big way. The same boat we ladies took to Windy Arm to stay at Carmen's cabin now belonged to me and Stan. Our friends Arne and Carmen had put her up for sale and I'd immediately bought her. It was a dream to have boat like that on Atlin Lake. She was diesel powered and used very little fuel, which was perfect for us. We took every opportunity we had to get out on the lake that summer after the school year ended. The lake had incredible recreational opportunities, with many hidden bays and coves, sandy and pebbly beaches and island campsites as well as great fishing. But it could also be very dangerous—winds could pick up and change the lake from mirror calm to raging waters in a matter of minutes. Many have lost their lives over the years from hypothermia from the frigid waters, but the beauty is so stunning, that it seduces you, sometimes blinding you to the possible dangers.

There were no charts for the lake as there are for travelling on the ocean. Most people have geological maps, and over the years every reef, rock, great campsite, etc. gets added. When we bought *Iota*, we purchased a map, which we called our chart, and copied all the info from someone else's map. This is how it was done, but with secret campsites often omitted so others couldn't find them.

Stan and I took many trips down the lake with family and friends, but the first trip with our family was the most memorable. We started out on a beautiful day with a good forecast on the horizon and crossed the lake to enter Torres Channel. This way, even if the wind did pick up for days, we never had to do the approximately eight-kilometre crossing of the lake again; we could actually go to the end of the lake and follow the shore back to Atlin if necessary.

Torres Channel is an arm of Atlin Lake bordered by the Coast Mountains on one side and Teresa Island with Birch Mountain on the other. Looking up at Birch Mountain, with its curlicue ice cream tip, reminded me of a helicopter flight we had taken to its peak when we first moved to Atlin. The flight was the result of another bet in the bar that I was not personally involved in, but I made out okay on this one—I got a free ride to the top of the famous Birch Mountain, getting a 360° view of the entire magnificent area.

The further we boated into Torres Channel the more magnificent it became. Cathedral Mountain loomed ahead, and its precipitous cliffs with waterfalls cascading down were magical. As we neared the south end of Teresa Island we had the choice to go through First Narrows around the island, or continue on to Second Narrows after Copper Island. We chose Second Narrows, and the water became greener and greener as a result of the influence of glacial silt, so different from the waters around the town of Atlin. The beauty was mesmerizing. Once we navigated through these narrows and arrived back in the main part of Atlin Lake, it was hard to decide where to go as there were endless bays and inlets to explore and camp in.

Choosing a favourite campsite from a previous trip, we motored to a little island with wonderful flat slabs of rock, some of which were laid out almost to the shore fashioning a walkway that beckoned you to enter. When you walked through a small stand of trees, the ground was lined with these rock slabs creating a patio effect. Hauling our camp kitchen from the boat, we placed it on a huge slab counter in the cooking area next to a table with benches. There was a path to an outhouse and to trails that led to all sides of the island down to the water. The kids played endlessly and built their own little niches. Over the years folks continued to enlarge the campsite area using these smooth slabs of different-shaped rocks, continually expanding on what had already been built. With the boys, we constructed smaller tables with bench-like seats, perfect for kids to eat at.

Continuing south the next morning, we had a choice to go into Llewellyn Inlet or head slightly east to a very narrow passage that opens up into a hidden inlet. This passage is lined with a rock face that seems to dive into the water, and at the head of the inlet is a white, sandy, tropical-looking beach. As this was our first time entering Lake Inlet, we tied our boat up, emptied our canoe and paddled in because we weren't sure we could navigate the narrow channel. We found out we could, but there was something so incredibly enchanting about paddling in the cool green waters and beaching on the glistening white sand that it seemed the natural way to see this area, so we paddled in again. Beaching the canoe, we took the boys on a path from the base of the inlet along a creek that opened onto Emerald Lake. There before us was truly the deepest, richest and most exquisite emerald-coloured lake. Travis and Brett wanted to go out to the small, thickly treed island that beckoned to us, but without our canoe it was impossible to get there. Instead we dipped our feet in the icy green waters, skipped rocks and explored the shoreline.

Our next stop at Royal Bay on Sloko Island yielded a deep royal-blue bay surrounded by cliffs and teeming with wildflowers. The boys and I hiked up the cliffs, the height magnifying the colour of the water when looking down and making *Iota* look so small on the pebbly shore of the bay. Motoring around the island, which was quite large, we found there was no end to the bays and inlets on this island and the many islands nearby. Cautiously entering many of them, we marked our charts with those that intrigued us the most so we could hopefully return and explore them more fully at another time.

One of the boys' favourite places was the sandy glacial silt and sand beaches. The silt seemed to pour out to the lake edges, creating an endless shoreline of shallow water to explore, splash and play in. Miniature lakes that were created in the sinks had become warm, enticing the boys to take off their clothes and jump in with their dad. Back in the boat and around the next bend was another glacial beach and then another, all spilling into the lake from the massive glacial field. The kids played non-stop on these beaches, never tiring of searching the area, inspecting the tracks in the sand and digging and building structures from it, along with their other finds.

Motoring farther south in Sloko Inlet, towards the end of the lake a bay appears with a peninsula that curves around, forming a "C" shape. It provided us protected moorage and the perfect camping spot, with late sun as well as early morning sun. Wild onions grow there, a unique phenomenon, and frogs of all sorts share this wondrous spot, giving Travis and Brett oodles of fun chasing and capturing them in miscellaneous containers. The lake continues to change colours from the influence of the glacier and Sloko Lake emptying into Atlin Lake so far south, and this bay was no exception. It was a rich turquoise blue. A pebble beach lined the inner side of the peninsula, the trees were gladed and waves lapped on the lakeside. It was another great place for the kids to explore and play in the long summer days. After setting up our tent and gathering firewood, we explored the area together.

At night, after a dinner cooked over the campfire, we readied ourselves for bed by caching our large cooler as far down the shore as we could and hanging the rest of our nonperishable food away from the sleeping area. There was no lack of evidence of the grizzlies that thrive in this environment. It was easy to spot the telltale signs—claw marks on the trees, grizzly fur stuck into the bark they have used to scratch their backs, and of course, their droppings. The fresher they are, the greater the concern. Fortunately, we did not see any fresh droppings around our campsite. But we didn't want to leave our cooler in the boat, as we had heard that bears will enter your boat and we did not want to have something happen to our newly purchased little trawler.

During our trip down the lake, we never had a run-in with a bear. We even saw black bears as we were motoring along in the afternoons, but never had one come into our camp (at least that we know about). Still, we were constantly on guard, especially since Stan and some of his crew had once rescued a woman on Lake Labarge whose husband had been killed by a grizzly in their campsite while she hid. She was on the shore frantically waving them down as they were motoring to the job site at Thirty Mile. In shock, she had managed to get her mauled husband's body into their canoe and covered him up, but they were still on shore. Stan and his crew had her board their boat and called the authorities, who met them back at the boat launch. It was a very unsettling experience for everyone and caused us to be extremely cautious and safe at all times.

Burning up the greater part of a week, we realized that it was not nearly a long enough time to explore and see all that Atlin Lake has to offer, but we had to start heading back, as provisions were getting low. Just northeast from our "end of the lake" campsite, there were a couple of bays with islands that also allowed safe moorage and great camping. We had heard from friends that this was their favourite place to camp but we were leery about entering, as we had no chart information. So we canoed from our campsite across the end of the lake and explored it ourselves. It was easy to see why it was their favourite place; there were little islands, a picnic table placed perfectly and a pebble beach—another piece of paradise.

Motoring north up the east side of the lake offered more intriguing places to explore and more magical campsites. Passing by Moose Bay, we stopped again at Janus Point off the mainland, just north of Griffith Island, for another night's sleep.

Making our way to Anderson Bay the next morning, Birch Mountain was captured in full view. We searched an old abandoned homestead with its cabin still partially standing. Inside we found scraps of hand-painted wallpaper, an old iron bed stand, yellowed newspaper stuck between old boards, dented enamel pots—all evidence of lives once lived there. From there, we slowly made our way to Pike Bay and on to Warm Bay, where the road meets the lake and overnight camping sites are available. Passing

Our cute little diesel crab troller, *Iota*, at a campsite on Atlin Lake.

Warm Bay, we were gently reminded that we were nearing the end of our trip down the lake.

Our boat trips on Atlin Lake were the most memorable times of our life in the North. To this day I have never seen a more stunning area. The snowy mountains lining the shores, glaciers reflecting the sun spilling into the lake, aqua-blue-green pristine waters and wildlife everywhere—for me, Atlin is a piece of heaven on earth.

As summer drifted to an end, friends of ours from Sawyers Bar came to visit. Two of the four men were African American, which was an unusual sight in Atlin. Being travellers and used to camping anywhere, they set up their tents in the front yard of our teacherage in downtown Atlin, becoming the talk of the town. They were a focal point for a week as they cruised the town taking in the sights and photographing the beauty of the area. Then we all set out to Little Atlin for the weekend.

The following weekend our four guests, Travis and Brett, and Stan and I packed up for another trip down Atlin Lake to the Llewellyn Glacier on *Iota*. Since *Iota* only went a few kilometres per hour, it took about eight hours to get to our destination. We chugged along, admiring and photographing the spectacular scenery. But with eight people on a boat not even big enough to sleep two adults, it was pretty cramped, even though we towed all our gear behind us in our canoe. It felt like we were playing musical chairs in slow motion. We could either sit in the back with Stan, who was steering using the rudder, or we could sit on the bow or on the top of the boat. Everyone just kept switching around, changing positions continually. The guys had it pretty easy as far as having to relieve themselves, but it was a different story for me, the only woman. It meant going to shore, jumping off the bow, running into the bushes and then climbing back up on the boat. Needless to say, I drank very little.

Arriving at the Llewellyn Inlet, we turned south and motored into the bay. Mountain goats appeared on the steep-sided ledges to the east, as if to welcome us. The water took on a surreal turquoise colour and numerous waterfalls cascaded into the inlet. Reaching the end of the bay, we shut off the engine and let the momentum carry us up until we stopped on the pebbly shore near the campsite and trailhead to the glacier. Anxious to make camp, have dinner and explore a bit, we leaped out of the boat, set up our tents and got a fire going.

Awaking early, we broke camp and started down the trail to the glacier. It was absolutely incredible that we could boat to this inlet, hike a short trail through the woods, cross a creek and walk easily over cotton grass-covered meadows of glacial silt to the glacier-fed lake and then actually climb onto the Llewellyn Glacier. The creek had overgrown vegetation and we had to push our way through to see the rocks we needed to step on in order to cross, but our biggest concern was keeping an eye open for grizzly bears, which usually abound there. At this point I had asked the guys to start singing, which was common practice in the North to try and warn the bears of our presence so as not to startle them; however, the guys weren't buying into it.

Entering the clearing, the reward was breathtaking. We could see the glacier's face where it actively calves, breaking off huge chunks of ice into glacial Lake Llewellyn, forming a flotilla of small icebergs glistening in the sun.

The Llewellyn Glacier is a tongue of the vast icefield from Juneau that flows into the tip of Atlin Lake. It reaches 161 kilometres from the lake to the Pacific Ocean. Walking up onto the glacier is fairly safe, but going any great distance can be dangerous with the many crevasses and hazards of travelling on ice. However, many expeditions have crossed this glacier to Juneau over the years, both by cross-country skiing and snowmobiling.

Sitting on a hillside looking down onto the lake, with the cool winds blowing off the surface of the glacier onto our faces, the view took our

Our friends from California with Stan and the boys looking out at the glacier.

breath away. It was a magnificent natural wonder that our kids and friends were able to experience. Taking in the scene before my eyes of the lake, the glacier and the mountains, I felt blessed sitting in this monumental sanctuary with everything you need to learn at its doorstep through observations and experiences, teaching respect, appreciation, love and living together in harmony.

We hiked back mostly in silence, our bodies filled with the raw, wild wilderness, our minds still seeing the images of the massive icecap, our nostrils taking in scents brought to us by the gentle breezes flowing off the glacier.

The trail we'd hiked in and out on would eventually be seriously flooded in late summer of 2011 when the glacier's recession caused another lake to drain into the one we'd just visited, causing it to overflow and sending a wall of water, ice and debris that uprooted trees, cascading down towards Llewellyn Inlet. But that day, we were joyfully oblivious to the possibility of an event of such magnitude happening while we were there.

Jumping on the boat and motoring north back up Llewellyn Inlet in the late afternoon, we bypassed Sloko Inlet and headed for our next camp on the very small island in between the entrances to the first and second narrows. We were pleased to find it unoccupied. In fact, so far on our trip, we had not passed one other boat on the lake, reinforcing my feelings of being one with this grand wilderness.

This island campsite was a perfect place for the boys to explore, allowing them to run from one side to the other, climbing over the scattered rock outcroppings and exploring every nook and cranny without being worried about bears. We knew bears swam in these frigid waters—in fact Stan and I, out with a friend on his boat when we first moved to Atlin, witnessed a grizzly swimming from the narrowest point on the north end of Teresa Island across Torres Channel towards the mainland. But this small island had nothing much to entice any kind of bear, which made me sleep much better at night.

The next morning we continued up the east side of Atlin Lake, making a few stops to take a break, walk the shoreline and have our lunch. At Pike Bay, we hiked a short distance on the old Telegraph Trail, part of a 265-kilometre stretch that still survives between Telegraph Creek and Atlin. We were rewarded by Stan finding an old glass insulator nearly buried in the bush near an old telegraph pole stump. Continuing on, we passed Warm Bay and cruised north towards Five Mile Point. Gazing at the expanse of white sandy beach on Teresa Island, a kilometre or so off our port side, we were tempted to cross the lake, but resisted the urge as the wind was picking up.

Docking our boat at the community dock in Brewery Bay in front of the Glaciological Institute, formerly the town's tiny hospital, we unloaded and made a quick stop in town before heading to Little Atlin. Our friends were ecstatic with their first trip into the Atlin Provincial Park and so appreciative of the chance to experience this magnificent country by boat. One friend, John, had taken hundreds of photos and couldn't wait to get them developed to share this memorable trip with others, and to enlarge, frame and possibly sell some of them. Years later, our friend Steve would repay us for this extraordinary trip by taking our family on a weekend outing into the Marble Mountain Wilderness in northern California on pack horses.

THE UPS AND DOWNS OF HWY 37

Having your own child in your classroom for one year isn't so bad, but teaching my smart, rambunctious, over-active, independent kid for three years could be extremely trying at times. Travis took it upon himself to start calling me Mrs. Milos instead of Mom several months into my first year of teaching him in a split grade three-four class. This worked better for a period of time, but I couldn't stop myself from giving him "the look" at times or sharing my frustrations with his father. Looking back on it now, I realize that he was very eager to learn as well as energetic. I should have embraced his keen awareness and high energy, but it drove me crazy at times because he was my son and he was not the only one in the class that was so lively.

A quick learner, Travis was reading all the grade one readers in kindergarten. It was good to have students that excelled, and I provided for the different styles of learning and levels but Travis seemed to be livelier, more determined and more zealous than any of my other students.

In the winters when we were at the teacherage in town, he would jump on his cross-country skis and skate ski to school over the alkali flat and arrive at school raring to go. One morning, after taking attendance and beginning my lesson with my grade four-five class fully focused, Travis walked in late. I knew he had left in plenty of time to get to school, and was usually early so he could skate on the rink, so I was irritated that he arrived late. Running into the room, throwing his pack down and disrupting everyone who was pretending to listen to me, he excitedly told the class he'd caught a rabbit in his snare on the way to school, and asked if they wanted to see it. As he grabbed his pack and began opening it, half the class jumped up and ran over to him, against my protests. Travis stuck his hand in his pack, pulling out a dead rabbit, and if that wasn't bad enough it had little flea-type bugs jumping all over it and out of the bag. That was it! Pointing towards the door and using my "mother voice," I sent him to the principal's office.

A few minutes later, the principal opened the door to my room saying, "Excuse me, but I believe Travis has a rabbit in his pack that he snared this morning. Travis, go and get your pack and take it out back beyond the schoolyard and gut it. You can't leave it like that all day. Do you need a knife?" Turning to me, he said, "The boy got his first rabbit, and he needs to deal with it. If he is going to trap an animal, he needs to take responsibility for it. It won't take him long. I'll keep an eye on him and make sure he's back here shortly."

I think I stood there with my mouth open for a minute, then said, "Okay," and that was it. But that wasn't it. Travis's passion for just about everything kept me on my toes both in and out of the classroom.

After three years, Travis moved onto the next grade with another teacher, but then I had Brett in my class. His personality was completely opposite from his brother's, but once again, I found myself using my mom voice, getting upset more than I would have with another student, and possibly even demanding more because he was my son. Four years of teaching my sons was enough for me, so I looked at the possibility of moving into the learning assistance position that was being temporarily vacated the following year.

In order to meet all the criteria for this position, I needed to take some additional university courses. I was hired for the next school year, beginning in the fall of 1990, on condition that I complete a course in the late summer to be ready for September. The course I needed was being offered in Terrace, BC, where my girlfriend Darlene had moved. It presented a perfect opportunity for a visit.

In July, my cousin Lynda, her husband Bill, and their two teenaged sons from Florida came to visit. For the second time that summer, we packed up *Iota* and headed down Atlin Lake to the glacier. Camping along the way, the boys fished at every opportunity and we feasted on fresh grayling as well as lake trout. We stopped at the campsite of a man from Atlin to say hello, and were surprised to find that he and his wife had a special visitor, Irene Coleman, a long-time resident of Atlin who was celebrating her seventy-fifth birthday by taking a skinny dip in the icy waters of Atlin Lake. We loved it! Evidently she celebrated many of her birthdays this way.

Entering Llewellyn Inlet trail, we saw fresh claw marks on a tree and fur lodged in the creases of its bark. The fur was a blonde-brown, signifying a grizzly, so the more noise we made, the better. When the boys were younger, I laced small jingle bells into my kid's runners when we took hikes in remote bush areas but got tired of the constant ringing so I took them out and never put them back in—now they were old enough to be more bear aware and they definitely had the ability to be loud.

We saw the shape of a huge grizzly in the distance on the flats so we kept close to the trail and saw no other signs of bears. We lazily explored the area and returned to Atlin. After another successful trip down the lake, I said goodbye to my cousin and her family, who were leaving to continue their exploration of BC. I was scheduled to take off for Terrace.

Leaving the boys with Stan, I packed up the van with a huge variety of veggies from the garden and greenhouse, and with notebooks and binders in hand, began the eighteen-hour journey to Terrace. Driving east from Jake's Corner, I turned south on Highway 37, also known as the Stewart-Cassiar Highway, just before Watson Lake on the Alaska Highway. I was cruising along at about 105 kilometres an hour listening to some tunes and enjoying a beautiful August day when all of a sudden my world turned upside down... literally.

There was a loud sound and the van leaned dramatically towards the passenger side, which sent it perilously near the edge of the road, threatening to leap off into the ditch or beyond. Frantically yanking the steering

The greenhouse with sitting room attached produced an abundance of vegetables, as did the gardens behind and the rhubarb and berry patch on the right. White Mountain is in the background.

wheel yielded no change in direction. Slamming on the brakes had the same response—nothing. Eyes wide open, bracing myself, I flew off the road and collided with the ground with tremendous force, throwing me up in the air and pressuring me against my seat belt. The van hit the ground once more and bounced, then started to roll. I closed my eyes as the windshield began disintegrating, throwing little cubes of glass everywhere. In an instant, my eyes opened again as the van began a second roll. This time I was slammed with vegetables from behind and heard loose gear hitting the roof, then the floor. Feeling the belt severely tightening on my shoulder once more, I wondered how in the world I could last through yet another roll as I began spinning one more time. I felt like I was being whisked around, like the van was the bowl and I was the contents. Trees appeared upside down in front of me and crunching sounds emerged from all directions. I tried to hang onto the steering wheel to brace myself for the inevitable abrupt stop I knew would come when I hit the line of trees rapidly approaching. I saw myself rolling in slow motion, feeling horror mounting and then all of a sudden it stopped, and there was complete silence. I was upright, looking at the forest through the opening where the windshield had been. Only jagged glass remained attached to the edges.

I sat for several moments in a daze, just staring straight ahead. I moved slightly and nothing screamed out. I gently turned my neck to look around, and did a bit of a body check to make sure all my parts were still attached and functioning. I unbuckled my seat belt. The door opened only slightly, and I squeezed myself out and looked through the back window of the van, which was devoid of glass. The middle seat where the kids were always buckled in was lying upside down, ripped from the bolts, the jack-all on top of it. I felt sick inside—not from what had just happened to me, but thinking about what could have happened to the kids if they had been with me. I looked around the van, surveying the damage. It was totalled, and the back left wheel and axle were gone. Glancing back to where I went off the road, I saw vegetables and books and clothes all strewn across the highway allowance, cut generously far from the highway itself, which had allowed my van to roll so many times without hitting the dense, unbroken wall of trees in front of me.

I didn't know what to do. I was in shock. I gathered my purse first, and then a couple of belongings, and walked back to the highway where I sat down next to the road on a boulder. There I sat for I don't really know how long. It seemed like forever, and I was just peering around me in a daze. I looked back at the van and could see that the right back wheel was gone. At that time, I didn't realize that the back axle had broken, causing the wheel to come completely off, which made the back of the van drag on the highway. Hearing the noise of a car, I turned and looked south but was unable to stand up to flag them down. They slowed, and then stopped. The woman in the passenger seat jumped out and ran over to me, asking me if I had been in "that accident."

I replied, "Yes."

"Are you okay?" she asked, bending over me as her husband came to my side.

I looked up and answered, "I think so."

Standing up, I realized that I really was okay. I had only a small cut and terrible bruise starting on my shoulder where the seat belt had dug into me. I felt a bit sore all over but could walk and talk so I knew I must be okay. The folks that stopped were on their way to Watson Lake and offered to take me to wherever I needed to go. They helped me gather the important things from the van, I slowly got into their car and we headed back up the highway.

I was stunned as I began fully grasping that I had managed to survive a three-time rollover that began at 105 kilometres an hour. Not only had I survived, but I had not sustained any serious physical injuries. Deciding that I still needed to attend my course in Terrace, I asked to be dropped at the lodge at the junction of the Alaska Highway and the Stewart-Cassiar Highway where I would call my husband, make plans to get the van towed and find a way to continue to Terrace. The folks at the lodge were very kind, offering me a back room to store my gear, the use of a phone and some tea to drink. I phoned Stan with the news and he said he would be there ASAP, after making arrangements for the boys at a friend's house. And then I sat... and sat... for the six hours it took for him to arrive, my mind still tumbling with thoughts about the accident, my kids, what we were going to do about a vehicle and how lucky I was. I felt exhausted but thankful to be alive and to be sitting in a café instead of a hospital somewhere.

Late that evening, close to dusk, Stan arrived. He pulled up in our truck and he and a friend Dave hopped out of the car, rushing to meet me as I walked down the stairs. I knew immediately that they had been drinking, but I had to ask, disbelief in my voice, "Are you guys drunk?"

"No, no, we just had a few beers. I was so upset when I got your phone call I grabbed Dave and we picked up a case of beer and raced here. I am so glad you are okay," Stan replied.

I stood there motionless, disconcerted, as Stan hugged me. "I… I can't get in the truck with you," I said. "Not like this. I'm too upset and shook up to drive with you when you've had so much to drink."

Taking a few seconds to respond, my husband replied, "Well, that was our plan, for you to drive… to get you back in the saddle. That's the best thing when something like this happens." I could have killed him, I was so mad, but instead I shook my head and pointed to my belongings, which they loaded in record time, got in the driver's seat and turned the truck out onto the highway, heading south. I stared ahead, refusing to enter into the conversation they were having about what a good plan it was to have me drive, to know I could, and about how tough I was and how I could handle anything and how everything would be all right.

As I drove down the Stewart-Cassiar Highway once again, I was upset. Old feelings were surfacing, reminding me of a time years ago when I was given the task of putting tire chains on our van in the middle of a snowstorm on a highway. Stan had the idea that I needed to learn how to do it by myself, not realizing it was poor timing or being sensitive to my need of more support. I knew Stan stilled loved me, but these feelings of frustration were now starting to become a wedge in what I thought was my special relationship with my husband. He just didn't seem to understand many of my feelings. It was as if we were on different paths.

From the lodge I had phoned the school district in Cassiar and asked if we could spend the night in one of the empty staff trailers in town. We arrived after dark, making our way to the assigned trailer. Walking in, I found a kind note, a sachet of fragrant bath salts and an airplane-size bottle of white wine left by a woman on staff at the school district. I walked straight to the bathroom, drew a tub of hot water laced with the bath salts and sipped my wine while having a long, hot bath, feeling grateful to be alive.

After tossing and turning off and on through the night, I woke up sore and bruised but in relatively good shape. We drove to Terrace, the guys eager to please me. I rode in the passenger seat this time. When we arrived at Darlene's, I said goodbye and the guys drove back to Atlin. By that time I was glad to be free of them. Even though they had driven the distance to get me and were genuinely concerned about me, I felt almost betrayed and hurt. I just needed to be alone and looked forward to being able to visit with my friend so I could tell her my thoughts and frustrations, and we could share stories of our children's lives, how our gardens were growing and our plans for the future.

After I completed my course, I caught an Alaskan State Ferry from Prince Rupert, just down the road from Terrace, and had a marvellous trip back to Skagway through the Inside Passage. I heard that early the next morning the humpback whales were going to be feeding in the area we were cruising though, so I awoke at 4:45 with a group of others interested in viewing this incredible sight. We were not disappointed. Unaffected by the huge ship slowly navigating by, we watched the pod of baleen whales, that only feed in the summer, repeatedly dipping their heads, gathering huge mouthfuls of ocean water, then spitting it out, trapping the tiny shrimp-like krill, plankton and small fish. These humpback whales were on their way to more tropical waters to breed and give birth in the winter, when they fast and live off of their fat reserves. We also witnessed their massive tail fins or flukes propelling them through the water and breaching. How spectacular to see and be near these magnificent creatures!

I began as the learning assistant teacher at the Atlin Elementary Junior Secondary School that fall, which made for a much happier family—the boys were now in the hands of other teachers.

My first teacher's workshop was in January 1991 in Cassiar, BC. When I was on my way there with Martin, the new Atlin School principal, and my teacher's assistant Brenda, we took an unplanned side trip that proved to be a mid-winter escapade. In those days, Cassiar was a small, company-owned mining town and the home of School District 87 Stikine; the town was eventually forced to close down, and is a ghost town today. While based in Cassiar, the district often hosted meetings and workshops that teachers and administrators travelled to from the outlying communities. Sometimes we flew there, or if only a few of the staff were attending, we would drive. On this particular occasion, the three of us were driving in my Subaru, and on our way, we planned to stop at Lower Post to visit the principal of the school there, an Atlinite named Lynn who at one time had been a member of our staff in the Atlin School.

Watson Lake is about a five-hour drive from Atlin on the Alaska Highway just beyond the Highway 37 turnoff, which we would have taken if we had been going straight to Cassiar. Lower Post is located about a half an hour's drive beyond Watson, just below the BC-Yukon border, at Mile 620. Once known as Fort Liard, it was the lower of two Hudson's Bay Company trading posts on the Liard River and is home to the Kaska Dena.

After arriving at Lower Post and reconnecting with Lynn, we had a tour of the tiny Denetia School and settled in for a visit. We shared stories and were catching Lynn up on all the happenings when someone mentioned the Liard Hot Springs. I do not for the life of me know how we got from talking about the hot springs to actually going there, but I think Brenda mentioned that it really wasn't that far. So the three of us ended up back in the car with a partially full bottle of Lynn's scotch in anticipation of submerging ourselves in the exquisite warmth of the hot springs on a cold winter night. We were supposed to be going from Lower Post to Cassiar that evening, only a short distance south on Highway 37, to be ready for a 9:00 am workshop session, but instead we were headed southeast on the Alaska Highway towards the Rocky Mountains. However, this didn't bother us too much at all, even though it meant driving 193 kilometres to get to the hot springs, having a soak, driving back and returning late to Lower Post, spending the night at Lynn's and then getting up very early to get to our workshop.

To this day, I am not sure what we were thinking, but we were all much younger and with a lot more energy then. The farther away from Lower Post we got driving the lonely, often icy highway, the more we began to question our choice, but after reaching the halfway point, we knew we were committed—there was no going back!

The Liard Hot Springs are the second-largest hot springs in Canada. The park is undeveloped and is kept as natural as possible. There is a boardwalk that passes through a warm-water swamp and boreal forest, where moose are often seen, which never freezes due to the continual influx of warm water. The boardwalk ends at a simple "his" and "hers" change room at the lower pools. The water in the springs ranges from 42°C to 52°C, which sounded luxurious at such below-zero temperatures. It was an adventure I was looking forward to, as I had never been there in the dead of winter.

We arrived and not a soul was there, not even in the campground. We had one flashlight, towels Lynn had given us, and that was all, except the half-filled bottle of scotch. As we started down the boardwalk, it felt mystical, with steam rising all around us, the trees and bushes trimmed with frost illuminated by the moon. Each twist and turn of the boardwalk offered new scents and a different view of the lush plant life. We heard only the water flowing into a pool and various night creatures, but not another human sound.

The boardwalk led us to the first pool, the Alpha Pool, where the change house with composting toilet was located. The change house was not really a house, but a shelter with a few walls where you could change into your swimwear. We were not prepared to be in the water, so none of us had bathing suits, but it was dark so Brenda and I went in wearing our bra and underwear. I threw on Martin's T-shirt and he went in wearing only his undershorts. After changing very quickly in the close to minus-thirty weather, the water felt like heaven—in fact, the entire place looked like heaven. The hoar frost from the warmth of the water enveloped everything in white crystals. It was like something out of a movie. I couldn't believe we were there, and I couldn't believe Brenda had agreed to come! She was such a good sport. She had worked with me for many years but I didn't really know her that well. Brenda was always so agreeable and helpful at school, and even now, she hadn't balked at going to the hot springs. She was a true Northerner.

Easing into the hot water and being submerged up to our chins in the middle of absolutely nowhere, surrounded with snow-laden banks while the moon shone brightly, was surreal. The bottle of scotch was floating upright in the water, bobbing around with us, ready to drink. We looked at each other and I asked, "Okay, any volunteers to be the designated driver?" Well, no volunteers, so we all had a few swigs. I was careful, though, as it was my car, so I would be driving.

The Liard Hot Springs, shown here in the summer, are located in the Liard River Hot Springs Provincial Park and open year-round.

After a glorious time, we had to start heading back. Getting out was a hundred times harder than getting in. We raced to the change room, threw on our now-chilled clothes and started back down the boardwalk. We felt freezing cold and warm at the same time! The tips of my hair and Martin's moustache quickly began to freeze. We jumped in, I cranked up the heater, and we began the drive back to Lower Post, which seemed twice as long now. The road had many twists and turns over the mountain passes, and no other cars were driving in these cold temperatures. In fact, we only passed one car on the Alaska Highway during the entire drive.

We crawled into our beds at Lynn's at about two in the morning and slept like babies. We were awakened early in the morning by the smell of bacon and coffee. Lynn, who is a wonderful person, had gotten up at 5:00 am to prepare breakfast for us, knowing that we had to be on the road around 6:00 am or so. What a gem she was, and what a fun and memorable visit we had.

We made it to Cassiar on time and headed straight for more coffee. Fifteen minutes after arriving there, Martin was pulled aside and informed about an urgent issue at Atlin School that needed his prompt attention. The next thing I knew, he and the school trustee were gathering their things, as they had to return to Atlin. Brenda and I spent the day in workshops, and in the evening, the director of curriculum hosted a party. We were all having a pretty good time. Brenda left early and went to bed while I stayed with the rest of the group and continued socializing. Unfortunately, someone made a very inappropriate comment regarding our school and I took offence, thinking it was a huge insult to our entire staff.

The situation was sensitive, particularly as it involved a child, and the remark left me feeling extremely uncomfortable staying at the party or even staying in Cassiar for the night. So, in a moment of anger, I made a quick decision to leave. The director, a woman whom I considered a friend, tried to stop me but I proceeded to get into my car, drive back to where we were staying and wake up Brenda. I told her to pack up because we were leaving. I was that mad. I hardly ever got mad, but the line had been crossed.

Brenda, bless her heart, said sleepily, "Okay, Terry, whatever," and got up, got dressed, packed and jumped in the car with me. We drove north up Highway 37, the same highway I rolled my van on, until we came to the junction of the Alaska Highway. It was very, very late and I was too tired to drive any longer, so we stopped at the lodge parking lot to try and get some sleep. Brenda took the back seat, I took the front, and we tried to sleep but it was *freezing*. We tossed fitfully in our sleeping bags, which were simply not warm enough for such cold conditions. I woke up about every half an hour and turned the car on to warm it up, then slept for a while longer and woke up to do it again. Needless to say, it was a long night. Finally, I couldn't stand it anymore, so I started driving again. When I got to Teslin, Yukon, I called the school and told Martin what had happened and that I was heading to Atlin early. He advised that since I wasn't at the workshop, I'd better come to the school. I raced home, dropped off Brenda, stopped at my teacherage to get changed and went straight to school. It was not only a long night but also an extremely long day!

As the school year continued, I got to be good friends with Martin and his wife Carrie. I'd been a little worried about meeting Martin's wife when they first moved to Atlin, as my girlfriend and fellow teacher Rose and I had sat on the hiring committee with the out-going principal to help select the new principal. Martin fit the bill completely, having had teaching and administrative experience at all grade levels and alternative school experience. He and his wife also owned an acreage in Atlin bought years ago, after visiting and falling in love with the area. This was a real plus.

The committee, having quickly made its decision, informed the applicants immediately of the results, announcing that Martin had been the successful applicant. As with most celebrations in Atlin, there was only one place to go to—the Atlin Inn—so the hiring committee, Martin, our trustee Michael, Rose and myself, with the unsuccessful candidates in tow, all headed there to celebrate. While having a few toasts, Martin, who was happy with the outcome, decided to call his wife and share his excitement with her. Leaving the bar and phoning from the antique phone booth down the hall, he was talking to his wife Carrie when Rose and I barged into the phone booth and told Martin we wanted to talk to her. We elbowed him aside, grabbed the phone and babbled on to this poor woman we didn't know about how great it was that Martin got the job and how happy we were that they were moving to Atlin and on and on while Martin was standing there looking perplexed. That was Carrie's first introduction to two of Martin's new staff.

I am sure that Carrie had some doubts about me, but they were short-lived as we became really good friends, as our kids did too. That summer our families went on a camping trip together down the lake on *Iota*. Their two boys and our two boys were best of friends and never stopped inventing games, playing and paddling around in the canoe we towed behind. We motored to many of our favourite places, wanting to share the magnificence of the area with our good friends. We camped at the little island with the rock-slab patios and furniture and motored in to our favourite bays and inlets.

The weather was terrific for most of the trip until we headed home. We had stopped south of Atlin at Pike Bay, noted for its black sand, when it started pouring. We managed to set up camp but it was instantly apparent that the rain was not going to let up and we were not going to stay dry. After a cold dinner, we herded the kids to the boat and tucked the four of them into the bow bunk. It was a tight squeeze, but they all fit. The rest of us crawled into our sleeping bags, Martin and Carrie under a tarp, and Stan and me in our tent. Sometime in the middle of the night I was so wet and miserable I just couldn't stay in the tent, so I made my way to the boat seeking a dry space. There was no way I could squeeze into the bed with the boys so I curled up on the floor between the steering station and a cabinet, a space probably about two by four feet. That's where Stan found me in the morning. I was stiff, cold and tired but drier than the rest of the crew.

Our glorious weather nowhere in sight, we cruised back to Atlin, glad at least that we had a few good days to seek out the sights and spend time together; we made a pact to do it again, and now, more than twenty years later, we are still taking these trips together and having adventures.

Martin's family and ours spent a lot of time together the next year, and we became very close. Our boys were the best of friends and often had sleepovers, rode bikes and went grouse hunting together, and played sports and games with each other. One memorable night, Martin, Carrie and their boys stopped by Little Atlin on their way home from a Whitehorse shopping trip. As they got up to leave, we opened the front door to wander over to their van with them and say our good-byes, when we were nearly blinded by the brightest pink sky I have ever seen. Not being dusk, it surprised us, but instantly we recognized the dancing of the northern lights, this evening more brilliant than ever before. Northern lights are usually greener in colour, but these shone wavy streams of pinks and purples. We stood mesmerized, entranced, the entire yard and lake bathed in pink. I felt like I was in a dream and someone had painted the entire scene a dazzling pink. Martin told us later that after they left, it was so bright that he drove a long section of the Atlin Road with his headlights off. At one point, the lights flared and they stopped the truck and got out to have another look. The chrome on his van, he said, glowed pink like molten metal. I also learned that Jamie, the

The Blakesley and Milos families during their boat trip down to the south end of Atlin Lake exploring one of the many islands dotting the area.

pilot in Atlin whose Hallowe'en party we had gone to at the hangar, jumped in his plane, taxied down the runway and flew into the unprecedented array of northern lights. It was truly a night to remember.

Four years earlier, I had applied for a Deferred Salary Leave. One fourth of my pay had gone into a fund so that in the fifth year, I would have a leave with full pay. The time had come for my leave and the end-of-the-year field trip for Travis's grade five-six class was the last school function we would attend before my leave began. It was a wonderful opportunity provided by the school district to allow teachers to pursue other interests, travel, or just take a break from teaching. I wanted our family to travel to the United States to visit family and friends and to explore the countryside.

As a learning assistance teacher, I was asked to be one of the supervisors for Travis's field trip, which was a two-night trip into the wilderness by canoe. The class travelled from Atlin to Palmer Lake, located approximately nineteen kilometres south of Atlin on the Warm Bay Road. After launching the canoes filled with supplies from the boat launch, we paddled approximately a kilometre before encountering our first beaver dam at the southeast corner of Palmer Lake. One by one the canoes navigated up to the narrowest part of the channel until we were unable to paddle any farther. With the assistance of the teacher, Mr. Markley, the students all got out of their boats wearing their rubber boots and helped drag the canoes over the ledge of sticks and branches creating the dam. Carefully reentering the canoes, we paddled across a small lake to the next dam, a little less than a kilometre, and then repeated the process on the second, bigger dam, to get to the beautiful little lake with a wonderful camping spot that was our destination. We couldn't have ordered more perfect weather, and the kids were excited.

The trip was expertly organized and as soon as we arrived at our campsite, the students knew exactly what to do. They had already practised putting up their tents on the school grounds and knew their sleeping groups so they only had to find the perfect spot to set up their tents. A main campfire area was already established. The entire camp looked out over the water where a large rock was perfectly situated a safe swimming distance from shore.

The trip was not only for fun, but was educational too. There were several adults, other teachers, parents and even the local RCMP officer. It really helps to have the child of an RCMP officer in your class when you go on a trip such as this. His participation meant we not only had radio access in case of an emergency, but we also had someone with a rifle that could keep away or shoot a bear if absolutely necessary.

Each adult had specific subject matter to teach. I was to teach bush art, the local nurse was to teach first aid, the grade five-six teacher was to teach canoe skills, a science person was to teach plant identification, and survival skills as well as some history were also taught. First aid was very important, so that was first with practice sessions. Little did the kids know, but at a pre-planned meeting with the adults, we were each to pretend an injury, unannounced to the students, during the two days to see how the kids would deal with it. I'll never forget when I was out with a group of kids gathering flowers and I "accidentally" tripped in a ravine. I made moaning sounds and held my leg and said I couldn't get up. The kids ran to me in concern, thinking I had really hurt myself. One ran back to camp to get the nurse. I kept saying I thought I'd broken my leg. The nurse instructed them to do whatever was necessary, just like they had been taught. That is when I think it started to click and they started understanding that it was staged. I actually felt guilty. The concern on their faces was genuine. I had taught most of these kids for three or four years and we had become quite close.

From then on the kids were right on it. Something would happen and they would go into it saying, "Okay, who remembers exactly what to do?" There were burns and bee stings, broken arms, cuts and concussions. It was an ingenious way to teach first aid.

Ice pushed up on the shore of Little Atlin Lake from wind during the spring break-up. While flowers are blooming profusely on land, the lakes are still melting in late spring.

My first art project was flower pictures. It was spring, and the wildflowers were profuse. I was able to infuse some plant identification during our wildflower collection hike. We set aside a spot on the sandy beach as our gallery. Each student, with a partner or by himself or herself, was to create a solid flower composition. After thinking about their composition and collecting their flowers, they gathered sticks to make a frame. They then used the flower parts for their design. The lupines were plentiful so there was ample blue-sky material; yellow flowers were also in abundance, so many of the compositions had a sun in them. A flower that had gone to seed produced white cotton material that made wonderful clouds. Each picture was unique to the artist and an incredible display of colour. One student put little sticks in to make a raft on a lake with stick figures; another used the yellow daisy-like petals, red paintbrush and orange flowers for a magnificent sunset over mountains, and others created non-landscape scenes such as a sports car, etc. They were so special and the fact that the wind was not blowing and they could remain on display throughout our trip was a real bonus. The flower pictures on the sandy gallery of the shore were a hit with the kids and adults alike.

While I was working with a group on art, another group would be out on the lake learning paddle strokes and rescue manoeuvres with a different instructor. The kids swam and played "King of the Rock" endlessly. One afternoon we hiked to the top of Strawberry Hill, which gave us a glorious view of Atlin Lake and the Coast Mountains with the glaciers behind.

One of the features of this campsite was a bald eagle nest right in its midst. I am sure the eagles did not count on having twenty or more kids running around below their nest. Every once in a while someone would yell, "You can see them, look!" and we would all stop what we were doing and look up to see little heads poking out of the nest. It was awesome.

Food preparation went fairly well—I have never seen kids eat so much. Around the campfire there was guitar-playing and songs were sung and stories told. A contest to see who could tell the scariest story had one or two kids up late at night—not from monsters or goblins or zombies, but from grizzly bear stories. It didn't help when our fine outstanding RCMP officer/ father faded away without anyone knowing and pretended to make bear noises in the bush. Of course everyone looked to him just in case there was a bear, but we were unable to find him. How ironic that he was the one making the noises.

Everybody was exhausted when we headed back. Many of the students had their grass weaving with them to take home and hang on a wall or give to their folks. I took snapshots of all the flower pictures to give to the kids later. The paddle back was less energetic than the paddle two days before, but fond memories thrived. It was an enjoyable trip and a great way to end the school year and start the summer. For Travis and Brett and I, it also meant the beginning of a year off from school and another adventure.

LEAVING THE NORTH

In the end, living in the North took a toll on my relationship with my husband. I was busy teaching school full-time, cleaning campgrounds and selling women's clothing to make ends meet. I was also an active mother in raising my kids and surviving off the land. Stan's work was seasonal and even with his artwork, he was not always able to contribute as much as he would have liked to financially. Slowly our lives began to take different paths. With the realization that we no longer loved each other came the realization that our boys were the glue holding us together. Stan loved our boys more than anything and was the best dad he could be, but in the end it just wasn't enough, and we took a break from each other.

In the summer of 1991 we began preparing to head south, as my deferred salary leave began that fall, and Stan and I were on extremely rocky ground. Our family had planned to explore the southwestern US, visiting as many of the national parks as possible, camping along the way and then heading east to visit relatives in West Virginia and Florida. Because the kids were so excited and we had planned it for such a long time, I decided to continue with our plans as a family and make the best of it.

I was responsible for their schooling while we were away, and it was not always easy. I don't blame the kids for not wanting to study or complete schoolwork while sitting on a beach somewhere, in a campground or at some other exciting place they wanted to explore. We stayed with relatives for a period of time and it allowed the boys and me to get into a bit of a routine, but they were losing ground and I was losing the battle.

After five months of travelling, we ended up in Arizona, and Stan and I made the decision that I would return to Atlin and put the boys back in school while he drove back to California to look for work. Travis, Brett and I hopped on a train from Phoenix, AZ to Seattle, WA, busing on to Vancouver. With the help of a friend, I bought a four-wheel-drive truck in Vancouver for the drive home. The boys and I made the long journey in January's frozen weather up the Alaska Highway. I had driven the highway many times, but had never driven it alone in the dead of winter. I was worried about the cold temperatures, knowing that when it hits minus-forty, vehicles start freezing up, steering is affected and you need to have a battery warmer and oil pan warmer, neither of which I had. They were to be installed when I returned home. Fortunately, the temperatures didn't drop below minus-thirty. I drove long days and we stayed in motels for two nights. I would wake up in the middle of the night a couple of times to start the truck so it wouldn't freeze up completely.

Driving endless kilometres in snow-covered scenery can be mesmerizing. Every turn of the road and every new mountain pass produced yet another magnificent scene. Little creeks yielded hoar frost, making the trees and shrubs look like someone had sprayed white ice crystals on them; larger rivers and streams looked like roller coasters with water running rapidly up and down the rocks and ice, and snow stuck firmly to fir forests, which made them look like enchanted forests out of a fairy tale. We could see the ice crystals in the air when the sun shone on the very cold days. The Rockies were glorious with their snow-capped mountains and glaciers. The boys marvelled at all the wildlife. We passed very few cars on the highway except near the larger cities.

Soon Travis and Brett were happily back in school with their friends, but I was getting cabin fever. I was staying in the teacherage in Atlin so the boys were near school, but I was not working and the days were long. Now fully realizing how unhappy I was, I once again began a deeper evaluation of my marriage and of my life in the North. Nineteen years was a long time, and I had begun to feel like my life needed a change.

In March I was given an opportunity to go south again. Friends were moving to Vancouver Island and needed someone to drive their old mail truck with the majority of their belongings down Highway 37, the Stewart-Cassiar Highway. There are only two ways to drive north or south from the Yukon—the Alaska Highway or the Stewart-Cassiar Highway. In the old days, there was a lot of logging off the Stewart-Cassiar and you never knew when a huge logging truck was going to round the bend. In fact, it used to be a private road and tourists could only travel on weekends when the trucks weren't running, but it was safe to drive at this time and a nice alternative to the Alaska Highway. Knowing my marriage was over, I hoped that this trip would give me a chance to find somewhere to begin a new life. I asked Stan to return home from my brother's in California to care for the boys and he did. We had a difficult few days together, Stan not happy with the possibility of me moving south with the boys, but I needed to explore my options and I left for Vancouver.

It was tough driving the old truck, but I did. My friends and I started out together but they ended up stopping at the town of Smithers to ski, so I kept on going by myself, driving the boxlike, rough-riding mail truck all the way down the highway. We rendezvoused at their new home on Vancouver Island and they loaned me their SUV to tour around and see if I could find a place to move to and explore job opportunities.

I travelled from school district to school district on Vancouver Island without one of them even accepting my resume, since none were doing any hiring at all, and especially not of anyone from out of the area. By ferry, I cruised across the Strait of Georgia to Powell River on the northern Sunshine Coast. Hopping another ferry, I landed on the southern Sunshine Coast. A short drive after leaving the ferry terminal, I passed two beautiful fresh water lakes dotted with islands, the mountains towering behind. I caught glimpses of the ocean and the mountains in the distance on Vancouver Island through the lush forest bordering the road. Fishing boats lined the docks of Pender Harbour, selling fresh crabs and prawns, sitting next to wonderful classic pleasure boats of all shapes and sizes, many with kayaks perched on their bows. Pink blossoms coloured the tips of trees, and spring flowers were showing their faces from pots and flowerbeds everywhere. I was drawn to this new land and fell in love with it immediately. I was anxious to get my feet in salt water and see the creatures of land and sea that lived in this area, to hike in the mountains and swim in the lakes. I knew that this was a place I could live; I felt it in my heart.

At the School District #46 office in Gibsons, BC, the assistant superintendent not only looked at my resume, but also spoke to me personally and sent me to the schools to introduce myself and let the principals know I was thinking of relocating. One of the principals that I met with told me straight out that I would probably not have a chance of getting hired, as good as my resume was and even with all the experiences I'd had teaching multi-grade levels, unless I actually moved to the coast and began substitute teaching in the schools. So that's what I did. I bussed back home, packed up the kids, since it was spring break, and the three of us drove back down the Alaska Highway.

I began subbing as spring break ended and soon after was offered a full-time job teaching grades three and four at West Sechelt Elementary School in Sechelt on the Sunshine Coast the following fall. The kids made new friends and were temporarily contented. A wonderful old house on the ocean came up for rent and we moved in. Stan came to visit and see our new surroundings, but returned north shortly after, realizing that our marriage was over. I had a separation agreement drawn up (that was uncontested by Stan) allowing us to get a divorce and move on with our lives.

Travis, Brett and I made a new life for ourselves on the Sunshine Coast, but the boys continued to regularly travel north to spend time with their dad too. In fact, both boys ended up moving to their childhood roots as they grew older, missing the lifestyle and what the spectacular north offers. I spent some time on my own before meeting Mike, whom I've lived with for more than twenty-four years in the wonderful homes we've built together on the Sunshine Coast and in Lake Havasu, Arizona.

No matter where I live, I will always remember and cherish my time in the North. It taught me many lessons and helped to create who I am. My experiences there embedded a love and admiration for beauty of the land and its creatures while helping to shape my spirit and those of my children. They also forced me to draw on my deep reserves and further develop courage, independence, and strength of character, which will always be a part of me. There was never a time I felt it was too difficult or I couldn't handle the lifestyle. I loved the adventures as well as the challenges the North presented me, and for those I will be forever grateful.

The relationships I formed in my nineteen years of living and working in Atlin and a variety of northern communities have held fast through the years, and the depth of our connections will remain for the rest of our lives. My friends Carmen and Arne also moved to the Sunshine Coast, enabling us to continue to share our lives, and our sons Travis and Eri are now living near each other outside Whitehorse. My good friends Martin and Carrie live a ferry ride away in the Gulf Islands not far from their kids and grandkids. A mutual friend Rose and her son live on Saltspring Island as well. Martin, Carrie and I see each other whenever we can, engaging in wilderness adventures together at every opportunity. I paddle often with Martin and Carrie on the BC Coast and in Arizona, and only last year as I write this, Marilyn, the woman I met in the hospital when we had our kids, and I paddled the Yukon River from just north of Whitehorse to Dawson City together. I also recently visited with Dick and Holly, who have a home in Arizona, and Susan, from the north end of Atlin Lake, was staying with them, allowing us all to reminisce about the old days. I connected with Bonnie and her sons in the Yukon. The fact that our boys and other Atlin young people have remained friends and followed the happenings in each other's lives continues to warm my heart.

One of the biggest joys in my life now is my reconnection with so many of the students I taught over the years in Atlin. Some I have connected with on the internet, others I've seen on my visits to see Travis. On a flight from Vancouver to Whitehorse not long ago, I sat across the aisle and slightly behind a woman who looked and sounded very familiar. As the plane was about to land I reached up and touched her arm and asked her if she was a Jack, a large family I knew from up north. She turned and looked at me, eyes wide open, yelling excitedly, "Mrs. Milos?" The plane touching down momentarily disrupted our exchange, and we stared and smiled, holding each other's hands. The moment we were able to remove our seat belts and get up, we were in each other's arms, crying and laughing and jumping up and down, drawing so much attention to ourselves that those around us cheered at our reunion. These kids, including my students Brad and Zandra from my first year of teaching in Atlin and my former foster child Robert amongst them, are not really kids any more but fine young adults, all now a part of my big, extended family.

These strong connections reached to the core of my being, touched my soul, and helped to ease the unfathomable loss of my son Brett, who, at age eighteen, died in a workplace accident in Alaska. This loss so hugely impacts every thought, every action, every word, every day of my life that I am not the same person I was. I am eternally grateful that I had my son for the short but precious time I did, and that he was raised in such a magnificent place, surrounded by so many amazing people, all contributing to the fine, kind, young man he grew to be, his memory remaining forever alive in all our hearts.

All those years ago, I dreamed of living a simple pioneer lifestyle in harmony with nature, yet filled with adventure. I found what I was looking for and more in the North. My soul was filled with the incredible vastness of the wilderness, its raw beauty, its power and gentleness, the endless gifts it had to offer. Anxious to learn what mysteries and adventures lay around the next corner in the road, over the next hill, in the bay behind the next point of land, I felt myself drawn to them. And I still am. Both Travis and Brett felt this too, the north embracing them, and whenever they left it, they felt it drawing them back to live their lives. And now Travis has a family and will share this grand land and all it has to offer with his kids. To this day, when I take a flight to the Yukon, the moment I step off the plane, I feel like I am home.

The author and her sons, Travis and Brett, sitting in their home on Little Atlin Lake. The old wood cook stove is in the background.